SAMUEL BECKETT AND THE IDEA OF GOD

Also by Mary Bryden

WOMEN IN SAMUEL BECKETT'S PROSE AND DRAMA

Samuel Beckett and the Idea of God

Mary Bryden
Senior Lecturer in Department of French Studies
University of Reading

First published in Great Britain 1998 by
MACMILLAN PRESS LTD
Houndmills, Basingstoke, Hampshire RG21 6XS and London
Companies and representatives throughout the world

A catalogue record for this book is available from the British Library.

ISBN 0-333-64076-4

First published in the United States of America 1998 by
ST. MARTIN'S PRESS, INC.,
Scholarly and Reference Division,
175 Fifth Avenue, New York, N.Y. 10010

ISBN 0-312-21285-2

Library of Congress Cataloging-in-Publication Data
Bryden, Mary, 1953–
Samuel Beckett and the idea of God / Mary Bryden.
p.   cm.
Includes bibliographical references and index.
ISBN 0-312-21285-2 (cloth)
1. Beckett, Samuel, 1906– —Religion.   2. Christianity and
literature—Ireland—History—20th century.   3. Christianity and
literature—France—History—20th century.   4. God in literature.
I. Title.
PR6003.E282Z57878   1998
848'.91409—dc21   97–41062
                                                                   CIP

This book is printed on paper suitable for recycling and made from fully managed and
sustained forest sources.

10   9   8   7   6   5   4   3
07   06   05   04   03   02   01   00   99

Printed and bound in Great Britain by
Antony Rowe Ltd, Chippenham, Wiltshire

Contents

Acknowledgements

In 1994, the award of a one-month Andrew W. Mellon Foundation Fellowship allowed me to consult, in preparation for this study, a wide variety of manuscripts at the Harry Ransom Humanities Research Center, Austin, Texas. Much of the fruit of that research has been incorporated into this book, and I am extremely grateful to the staff of HRC and to the Andrew W. Mellon Foundation for making this opportunity available. I would also like to thank the personnel of the Ohio State University Library, at Columbus, for their helpfulness, and to acknowledge an additional travel grant from Reading University towards the cost of that visit.

In the fields of theology and spirituality, I am very fortunate in having been able to draw for advice upon the expertise of a number of specialists. I would like to thank Rev. Dr Michael Child for much information concerning classical, scriptural, theological, and spiritual sources, as well as for books lent and given; Rev. John Buckley for handling with typical good humour some detailed enquiries relating to Ireland; Sr Teresa Benedicta of the Holy Spirit ODC and Iain Matthew ODC for help in locating references to St Teresa of Avila, St John of the Cross, and Julian of Norwich; Tony Corley of the Library of Heythrop College, Sr Teresita ODC, and Br Jamie Glackin for valuable assistance with queries.

I am grateful to the staff of the Manuscripts Department at Trinity College Dublin, to Susan Schreibman, and to Anna McMullan for her friendly presence during my research visit to TCD in 1996. Among my colleagues at Reading, I am greatly indebted to Walter Redfern, for his conscientious guidance, constructive suggestions, and meticulous reading of my drafts. James Knowlson gave me crucial assistance with respect to Beckett sources and materials, and, as always, offered support and encouragement.

Thanks are due to the Samuel Beckett Estate, to the Harry Ransom Humanities Research Center at The University of Texas at Austin, and to The Board of Trinity College Dublin, for permission to quote from unpublished sources. Parts of the material on Dante and on Pseudo-Dionysius and Eckhart have appeared in modified form in the *Romanic Review* and in *Representations of Belief: Essays in Memory of G.V. Banks*, ed. Elizabeth Fallaize, Ron Hallmark and

Ian Pickup (Birmingham: Birmingham Modern Languages Publications, 1991), and I am grateful for permission to re-work some of that material here.

MARY BRYDEN

List of Abbreviations and Editions Cited

Throughout this study, quotations from Beckett's works are given in the language of the original composition. Where the translation is referred to, indication is given in the text.

Works of Beckett

ASWT	*As the Story Was Told* (London: John Calder, 1990)
BT	*The Beckett Trilogy* (London: Picador, 1979)
CC	*Comment C'est* (Paris: Editions de Minuit, 1961)
CO	*Compagnie* (Paris: Editions de Minuit, 1985)
CP	*Collected Poems 1930–1978* (London: John Calder, 1984)
CSPL	*Collected Shorter Plays* (London: Faber & Faber, 1984)
CSPR	*Collected Shorter Prose 1945–1980* (London: John Calder, 1986)
DBVJ	*Dante...Bruno. Vico.. Joyce*, in *Disjecta*, ed. Ruby Cohn (London: John Calder, 1983)
DFMW	*Dream of Fair to Middling Women* (London: Calder Publications, 1993)
EAG	*En attendant Godot* (London: Harrap, 1966)
EG	*Endgame* (London: Faber, 1964)
E	*Eleutheria* (Paris: Editions de Minuit, 1995)
FP	*Fin de partie* (Paris: Editions de Minuit, 1957)
HD	*Happy Days/Oh les Beaux Jours*, bilingual edition ed. James Knowlson (London: Faber, 1978)
HI	*How It Is* (London: John Calder, 1964)
HW	Human Wishes, in *Disjecta*, ed. Ruby Cohn (London: John Calder, 1983)
LD	*Le Dépeupleur* (Paris: Editions de Minuit, 1970)
LI	*L'Innommable* (Paris: Editions de Minuit, 1953)
MAC	*Mercier and Camier* (London: Picador, 1988)
MC	*Mercier et Camier* (Paris: Editions de Minuit, 1970)
ML	*Molloy* (Paris: Editions de Minuit, 1951)
MM	*Malone meurt* (Paris: Editions de Minuit, 1951)
MP	*Murphy* (London: Picador, 1973)

MPTK   *More Pricks Than Kicks* (London: Calder & Boyars, 1970)
MVMD   *Mal Vu Mal Dit* (Paris: Editions de Minuit, 1981)
NO   *Nohow On* (London: John Calder, 1992)
NTPR   *Nouvelles et Textes pour rien* (Paris: Editions de Minuit, 1958)
P   *Proust, and Three Dialogues with Georges Duthuit* (London: John Calder, 1965)
PS   *Pas, suivi de Quatre Esquisses* (Paris: Editions de Minuit, 1978)
TM   *Têtes-Mortes* (Paris: Editions de Minuit, 1967)
TD   *[Proust, and] Three Dialogues with Georges Duthuit* (London: John Calder, 1965)
W   *Watt* (London: John Calder, 1976)
WFG   *Waiting for Godot* (London: John Calder, 1965)

Works by Other Authors

Note: All Bible quotations are from the King James Bible.

CONF   St Augustine, *Confessions*, trans. E.B. Pusey (London: J.M. Dent, 1907)
IMI   Thomas à Kempis, *The Imitation of Christ*, trans. E.M. Blaiklock (London: Hodder & Stoughton, 1979)
INF   Dante Alighieri, *The Divine Comedy: Inferno*, trans. Mark Musa (Harmondsworth: Penguin, 1984)
OSU   Ohio State University
PAR   Dante Alighieri, *The Divine Comedy: Paradise*, trans. Mark Musa (Harmondsworth: Penguin, 1986)
PUR   Dante Alighieri, *The Divine Comedy: Purgatory*, trans. Mark Musa (Harmondsworth: Penguin, 1985)
RUL   Reading University Library
TCD   Trinity College Dublin
UTA   University of Texas at Austin

Introduction

This study has grown out of a long-lasting fascination with the barbs, clouds, and dungheaps of Beckett's religious landscape. Its initial working title was simply 'Samuel Beckett and God'. I soon discarded this as unsatisfactory, since the particle 'and' seemed to suggest, deceptively, that it was linking two comparables, co-existents, or co-locutors. Eventually, I settled for 'Samuel Beckett and the Idea of God'. The two elements were now indeed co-existent. Even when repeatedly stamped upon, the *idea*, or hypothesis, of a Godhead keeps growing back in Beckett's texts. Sometimes, it is kept at bay, rooted out with anger or indifference. At other times – in texts such as *Comment C'est*, or *L'Innommable* – it clings like bindweed. After all, the Latin root of religion – *religare* – itself means 'to bind'. No wonder Estragon asks fearfully in *Waiting for Godot*: 'We're not tied?'

The focus of my analysis is primarily directed at Beckett's texts. Of Beckett's own religious positioning or non-positioning, 'evidence' (if such is ever conceivable, for anyone) is inconclusive. Faith, non-faith, and partial faith are organic matters. They may expand or recede at different stages in life; they may not necessarily ever pose themselves at all. Beckett's own statements on the matter – (those at least which are in the public domain) – tend towards the negative. In a 1935 letter to his friend Thomas MacGreevy, Beckett wrote of himself as one who has seemed 'never to have had the least faculty or disposition for the supernatural'.[1] Later, in 1961, he said something similar in an interview with Tom Driver: 'I have no religious feeling. Once I had a religious emotion. It was at my first Communion. No more'.[2]

This was also the man, however, who, in answer to a defence counsel question in 1937 (during the trial of his uncle) as to whether he was a Christian, Jew, or atheist, is reported by James Knowlson to have replied: 'None of the three'.[3] Moreover, when Charles Juliet enquired in 1977 whether or not he had been able to rid himself of the influence of religion, he replied enigmatically that this was the case 'dans mon comportement extérieur, sans doute.... Mais pour le reste...' [in my external behaviour, no doubt.... But as for the rest...].[4]

1

What is not made clear by the ellipses is whether a complete clearing away of all religious baggage is considered to be a desirable project, or not. On a literary level, Beckett continued to be responsive to the beauty of the King James Bible, its verses often throbbing below the surface of the Beckettian text, or being moulded or perverted to suit the author's purpose. What also emerges from Beckett's oeuvre is a familiarity with Christian belief and practice, and a wide knowledge of theological and spiritual writers. Early notebooks testify to his close and careful reading of St Augustine, of Thomas à Kempis, St John of the Cross, and others.

Yet the hypothesised God who emerges from Beckett's texts is one who is both cursed for his perverse absence and cursed for his surveillant presence. He is by turns dismissed, satirised, or ignored, but he, and his tortured son, are never definitively discarded. If God is not apprehended in the here-and-now, there is nevertheless a perceived need, a potential opening, for a salvific function which a Deity could fulfil. This might be compared with the concept of an anticipated *parousia*, the Final Coming of Christ, the climax of the redemptive process. Within Dante's *The Divine Comedy* – that text so thoroughly known and admired by Beckett – the *parousia* is (in accordance with much Patristic writing, and also with St Bernard, who leads the Pilgrim in the final stages of *Paradise*) the last component of the *triplex adventus*, or Threefold Coming of Christ. The First Coming – the historical Jesus-event – is also recognised intermittently within Beckett's texts. What is absent, however, is the central experience: the Second Advent, the daily communion with Christ within assenting individuals, signalled in Canto 8 of *Purgatory* by the descent of angels. It cannot be said that Beckett's people show much aptitude for religious faith as conventionally understood, but what they are never healed of is a faint hope/misgiving that, as Hamm puts it: 'We're not beginning to...to...mean something?'.

Throughout the book, I have tried to avoid dealing lengthily with issues already extensively treated within existing criticism. The first chapter of the book focuses upon Beckett's early essays and reviews. These justify treatment in their own right, partly because they are sometimes neglected, and partly because of my contention that the tastes and distastes they reveal demonstrate affinities between what Beckett is rejecting in art and literature on the one hand, and, on the other, what he is rejecting in organised religion.

Chapter 2 deals with Beckett's early fiction, and Chapter 3 with his drama and later fiction. Both chapters have a tripartite structure: Uses of the Bible; Priests, Prayers, and Popular Piety; Theology and Spirituality. The last two chapters of the book are overarching studies, not limited in span to any stage or genre of Beckett's output. Of these, Chapter 4 deals with the invasive forces of pain and cruelty (including the intertextual resource of Dante's *Inferno* and *Purgatory*), as they appear in Beckett's oeuvre. Chapter 5, in contrast, considers what mitigating elements are available to Beckett's people, including solitude and silence. It ends with some reflection upon the relevance of the mystical tradition within Beckett's writing. I considered calling these last two chapters 'Darkness' and 'Light', respectively. This idea was, however, soon abandoned as potentially misleading. Both darkness and light, and especially twilight, provide refuge or inspiration at different times within the Beckettian world. Darkness can by no means be allied with negativity (unless it is the desirable darkness of the *via negativa*). As the narrator says of Murphy's mind: 'It felt no issue between its light and dark, no need for its light to devour its dark. The need was now to be in the light, now in the half light, now in the dark. That was all' (*MP*, p. 63).

Following this Introduction, quotations from Beckett's work are given in French or English, depending upon the language of original composition of the text in question. Quotations from the translated text are only given for specific purposes. For instance, Beckett's works are quoted consistently in English in the 'Uses of the Bible' sections of Chapters 2 and 3, so as to allow their parallels with the King James Bible to emerge. In the case of French quotations from other authors (Weil, Bataille, Juliet, etc.), each extract is followed by a translation into English. These translations are my own.

At various stages of this study, Beckett's work is compared with, or differentiated from, a range of theological and spiritual sources. For example, it seemed to me that Jean Claude Bologne's analysis recommended itself for the purposes of this project. Considering himself to be an 'atheist mystic', Bologne defines mysticism not in relation to fervent and faith-filled transports, but as the 'expérience de mise en contact directe et inopinée avec une réalité qui dépasse nos perceptions habituelles, et qu'on peut ressentir selon le cas comme étant le vide ou l'infini' [experience of direct and unexpected contact with a reality which exceeds our customary perceptions, and which may be felt, as the case may be, as void or infinity].[5]

Bologne's definition of atheism is also an expansive one: 'Il s'agit pour moi d'un état (je constate que je n'ai pas la foi), et non d'une prise de position (je ne me prononce pas sur l'existence d'un dieu et n'ai aucune agressivité vis-à-vis de la foi). Si je considère que le mysticisme est athée, c'est dans la mesure où il se situe *en dehors* de Dieu, pour le croyant comme pour l'incroyant' [For me it is a matter of a state (for the record, I do not have faith), and not a statement of position (I do not pronounce upon the existence of a god and have no bone to pick with faith). If I consider that mysticism is atheistic, it is insofar as it situates itself *outside* God, for both believer and non-believer] (Bologne, p. 126).

Both of these careful but spacious definitions allow the reader to travel some distance along the exploratory path of Beckett and mysticism. Yet it must also be added that, just as Bologne embraces modes or states, rather than barricaded positions, Beckett's work must also in the last analysis be released from any over-insistent template. As Shira Wolosky rightly remarks: 'Beckett's work frequently invokes religious materials, but it resides within none of them'.[6] Indeed, as the French spiritual writer Simone Weil notes, in observations concerning 'Decreation' which are equally applicable to the Beckettian dynamic: 'Prendre le sentiment d'être chez soi dans l'exil. Etre enraciné dans l'absence de lieu. Se déraciner socialement et végétativement. S'exiler de toute patrie terrestre' [One must take into exile the feeling of being at home. Be rooted in the absence of place. Uproot oneself socially and vegetatively. Exile oneself from every earthly country].[7] If Beckett was in exile from heaven, he was also in exile on earth. He was, as one of his 'mirlitonnades' proposes, 'chez soi sans soi' (*CP*, p. 72). His home was in the border country.

1
Writing on Writing

to and fro in shadow from inner to outer shadow
from impenetrable self to impenetrable unself by way of neither
(from Samuel Beckett, 'Neither' [*ASWT*, p. 108]).

When the distinguished American composer, Morton Feldman, was preparing to write an opera based upon Beckett's short text 'Neither',[1] he felt the need to find out more about the author of those lines, before embarking on the project. Since it was impractical to re-meet Beckett, he set about reading his early essay, *Proust*. The text did yield the kind of experience which Feldman sought. He said later in an interview: 'It told me a lot about him'.[2]

It may be wondered why *Proust* was chosen for this purpose, rather than Beckett's fiction, drama, or poetry. Admittedly, the text does close with some revelatory remarks upon music, and more specifically upon opera. Yet they occupy only a very small proportion of the whole text, which is an extended engagement with other overarching preoccupations to be found in Proust's writing, including Time, Habit, Love and Memory.

I would suggest that (consonant with Feldman's perception), Beckett's early essays on, and reviews of, the writing of others do provide privileged insights into the evolving viewpoints which were to underlie some of his later fictional writing, including his attitudes towards the hypothesis of God, and towards organised religion. I would also suggest that, contrary to the view famously propounded by Matthew Arnold – that the function of literary criticism is 'to see the object as in itself it really is',[3] – the factor of *selection* speaks (more voluminously than volumes) of the seer, in equal measure to the seen.

Of course, reviewers do not always initiate their review project or choice of review text. (Beckett's early review of Leishman's translation of Rilke for *Criterion*, for example, may well have been T. S. Eliot's choice of text rather than his own).[4] However, even if this is the case, the selection of those elements of the focus text to be considered and commented upon is itself significant. Reviews are by their nature gregarious (they josh, and rub shoulders with, other reviews of the same text) and impressionistic (they are seen through particular eyes). They might also be said to be temporally mobile, and at least partially retrospective. They re-view (Lat: *revidere*); they reflect back upon a reading previously undertaken one or several times before. To that extent, they are at an interface where 'the object as in itself it really is' negotiates with 'the object as in itself it really *was*'. As Beckett writes tellingly in *Proust*: 'The observer infects the observed with his own mobility' (*P*, p. 17). Perhaps Beckett would even have accorded in this respect with the view of Giambattista Vico (to whom he had already devoted disproportionate attention in his essay *Dante...Bruno.Vico..Joyce*) that memory 'infects' those other spheres of creativity – imagination and invention – which are often regarded as autonomous: 'Memory thus has three different aspects: memory when it remembers things, imagination when it alters or imitates them, and invention when it gives them a new turn or puts them into proper arrangement and relationship'.[5]

For all these reasons, it is difficult to see how reviews can be considered to be objective, definitive, or fully comprehensive. Thus, their constitution in itself contains indications of the critical assumptions of their propagator. It is evident that differing degrees of self-revelation are to be found on the part of reviewers. Some reviewers lean towards self-anatomisation. They lay out on the critical table their own recognised prejudices and mind-machinery. In the case of others, these parameters can only be deduced.

In his early critical writing, Beckett rarely addresses theological or religious issues lengthily or even explicitly. Moreover, when he does, it tends to be in a non-systematic, tangential manner. Yet his remarks, however throwaway, rarely succeed in throwing away their content or import. The result is that, the more one reads these passages and their subtexts, the more one begins to discern recurrent perceptions and concerns which have a bearing upon Beckett's uneasy relationship with religious practice and belief systems. These all contribute to an impression that what Beckett is rejecting in 'art', in its widest sense, is very similar to what he is also rejecting in organised religion.

Clearly, one should not overestimate the importance of Beckett's self-positioning in matters of religious belief, at the expense of other burgeoning concerns in the mind of a developing writer. A weighty theological agenda should not be supposed on the basis of a glancing reference. Yet that glance should not be dismissed, on the part of a writer who opined in his review of his devout friend Thomas MacGreevy's *Poems* that: 'Prayer is no more (no less) than an act of recognition. A nod, even a wink. The flag dipped in Ave, not hauled down in Miserere'.[6] In this he concurs with the French writer, Simone Weil, who writes that: 'Il devrait être reconnu publiquement, officiellement, que la religion ne consiste pas en autre chose qu'en un regard' [It should be publicly and officially recognised that religion is nothing more than a glance].[7]

In what follows, I have tried to distinguish, in Beckett's treatment of other writers, certain patterns of thought and reaction which have significance in the religious domain. The focus here – inevitably a selective one, when considering a writer who read so widely – is not so much upon theologians as upon those writers and artists with whose work Beckett was familiar.

* * *

For Beckett in the early years, not yet launched upon a publicly recognised literary career, a posture of scepticism or refusal seems to have offered as good a starting-point as any. The development and sharpening of critical faculties requires, after all, a recognition of what must be rejected as well as of what is to be welcomed and acclaimed. As the sage Imlac states in Johnson's *The History of Rasselas* – from which text Beckett copies out extracts in his 'Whoroscope' notebook from the 1930s[8] – 'I soon found that no man was ever great by imitation'.[9]

It is clear from the above-quoted remark concerning the notion of prayer as an 'act of recognition' that Beckett saw no difficulty in bringing together the domains of art and religion in certain respects. Indeed, the alignment is pursued repeatedly throughout the MacGreevy review, which begins: 'All poetry, as discriminated from the various paradigms of prosody, is prayer' ('Humanistic Quietism', p. 68). Beckett was to pursue the same idea in a letter to MacGreevy in 1935, where he refers to 'the depths where demand and supply coincide, and the prayer is the god. Yes, prayer rather than poem, in order to be quite clear, because poems are prayers, of Dives and Lazarus one flesh'.[10]

The comparison with Dives and Lazarus is at first startling, for these two names are, on one level, synonymous with two radically opposing identities. The parable – which, of the four Gospels, occurs only in Luke – concerns the poor man (Lazarus) and the rich man (Dives). Lazarus, needy and sore-infested, lies waiting for food-scraps from the richly-laden table of Dives. The latter, showily dressed and self-absorbed, ignores the destitute man at his gate. When Lazarus dies and goes to heaven, the roles are reversed. Dives, assigned to Hades, petitions Abraham for Lazarus to be sent with cooling water on the tip of his finger for Dives to lick. His request is refused. The realisation has come too late; Dives has persisted for too long in his obliviousness.

There is an urgency about this parable, with its chilling conclusion, and Beckett seems to have been especially drawn to it. Later, in *Murphy*, Neary plunders the parable in order to describe the torment of unrequited desire: ' "The love that lifts up its eyes", said Neary, "being in torment; that craves for the tip of her little finger, dipped in lacquer, to cool its tongue – is foreign to you, Murphy, I take it" ' (*MP*, p. 7). The comparison is more explicitly re-visited later: 'Then Neary met Miss Counihan, in the month of March, ever since when his relation towards her had been that post-mortem of Dives to Lazarus, except that there was no Father Abraham to put in a good word for him' (*MP*, p. 31).

In the 'Whoroscope' notebook, Beckett copies out twice, first in French and then in Italian, that part of the account (beginning 'Father Abraham' and constituting Luke 16: 24–6) which deals with the appeal of Dives and its subsequent rejection by Abraham. He prefaces the copied passage with a note that it constitutes a 'prayer from virtual to actual in entelechy'. The reference to 'entelechy' (the Aristotelian term to denote the perfect fulfilment of a function) seems to connect with an acknowledgement by Beckett of an irrevocable reversal. While on earth, Dives could have recognised his common humanity with Lazarus, and reduced the gulf between them by almsgiving. To that extent, the gulf was only 'virtual', or existential. Now in Hades, further choices are unavailable. The gulf, as Abraham confirms, is 'fixed' (Luke 16: 26). It is 'actual', or essential. (Beckett makes another glancing reference to the parable in his translation of *Textes pour rien V*, where it is stated that: 'Between them [the sky and earth] where the hero stands a great gulf is fixed' [*CSPR*, p. 86].)

Thus, the parable illustrates both an inversion and a progression. Fortunes are switched, but temporality gives way to infinity. On one level, there is satisfaction to be drawn; justice for the poor has been achieved. On another level, some grudging sympathy might be elicited for Dives in the throes of his eternal punishment. Not only has his sin been that of omission rather than commission, but he also makes a (fruitless) appeal on behalf of his brothers still on earth. In a review of poetry by Denis Devlin, Beckett terms the parable a 'conte cruel' [cruel story].[11] His perception of cruelty presumably derives from an apprehension of apparently disproportionate suffering allotted to Dives.

At the heart of this parable is what it promotes as a salutary contrast: between undeserved suffering for Lazarus – (although the circumstances leading to his destitution are not detailed) – and deserved suffering (or, otherwise put, punishment) for Dives. Nevertheless, as well as a contrast, it enshrines a parallel: both men have to endure the experience not only of suffering, but of indifference on the part of others (respectively, Dives to Lazarus, and Abraham to Dives) to their suffering. On this level, the *experience* of their suffering is not only closely allied, but is inextricably intertwined. It is this interdependency which fascinates Beckett, and, in drawing attention to the 'one flesh' of Dives and Lazarus (as he does in the letter to MacGreevy), he signals his attachment to the paradox of shared but solitary misfortune. In the later review of Devlin's poetry, he explicates this further: 'The Dives–Lazarus symbiosis, as intimate as that of fungoid and algoid in lichen (to adopt the Concise New Oxford Dictionary example). Here scabs, lucre, etc., there torment, bosom, etc., but both here and there *gulf*. The absurdity, here or there, of either without the other, the inaccessible other. In death they did not cease to be divided. Who predeceased? A painful period for both' ('Intercessions', p. 92).

This concern with 'gulfs', in states or fortunes which in other respects have much in common, provided a continuing preoccupation for Beckett. It is evinced in his careful copying into the 'Whoroscope' notebook, from the *Pensées*, of Pascal's insertion of infinite space between body, mind, and (divine) love (elements which, in other theological contexts, are presented as intimately enmeshed): 'La distance infinie des corps aux esprits figure la distance *infiniment plus infinie* [Beckett's underlining] des esprits à la charité: car elle est surnaturelle' [The infinite distance between bodies and minds represents the *infinitely more infinite* distance between minds and charity: for the latter is supernatural].[12] 'Charity' here denotes the dual Christian requirement of love of God and love of one's neighbour, and is thus relevant to what Beckett terms 'the Dives–Lazarus symbiosis'. He was to explore a similar theme in *Fin de partie*, when Hamm tells his story of being approached by a starving man, and of asking him about 'la situation à Kov, de l'autre côté du détroit' (*FP*, p. 72). The equivalent in the English translation is 'the situation at Kov, beyond the gulf' (*EG*, p. 36). The first-person narrator, secure in his possession of tobacco and granaries, interacts callously with the man who petitions him on behalf of himself and his son. Concluding his story, Hamm recommends: 'Prions Dieu' (*FP*, p. 75). The prayer is as unproductive as that of Dives, for Hamm subsequently reports the prayer dividend as having been 'bernique' (*FP*, p. 76).

When Beckett writes, then, that 'poems are prayers, of Dives and Lazarus one flesh', he is recognising on the one hand the circumstantial and qualitative differences between poems and prayers, but on the other hand their consubstantiality, their rootedness in a very similar dynamic. In Beckett's terms, prayer has to do with a glimpse, or a vision, akin to that available in poetry (just as Words, in the later play *Words and Music*, will adopt a 'poetic tone' to try to sing of the place where there is 'one glimpse / Of that wellhead') (*CSPL*, p. 133). What Beckett appears to reject, in both religion and art, is the idea of artifice or fabrication: Hamm's enforced prayer meeting, for example, or the 'cut-and-dried sanctity and loveliness' which Beckett, in a review of 'Recent Irish Poetry', attributes to those mainstream poets whom he terms 'our leading twilighters'.[13] Rather, both prayer and poetry should in Beckett's terms spark from that 'act of recognition' which stems from self-recognition.

Such self-awareness is for Beckett the only possible starting-point for art, as it was for Paul Valéry, who, in a preface to his *Monsieur Teste* (a work referred to by Beckett in his review of Leishman's translation of Rilke[14]), describes how a lengthy period of abstention from writing resulted from a felt need to privilege input over output (thus proving, he adds mischievously, that 'la théologie se retrouve un peu partout' [theology gets everywhere]).[15] Desirous of sidelining a preoccupation with the effect of his works upon others, he decided that the priority was 'de me connaître et reconnaître tel que j'étais, sans omissions, sans simulations, ni complaisances' [to know and recognise myself as I really was, without omissions, pretence, or compromise] (*Monsieur Teste*, pp. 8–9). A similar insight is manifested by Sir Philip Sidney, whose *Astrophel and Stella* is referred to by Beckett (together with Dante's *Vita Nuova* and Petrarch's *On the Death of Laura*) as one of 'the great publican poems' ('Humanistic Quietism', p. 68). In the first sonnet of that collection, the first-person narrator describes the writer's block which ensued when he tried to commit to words 'the blackest face of woe'. Release comes when he realises that the remedy lies not without, but within himself. The perception is encapsulated in a memorable last line: 'Foole, said my Muse to me, looke in thy heart and write'.[16]

In characterising Sidney's *Astrophel and Stella* as one of the great 'publican poems', Beckett is contrasting it with what he posits as 'the great pharisee poems' ('Humanistic Quietism', p. 68), under which heading he includes Goethe's 'Prometheus' and Carducci's 'Satan'.[17] Again, then, Beckett accesses a religious frame of reference – here, the parable of the Pharisee and the Publican in the New Testament – in order to make an aesthetic distinction. In bringing his categories into collocation by coining the formula of 'the publican's whinge and the pharisee's tarantara', Beckett is evoking on the one hand the deeply unpopular petty tax-collectors – (the relevant Greek word is translated variously as 'tax collector' or 'publican') – who yet could gain an insight into their own neediness, and, on the other, the self-appointed pillars of religious observance of a deliberately visible kind. Although comparisons between these groups are constantly drawn throughout the four Gospels, they emerge most clearly in the episode described in Luke 18: 9–14, when a publican and a pharisee both go to the Temple to pray. Whereas the pharisee proceeds to read the roll-call of his own upright conduct, the publican simply prays: 'God be merciful to me a sinner'. This aspiration – ironised by Beckett as a 'whinge' – is thus emphatically differentiated from the pharisee's 'tarantara' (evocative of the custom some pharisees had, when almsgiving, of having a trumpet sounded ahead of their approach, as described in Matthew 6: 2).

On the face of it, the application of this categorisation is somewhat curious. Given the prevalent biblical alignment of pharisaism with an excessive concern for the outward display of faith, it is difficult to reconcile that image of hypocrisy with, for example, the pure and stark demonic impulse of Carducci's hymn to Satan:[18]

Via l'aspersorio	Priest, chanting and sprinkling
Prete, e il tuo metro!	No succour shall find thee,
No, prete, Satana	For never shall Satan
Non torna in dietro!	Get him behind thee.

Yet, coming hard on the heels of Beckett's assertion that 'all poetry [...] is prayer', the publican/pharisee opposition emerges as a broad-based contrast between inner and outer, between insecurity and bold certainty. Of the two groups, it is only the publicans who remain accessible to doubt and self-scrutiny, within the biblical context. (They are tax collectors in favour of self-assessment). Beckett makes clear that both tendencies – the publican's miserere and the pharisee's 'tarantara' – may be productive of competent poetry. As with the Lucan contrast, the balance tips towards the publican, for he, after all, begins with himself, and not with externals. Yet the characterisation of his humility as 'whinge' enables Beckett to gravitate towards a middle ground between abasement and posturing. Hence, in the second paragraph, he is able to usher MacGreevy onto pre-prepared ground, for: 'It is with neither of these extremes that we have to do here' ('Humanistic Quietism', p. 68).

To MacGreevy Beckett attributes 'the grace of humility' of a kind that is not abasement or lowliness, for it is linked to a 'mind that has *raised itself* to that grace' (p. 68 [my italics]). Thus equipped with this self-enlightening humility, the poet, participating in 'the adult mode of prayer', is enabled to produce poems which are, in Beckett's unusually lyrical ascription, 'kindled to a radiance without counterpart in the work of contemporary poets writing in English' (p. 68). He goes on to quote, significantly, the opening lines of MacGreevy's poem 'Seventh Gift of the Holy Ghost': 'The end of love, / Love's ultimate good, / Is the end of love ... and / Light' (p. 69). He could equally well have quoted that poem's middle line, the lengthiest, which sets out an upward-tilted perspective of space and radiance: 'In a vast, high, light-beaten plain'.[19] The unexplicated Seventh Gift of the Holy Ghost is the quaintly-termed 'Divine Awfulness' (or fear of the Lord). Awe is, by its nature, contemplative. It incorporates that humility which (in the Beckettian understanding) is about lucidity rather than self-flagellation. Its status as the seventh gift (seven being, from ancient times and in many traditions, the figure denoting perfection or completion) endows it with a culminatory status. It is a perfect attitude of waiting, of receptivity and vulnerability. It is the gift of the publican. As such, it contrasts with the Sixth Gift of the Holy Ghost – that of righteousness, the territory commandeered by the pharisee.

Beckett accordingly goes on within the review to diagnose MacGreevy's poetry as springing from a 'nucleus of endopsychic clarity, uttering itself in the prayer that is a spasm of awareness' ('Humanistic Quietism', p. 69). He discerns those same pulses of self-awareness in Denis Devlin's poetry, which he deems to begin 'with himself on behalf of himself' ('Intercessions', p. 91), resulting in such lines – praised highly, almost gushingly, by Beckett – as: 'Till the forgotten matutinal colours flame / Various the rosewindows through...' (p. 93).

If any 'light of faith' be deemed conceivable for Beckett, it is not the clear and steady doctrinal light of Thomism, but the filtered radiance or naked spark of a MacGreevy or a Devlin. Here is to be found the 'self-absorption into light' which Beckett deems to be 'the adult mode of prayer' ('Humanistic Quietism', pp. 69; 68). This, in Beckett's mind, is in direct contrast to that critical stance which privileges clarity, to the extent that it dismisses 'as understatement anything and everything between brilliance and murk' (p. 68). Thus, to Devlin's 'priest uncertain among his mysteries when a bending candle-flame provokes forbidden images',[20] Beckett opposes that other aesthetic instinct which resorts to the 'solution clapped on problem like a snuffer on a candle' ('Intercessions', p. 92). Moreover, it is in the same Devlin review that Beckett sets out his oft-quoted perception that: 'Art has nothing to do with clarity, does not dabble in the clear and does not make clear [...]. Art is the sun, moon and stars of the mind, the whole mind' (p. 94). It is 'pure interrogation' (p. 91). As Giambattista Vico states in a complementary insight (which is explored by Beckett in *Dante... Bruno. Vico.. Joyce*[21]), poetry is to be distinguished from metaphysics in that it is concerned not with universals but with particulars, since 'the poetic faculty must submerge the whole mind in the senses' (*The New Science*, p. 314).

A poet, then, should be primarily concerned with asking questions rather than supplying answers, with demonstrating self-awareness rather than mastery. To that extent, Beckett would express the poetic aim in rather different terms from those used by Brian Coffey, in his Introduction to Devlin's poetry: 'Mastery of language is one abiding aim of the poet. Denis Devlin became a master of language' (*Collected Poems*, p. xiv). For Beckett, mastery is no more realisable a goal for the artist than is that of total possession of the beloved for the lover, for 'total possession [is] only to be achieved by the complete identification of object and subject' (*P*, p. 57).

In thus rejecting any professed designs upon 'clarity', Beckett is rejecting all modes of pronouncement and dogma. In this connection, he jots down in the 'Whoroscope' notebook – a treasury of, amongst other things, words and phrases which captured his attention – the French word 'stultologie' [the science of stultification], with a note that the word was applied by St Bernard of Clairvaux, at the Council of Sens, to the theology of Peter Abelard. Interestingly, it was Bernard who countered Abelard's powerfully intellectual recourse to reason and dialectic with the perception that prayer and knowledge of God must begin with self-knowledge. Nevertheless, it is unlikely that Beckett would have warmed to the penchant of the 'Mellifluous Doctor' for loquacious self-distancing from intellectual rivals.[22] In this he exemplifies the religious contentiousness of Milton, whom Beckett dismisses as a 'beastly bigot' in that essay on Ezra Pound which bears the splendidly punning title of 'Ex Cathezra'[23] – (a case, perhaps, of an irresistible title rather than a totally apt one, since Beckett characterises Pound as not so much dogmatic as 'galvanic' [p. 79]).

Thus, if (as Beckett asserts in the opening words of his essay *Dante... Bruno.Vico.. Joyce*), 'the danger is in the neatness of identifications' (*DBVJ*, p. 19), then his preferred aesthetic begins to emerge as one in which an impulse tends to be preferred to a system, a need to a statement, a cry to a promulgation. Of course, the undermining of one system may simply lead to the installation of another. For example, it may be argued that, in levering aside Descartes's machinery of physics, metaphysics, and theology, Vico simply imposed another tripartite grid – notably, the taxonomy based upon divine, heroic, and human – in its place (a characteristic to which Beckett, surprisingly, does not advert in his exposition of Dante's obsession with the number 3 at the close of the essay [*DBVJ*, p. 32]). Similarly, though Beckett tries in these early essays to strip away the 'stultology', to expose the bare bones of the artistic project, he sometimes undermines his own case by adopting a tone of self-righteousness or of impenetrable intellectualism. Though the careful sophistication of his analysis can often delight, and well repay the reader who has staying-power, the raw edge of Beckett's sensitivities is sometimes most memorably communicated in the simpler among his formulae. And, if Pontius Pilate could ask: 'What is truth?' (John 18: 38), Beckett has a ripe reply: 'La vérité? Le pet du plus grand nombre' [Truth? The fart of the majority].[24]

What Beckett does try to cling to consistently, throughout the vagaries of his exposition, is the rejection of notions of certitude and mastery, and the embrace of that 'adult mode of prayer' which is able to contemplate inhabiting a paradoxical zone of permanent transition. To do this involves – to use that recurrent image for Beckett – diving from the safety and solidity of the rocks into a moving and murky sea. What lies below is certainly unknown, possibly unknowable, and probably unignorable. Beckett was no doubt less impressed by physical manifestations of religious belief than by its inner dimension. Interestingly, he copies into his 'Whoroscope' notebook a quotation (in French) from the Book of Deuteronomy which extends circumcision beyond the foreskin (physical) to the heart (spiritual). Pascal also explores this theme in the *Pensées*, and this is probably why the passage appears in French in Beckett's notebook: 'Circoncisez donc la prépuce de votre coeur, et ne raidissez plus votre cou (Deutéronome X, 16)' [Circumcise therefore the foreskin of your heart, and do not be obstinate any longer]. Similarly, although no doubt alienated by the liturgical 'bells and smells' of Catholicism, Beckett could nevertheless state that: 'Irish Catholicism is not attractive, but it is deeper [than Protestantism]'.[25] Thus, art and religion have in common that, in both cases, 'the only possible spiritual development is in the sense of depth' (*P*, p. 64). Moreover, the 'sense of depth' is inextricably linked to that mobile image of choppy seas: it is a current (not a deposit) account. That deposit of faith which finds its expression on the surface, upon 'our carapace of paste and pewter' (*P*, p. 31) is therefore to be eschewed, together with the gestures and rituals which accompany it.

Accordingly, in his review of Rilke's poems, Beckett compares Rilke's Malte Laurids Brigge unfavourably with Valéry's Edmond Teste, on the grounds that Brigge was 'a kind of deficient Edmond Teste, [...] a Teste who had not "tué la marionnette"' ('*Poems*', p. 66). Valéry's eponymous Monsieur Teste is indeed referred to as a man of glass, a man whose limpidity of spirit derives from his having descended deeply into the depths of himself. Accredited with such thoughts as: 'Tu es plein de secrets que tu appelles Moi. Tu es voix de ton inconnu' [You are full of secrets you call Me. You are the voice of your unknown] (*Monsieur Teste*, p. 119), Teste is said to have 'tué la marionnette' (p. 18). He has 'killed the puppet' not only physically – he never waves his arms, puppet-like, when conversing – but also in every other domain of his life and behaviour. The puppet of nobody, Teste does not indulge in superficial politeness, for: 'Il ne souriait pas, ne disait ni bonjour ni bonsoir' [He neither smiled, nor said 'good day' or 'good evening']. Referred to by his wife as a 'mystique sans dieu' [a godless mystic] (p. 50), Teste is never happier than when plunging deeply into the seas of his own interiority.

Hence, for Beckett, Brigge is a 'deficient Edmond Teste' in that, sometimes at sea in these inner seas, he is constantly 'obliged to rise, for the purpose of breathing, at frequent intervals to the surface' ('*Poems*', p. 66). He is, Beckett seems to be saying, like a Teste in reverse: not so much diving for treasures below, as cushioning himself with the baggage acquired from his necessary forays to the world of externals.

This is not to say that Beckett is privileging a realm of ethereality, a kind of poeticised Manichaeanism in which the spiritual lords it over the physical within the artistic domain. On the contrary, Beckett liked his 'real' to be real. Despite reservations about the poetry of F.R. Higgins, Beckett did detect the Irish countryside in it. Not without irony, he acknowledged in it 'a good smell of dung, most refreshing' ('Recent Irish Poetry', p. 73). The 'reality' he seems to have responded to best in art was not a photographic or representational one, nor a symbolic one, but rather one which provided a direct encounter with shape, colour, stillness or fluidity, without the mediating filters of 'theme', theory or theology. Thus, his taste in crucifixion paintings was always for those in which Christ's objectification, his manliness and physicality, were apparent, rather than those which, foregrounding an evangelical sub-text, either emphasised the soteriological import of this bloody drama, or transformed victim into victor. This is suffering – actual, not pretended (and thus, incidentally, theologically sound) – but still at a remove, like that striking line from Devlin's *Intercessions*: 'My blood sounds like a scream in the distance' (*Collected Poems*, p. 101).

It is indeed in these terms that Beckett writes to MacGreevy of his repeated visits to see the Perugino Pietà which had just arrived at the National Gallery of Ireland. Ignoring its invitation to empathetic devotion at the sight of grieving mother and dead son, he writes of 'the lovely cheery Xist [Christ] full of sperm, and the woman touching his thighs'.[26] Further, what he discerns and admires in the clown-Christs of Rouault's paintings is precisely their 'choseté', their 'thingness', a characteristic which enables Beckett to link the Rouault Christs with Matisse's apples or Kandinsky's blocks of red.[27]

Such art has no truck with what Beckett elsewhere terms 'the grotesque fallacy of a realistic art' (*P*, p. 76). It makes no claim to incarnate the invisible – (Beckett's chief grievance against opera, which has figural designs upon music [*P*, p. 92]). Instead, in a space beyond guilt, imaginative empathy, and breast-beating, it simply exists, as did Bram van Velde's art for Beckett: 'Balayés les repentirs. Peinture de vie et de mort. Amateurs de natron, abstenez' [Repentance swept aside. Painting life and death. Those keen on mummification should abstain].[28]

Thus, the kind of art favoured by Beckett is that which does not cater for preservation or consummation. Rather, it is always provisional, always in transit. Again, this rejection of stagnation in art is reflected in Beckett's conception of the religious, for Beckett refers in *Proust* to 'a religious experience in the only intelligible sense of that epithet, at once an assumption and an annunciation' (*P*, p. 69). It is striking that Beckett should have chosen to exemplify the 'religious' by reference to two items – the first devotional, the second biblical – drawn from Marian piety. Both are kept as feast days within the Catholic Church. The annunciation constitutes the episode described in Luke 1: 26–38, when the heavenly visitor Gabriel announces to the Virgin Mary that she is to conceive a child. The annunciation is therefore an event associated with new life. The assumption, on the other hand, moves forward to the close of Mary's life, when tradition has it that she was translated body and soul into heaven, rather than being subject to the corruption of the grave.

Although not biblically-based (since the manner of Mary's life after her son's crucifixion is not detailed in the Gospels), evidence of belief in the assumption of Mary began to appear as early as the fifth century. For many centuries it was regarded as a tradition rather than a doctrine, and, interestingly, at the time when Beckett's *Proust* was written, it still retained this unratified status (even though it had constituted one of the solemn 'mysteries' of the rosary for many hundreds of years). Only in 1950, after widespread petitions from the faithful, was the tradition declared by Papal bull to be an article of faith.

Clearly, in citing these two feasts, Beckett is not participating in the cult of Mary. Given his lifelong interest in art, he was undoubtedly familiar with many depictions of those events in religious iconography.[29] Nevertheless, in associating them with 'the only intelligible sense' of the adjective 'religious', he is responding to them in a particularly attentive way. This derives, I would suggest, from his perception of them as moments of movement, intensity, transition. On the one hand, they centre around that interpenetration of life and death – the conception of Christ, the close of his mother's life – which is a feature of so much of Beckett's

writing. (He wrote in *Dante...Bruno.Vico..Joyce* of 'the consciousness that there is a great deal of the unborn infant in the lifeless
octogenarian' [*DBV*], p. 22]). In addition, the annunciation and the
assumption both constitute moments charged with suspense and
possibility. Luke's account of the annunciation implies that Mary's
consent is required. Accordingly, if her 'fiat' enabled the Incarnation, presumably her non-compliance would have averted it. More
importantly still, the annunciation and the assumption both involve
a temporary mingling of heaven and earth, divine and human
(symbolised in many religious paintings by the presence of angel
intermediaries). The assumption in particular, by virtue of its emphasis upon continuation rather than transformation, achieves
some kind of symbiosis between earthly life and life eternal.

It is significant, then, that Beckett should choose to endow an
early short story (published in 1929) with the title 'Assumption',
and, although this chapter is primarily concerned with Beckett's
reactions to other writers, it is apposite to consider it here. In the
story there is indeed an assumption, a kind of mysterious interface
between human and divine. In this case, the mystical experience
appears to be both closely allied to the sexual, and inimical to it. The
male central figure, fascinated by a woman in a green felt hat,[30]
nevertheless feels that each ecstatic encounter with the woman
drains away something of himself that 'he could not spare'.[31] Thus
he goes through repeated, debilitating cycles: troubled all day with
thoughts of her, 'only relaxing with twilight [another transitional
time], to listen for her coming' (p. 271), and then 'spent with ec-
stasy, torn by the bitter loathing of that which he had condemned to
the humanity of silence'.

The man's ecstatic release is said to occur when he is 'uncondi-
tioned by the Satanic, dimensional Trinity'. The notorious tension
which has long been associated with theological explanations of the
Trinity derives from the difficulty of communicating the idea of
three-in-one, or separate-in-same. Despite the overarching concept
of one Godhead – and, thus, Trinity rather than Tritheism – the
identification of three 'persons' inevitably suggests three person-
occupied spaces; it renders it 'dimensional'. The man's release,
however, which sounds like a robust sexual orgasm – 'a timeless
parenthesis' – is described as 'the blue flower, Vega, GOD'. Thus,
the trinity of dimension is replaced by a movement through intensities, which may themselves be seen as building up from desire
to culmination, and from singularity to plurality (1–3). First is the

blue flower (unitary symbol of romantic longing); then Vega (the white binary star, fifth brightest in the firmament, and made up of two stars revolving in different orbits around one another). (In his poem 'Vega', Lawrence Durrell also ascribes a mystical quality to Vega, referring to it as 'a candle burning high in the alps of heaven'[32]). The final element is a definitively upper-case GOD (the threefold community-of-persons, but also, in Beckett's rendering of Giordano Bruno, 'the universal monad, Monad of monads' [DBV], p. 21]).

The central figure in 'Assumption' very rarely manages to transcend the compartments which structure his self-evaluation and identity. Instead, he remains wrenched and tossed to and fro. In some kind of echoing of the Christ-event, he becomes an ever-renewed sacrifice: 'Thus each night he died and was God, each night revived and was torn' ('Assumption', p. 271). But, whereas the Christ-commemoration is infinite in duration, the man's tortured accommodation to his cyclical existence leads in the final paragraph of the story to his demise in a crescendo of sound, drowning in his own pulsing cry. He had dreamed, in what are perhaps the most memorable lines in a rather intractable story, of being 'irretrievably engulfed in the light of eternity, one with the birdless cloudless colourless skies, in infinite fulfilment'.[33] Yet the calmness of that mystical vision is displaced by the frenzy of the final paragraph and by the image of the 'wild dead hair' ('Assumption', p. 271) with which the story ends.

In the later novel Murphy, the central male character will also die explosively. By then, however, Beckett's absorption of Geulincx's Ethics will have contributed to a presentational change, in which the split which yawns at Murphy's core is allied to mind/body, or the world in re rather than the world in intellectu. At this point, the mystical referent can be sidestepped.

In his early reviews and articles, however, Beckett remains preoccupied with the interrelatedness and yet separateness of divine and human, transcendent and immanent. This inevitably encompasses the complex notion of Providence. Although, in the strict sense, 'providence' refers (Latin providentia) to God's foresight of events, the term has spilled forward into the domain of God's action and ongoing involvement. Moreover, when exemplified within biblical texts, this involvement may itself be understood on various levels, including creative action (Genesis), sustaining action (God accompanying human activity at all times, and not just at moments of crisis), and specific action (speaking to humanity through prophets, for example).

The controversial domain of miracles is also relevant, since the term 'miracle' attaches to a perception of a divine altering of natural events to achieve a goal or to strengthen faith. Many modern theologians, informed by evolving understandings of physics and of causality, have expressed uneasiness about the notion of miracle, relying as it does upon the idea of an interventionist God who upturns natural laws from time to time. Beckett appears to share this misgiving. Indeed, he copies out in his 'Whoroscope' notebook a remark of Pascal on the subject. After paraphrasing in English Pascal's contention that the age of miracles is over – 'Miracles necessary for accomplishment of prophecies (conversion of nations) no longer necessary' – Beckett cites, in French, Pascal's reasoning: 'car les prophéties accomplies sont un miracle subsistant' [for realised prophecies are an abiding miracle] (see *Pensées*, fragment 180, p. 110). A very similar perception occurs in the section on Prophecies (fragment 335, p. 163): 'La plus grande des preuves de J.-C. sont les prophéties. C'est à quoi Dieu a le plus pourvu; car l'événement qui les a remplies est un miracle subsistant' [The greatest proof of Jesus Christ is the prophecies. This is what God has above all provided for, for the event which fulfilled them is an abiding miracle]. Pascal's prudent treatment of miracles – not as one-off wonders, but as durable signs – is carried further towards scepticism on the next page of the 'Whoroscope' notebook, when Beckett notes from Spinoza's *Tractatus Theologico-Politicus* the view that: 'La réalité d'un seul miracle serait une irréfutable démonstration de l'athéisme' [the reality of a single miracle would be an irrefutable demonstration of atheism], for, in Spinoza's terms, an infinite God would not need to disturb the logical order of being by the execution of miracles within a finite domain. As Spinoza opines elsewhere in the work: 'If anyone asserted that God acts in contravention to the laws of nature, he *ipso facto*, would be compelled to assert that God acted against His own nature – an evident absurdity'.[34]

Giambattista Vico's reading of Spinoza's *Tractatus Theologico-Politicus* did not, in Benedetto Croce's view, tilt him towards a reassessment of the Hebrew prophets. Nevertheless, Beckett is guilty of an over-simplification of Croce's nuanced and immensely careful analysis of Vico when he asserts in *Dante...Bruno.Vico..Joyce* that 'it pleases Croce to consider [Vico] a mystic, essentially speculative' (*DBVJ*, p. 19). He goes on to expostulate: 'Croce [...] absolves

[Vico] from the utilitarian preoccupations of Hobbes, Spinoza, Locke, Bayle and Machiavelli'. Croce maintains in an important chapter of his *The Philosophy of Giambattista Croce* that: 'The two chief representatives of utilitarianism in the seventeenth century, whom Vico always keeps in view, are Hobbes and Spinoza: but in addition to them, he refers to Locke and Bayle and, in the preceding century, Machiavelli'.[35] Admittedly, Croce does then proceed to analyse the ways in which, having taken cognizance of them, Vico forges a path which diverges from these thinkers. Further, as the analysis continues, he will observe that: 'Utilitarianism was [...] strongly repugnant to Vico's observed ethics' (p. 120). Yet Croce demonstrates nothing if not his awareness of the paradoxes inherent in Vico's writing. Moreover, his understanding of historico-cultural heterogeneity leads him to discern that, at least within the Italian context, historical justifications could be, and were, enlisted in the nineteenth century to support views of Vico as both 'the Platonist, the mystic of the unknowable God', and 'the Vico of the rationalists, [...] the European philosopher to be set side by side with Descartes and Spinoza, Kant and Hegel' (p. 275).

Beyond this somewhat peremptory dismissal of Croce, however, the significance of Beckett's remarks resides in his characterisation of Vico as 'a practical roundheaded Neapolitan' (*DBVJ*, p. 19). It is in this rationalist light that Beckett surveys Vico's handling of the notion of Providence. Again setting his face against the miraculous, Beckett contrasts Bossuet's conception of a 'transcendental and miraculous' Providence with that of Vico, which is 'immanent and the stuff itself of human life, working by natural means' (*DBVJ*, p. 22). Thus humanity is infused with the divine, but in a collective rather than an individual sense, a cyclical rather than a pantheistic sense, and a creative rather than a quietist sense, for: 'Humanity is at work in itself. God acts on her, but by means of her. Humanity is divine, but no man is divine' (*DBVJ*, p. 22). Indeed, in contrast with St Augustine's 'city of God', Vico is concerned with the earthly city, the 'city of the human race' (see *The New Science*, Book I, 'Establishment of Principles', p. 102), just as Thomas MacGreevy's poem 'De Civitate Hominum', written under the white, cold shadow of war, centres its gaze upon the spoiled stumps and bones of humanity.

What Beckett is responding to in Vico, it seems, is his cerebral and slightly detached analysis of divine providence. This complements his distrust, expressed in his Rilke review, of the easy and warm intercourse which appears to operate between the poetic 'Ich' of

Rilke, and God: 'Such a turmoil of self-deception and naif dis-
content gains nothing in dignity from that prime article of the
Rilkean faith, which provides for the interchangeability of Rilke and
God' ('*Poems*', p. 67). Where all space is removed between divine
and human, maintains Beckett, 'there is no position here, no possibility of a position, no faculty for one. He changes his ground
without ceasing'. In seeking 'position', Beckett is not exhibiting a
nostalgia for immobility and quietism, but, rather, a need to reserve
the possibility of a still centre, or vantage-point. This may be temporary, but must be amenable to sole occupancy, unjostled by
competing viewpoints. As he will later observe in his *Three Dialogues with Georges Duthuit*: 'What is the good of passing from one
untenable position to another, of seeking justification always on the
same plane?' (*TD*, p. 140).

A sometimes searing awareness of different or sundered planes is
for Beckett infinitely preferable to an artificial and reassuring
synthesis of them. Hence his distaste for the fluidity of the ich/Gott
relation in Rilke's poetry. Just as Pascal sees no difficulty in siting
the response to God within the realm of emotion rather than that of
rationality – 'C'est le coeur qui sent Dieu et non la raison' (*Pensées*,
fragment 424, p. 192) – Beckett privileges art which does not rely
upon the structured zones of rationality. Thus, he praises the
painting of Bram van Velde for resisting that kind of studied and
reasoned manipulation of the viewer which he terms 'peinture
raisonnée'. This is the kind of painting which justifies itself, which
postures, or which peddles enthymemes (syllogisms in which one
premiss is suppressed: a kind of docked truism). Thus: 'La peinture
raisonnée, c'est celle dont chaque touche est un synthèse, chaque
ton l'élu d'entre mille, chaque trait symbole, et qui s'achève dans
des tortillements d'enthymème. C'est la nature morte au papillon'
[Reasoned painting is that in which each brush-stroke is a synthesis,
each shade selected from a thousand, each feature a symbol, and
which culminates in enthymematical contortions. It is still life with
butterfly] ('La Peinture des van Velde', p. 127).

The Beckett who emerges from these early reviews, then, is one
for whom there can be no overt, loving, acknowledged communion
between a hypothesised God and humankind. Neither, despite his
fascination for the *Pensées*, does Beckett show any sign of wishing to
lay money on Pascal's famous 'pari', according to which there is
nothing to be lost in opting for faith in God (where loss might result
from not so doing), but everything to be gained. The existence or

otherwise of God does not seem to preoccupy Beckett as much as his distrust of religious obligation, and his recognition of human need. Thus, the idea of trading in the spiritual futures market is repulsed in favour of an aesthetic directed towards an awareness of present indigence. Accordingly, Beckett speaks in the *Three Dialogues with Georges Duthuit* of his 'dream of an art unresentful of its insuperable indigence and too proud for the farce of giving and receiving' (*TD*, p. 112). In this, he departs from the grudging acceptance of Pascal's 'pari' by Denis Devlin, and his consequent co-operation with a God (or his representative) whom he likens to a 'tentacular sadist':

> There has to be give for take although that sweated labour
> Make us spit at the pictures of heaven we have painted
> At the merchant of honour granting will with sanctions
> Therefore let us bare our hold, let us
> Offer our passion to the tentacular sadist
> There is just one chance we dare not miss this chance.
> (From Denis Devlin, 'Communication from the Eiffel Tower',
> in *Intercessions*, pp. 103–4).

This does not, however, preclude a recurrent engagement with a religious frame of reference, since Beckett – as earlier discussion has examined – constructs many bridges between the domains of art and religion. Within Beckett's conception, both the aesthetic and the religious impulse must spring from an awareness not of obligation, but of need. As Faust declares in Valéry's play *Le Solitaire*: 'Souffrir, ne pas souffrir. Tout le reste est philosophie. Du luxe' [To suffer, or not to suffer. All the rest is philosophy. Luxury].[36] Hence, in his review of Devlin's *Intercessions*, Beckett draws the distinction between poetry which (like that of Devlin) arises from an 'inverted spiral of need' ('Intercessions', p. 91), and that which emanates from the 'gerimandlers' (i.e. the manipulators of need). In illustration of what he sees as the impulse animating the latter category, Beckett quotes an unattributed passage redolent (albeit rather charmingly) of self-satisfaction: 'He roasteth roast, and is satisfied: yea, he warmeth himself, and saith, Aha, I am warm' (p. 92). The passage is in fact from the Old Testament – Isaiah 44: 16 – and Beckett had previously copied it out, in that same King James translation, in his 'Whoroscope' notebook. The image is used within the book of Isaiah to present a scene not of security and plenty, but of its opposite. Those who make gods of transient joys 'have not known nor understood' (v. 18) that such things are, in this rendering, doomed to futility.

Hence, a life or a text in which need is suppressed or anaesthetised is one which, in Beckett's view, never penetrates the superficies. It is not surprising, then, that he writes in his 'Whoroscope' notebook a motto said to be that of Descartes: 'Bene qui patuit, bene vixit' [roughly translated: Whoever has been open/ vulnerable has lived well]. Pascal's complementary image is that of the human being as a 'thinking reed'. Mortal, and subject to outside assault, human life is reed-like in its fragility. Yet it is distinguished and ennobled by its consciousness of itself. Beckett was sufficiently struck by this image to copy Pascal's exposition of it into his 'Whoroscope' notebook: 'L'homme n'est qu'un roseau, le plus faible de la nature; mais c'est un roseau pensant. Il ne faut pas que l'univers entier s'arme pour l'écraser; une vapeur, une goutte d'eau suffit pour le tuer. Mais quand l'univers l'écraserait, l'homme serait encore plus noble que ce qui le tue, puisqu'il sait qu'il meurt et l'avantage que l'univers a sur lui. L'univers n'en sait rien' [A human being is merely a reed, the weakest in nature; but a thinking reed. It does not require the whole universe to arm itself to crush him; a vapour, a drop of water is enough to kill him. But, if the universe were to crush him, a man would be even nobler than that which is killing him, since he is aware that he is dying, and of the advantage that the universe has over him. The universe knows nothing of this] [*Pensées*, fragment 200, pp. 121–22).

Pascal goes on, in that same fragment of the *Pensées*, to sum up the significance of the reed image by the statement: 'Toute notre dignité consiste donc en la pensée' [Our whole dignity, then, derives from thought] (p. 122). Yet thought is multiform, and no doubt it was that image of the 'roseau pensant' which Beckett had in mind when, in his essay 'Les Deux Besoins', he characterises the opposite tendency as being that of the 'choux pensant et même bien pensant' [thinking cabbages, and even right-thinking cabbages].[37] These are the people who are rooted firmly in earth rather than water. They insulate themselves from the moisture of doubt, and 'ne laissent rien monter chez eux qui puisse compromettre la solidité des planchers' [let nothing rise up about them which might undermine the solidity of the floors] ('Les Deux Besoins', p. 55). Those, on the other hand, who acknowledge their own transience and vulnerability are not only recognising their need, but also their need to have need: 'Besoin de quoi? Besoin d'avoir besoin. Deux besoins, dont le produit fait l'art' [Need of what? Need to have need. Two needs, whose product is art] (p. 55).

Indeed, one of Beckett's early worries about his own art – and, in particular, his poetry – was his conviction that it was too 'facultatif' [optional], that it was not the product of that need which he discerns as the mainspring of the only kind of art he respects. In a letter to Thomas MacGreevy in 1932,[38] he complains that his poetry seems to him to issue from a 'writing-shed', and that it is 'nearly all frigged up, in terram', rather than manifesting itself as 'spontaneous combustion of the spirit to compensate the pus and the pain that threaten its economy'. Even here, Beckett accesses religious referents, characterising poetry which 'is an end in itself and justifies all the means' as 'Jesuitical', and concluding that: 'I suppose I'm a dirty low-church P[rotestant] even in poetry, concerned with integrity in a surplice'. (Beckett uses the first part of this phrase in both *Dream of Fair to Middling Women* and *More Pricks Than Kicks*, as the next chapter examines).

'Integrity' for Beckett is allied to that 'obligation to express' of which he will later speak in his *Three Dialogues with Georges Duthuit* (*TD*, p. 103). It is an imperative which overrides usefulness and appropriateness, like a hanged man's ejaculation. As Beckett states in the 1932 letter to MacGreevy: 'I'm in mourning for the integrity of a pendu's emission of semen'. It issues from unavoidable suffering, not optional pattern-making. A dying person sees the world differently. As Valéry's narrator says with regard to the death of Monsieur Teste: 'Le regard étrange sur les choses, ce regard d'un homme qui ne *reconnaît* pas, qui est hors de ce monde [...] appartient au *penseur*. Et c'est aussi un regard d'agonisant, d'homme qui perd la reconnaissance. En quoi le penseur est un agonisant, ou un Lazare, facultatif. Pas si facultatif' [The glance of a stranger upon things, that glance of a man who doesn't *recognise*, who is beyond this world [...] belongs to the *thinker*. And it is also the glance of the dying man, of the man who is losing the power of recognition. So that the thinker is a dying man, or a Lazarus, optional. Not so optional] (*Monsieur Teste*, p. 124). ('Lazarus' is on this occasion not the victim of Dives, but the brother of Martha and Mary, famously restored to life by Jesus in a pre-Passion foreshadowing of Christ's own resurrection). Whether the thinker is dying, or returning from death, s/he is at a moment of extreme vulnerability, when vision is hungry and acute.

In his *Proust,* Beckett cites 'the suffering of being' as being productive of 'the free play of every faculty' (*P,* p. 20). This is not, of course, to upgrade suffering to the status of a desirable good; it is to recognise its searing impact on human beings. Since acute suffering slices through the cushioning of habit, exposing 'the perilous zones in the life of the individual' (*P,* p. 19), the perception of the sufferer is thereby heightened. This is the enhanced perception which, for Beckett, is attainable by artists, for, as the opening words of 'Les Deux Besoins' somewhat grandiosely assert: 'Il n'y a sans doute que l'artiste qui puisse finir par voir [...] la monotone centralité de ce qu'un chacun veut, pense, fait et souffre, de ce qu'un chacun est' [It is doubtless only the artist who can eventually see the monotonous centrality of what each wants, thinks, does and suffers, of what each person is] ('Les Deux Besoins', p. 55).

In Beckett's terms, then, human life can neither be conceived of as a series of transactions with a guiding and beneficent Deity, nor as a state in which stability and regulation constitute goals. Instead, it is a movement through intensities, from one unfathomable darkness to another. As Valéry's narrator in *Monsieur Teste* remarks: 'Il s'agit de passer de zéro à zéro. – Et c'est la vie' [It's a matter of going from zero to zero. – And that's life] (*Monsieur Teste,* p. 123). In between onset and subsidence (birth and death) lies that *via dolorosa* of which the Beckettian organism is the all too pained and paining witness. There is no sense in Beckett's work in which that dolorous path can be viewed as a progressive and purifying one – as a *via purgativa* leading in due course to a *via unitiva.* Instead, there is, if not a transformation, then a rehabilitation of the purgatorial concept, such that it emerges as a place of movement and transition. Of the three books of Dante's *Divina Commedia,* it was undoubtedly to the *Purgatorio* that Beckett most repeatedly gravitated. Between the two stases of 'immaculation' [heaven] and 'viciousness' [hell], maintains Beckett in his *Dante...Bruno.Vico..Joyce,* Purgatory exists as 'a flood of movement and vitality released by the conjunction of these two elements' (*DBVJ,* p. 33). Thus, the 'purgatorial aspect' of Joyce's work finds expression in 'an endless verbal germination, maturation, putrefaction, the cyclic dynamism of the intermediate' (*DBVJ,* p. 29).

Given this privileging of the dynamic of the transitional space, Beckett recurrently shows evidence of a committed response to those writers and artists who exhibit an avoidance of fixed positions, who are less concerned with manipulation and culmination than with observation and experimentation. Indeed, Beckett's own fictional work overwhelmingly demonstrates not so much a denial of polarities, as an awareness of their relativity and of the intermediate space between them. Contemplating infinity, Faust declares in Valéry's *Le Solitaire*: 'Il y a énormément de rien dans le Tout' [There's an awful lot of nothing in the All] (*Le Solitaire*, p. 382). Similarly, Pascal's characterisation of mankind in the world is: 'Un néant à l'égard de l'infini, un tout à l'égard du néant, un milieu entre rien et tout' [A nothingness with regard to infinity, an all with regard to nothingness, a middle ground between nothing and everything] (*Pensées*, p. 116).

Several years before the term 'existentialism' became common currency, and before the appearance of Sartre's major philosophical works, Beckett could use it, in his essay 'Recent Irish Poetry', to describe the dynamic he discerned in Thomas MacGreevy's poetry. Maintaining that, in MacGreevy's poetry, 'it is the act and not the object of perception that matters', he terms MacGreevy 'an existentialist in verse' ('Recent Irish Poetry', p. 74). Without maintaining that there is nothing to be seen, Beckett articulates the perception that, as with Dante's Pilgrim, seeing is progressive. And, *en attendant*, the waiting for the vision is no less important. Designating MacGreevy's poems as 'elucidations', Beckett asserts that MacGreevy 'knows how to wait for the thing to happen' (p. 74).

Indeed, MacGreevy, like his fellow Catholic, Giambattista Vico, does not look for static and universal essences in humanity but for movements and impulses towards understanding. In his essay 'The Catholic Element in *Work in Progress*', he observes that: 'Purgatory is not fixed and static like the four last things, death, judgment, heaven and hell'.[39] And if MacGreevy 'knows how to wait' in a way preached by Vladimir to Estragon but seldom practised by either, this does not exclude a preoccupation with the yawning and obscene gap between fulfilment and frustration. Long before Pozzo, in *Waiting for Godot*, is given the line: 'That's how it is on this bitch of an earth' (*WFG*, p. 38), MacGreevy had already used the phrase 'our bitch of a world' in his poem 'De Civitate Hominum' (*Poems*, p. 4). In a world of 'black spots in the whiteness' (p. 4), MacGreevy's cry, like that of Job, is: 'How long?'.[40] Moreover, his cry is extended towards a God who, like Godot, is always in the wings. Meditating on the dreadful death of wartime pilots, MacGreevy's 'De Civitate Hominum' ends with the lines: 'Holy God makes no reply / Yet' (p. 5), just as, when at the close of the failed prayer meeting in *Endgame*,

Hamm rants that God is a bastard for not existing, Clov replies, 'Not yet' (*EG*, p. 38).

Within the 'existentialist' context favoured by Beckett, waiting can never be entirely static, since circumstances and individuals are constantly on the move. Thus, although Beckett experienced many reservations and frustrations in reading Proust – he wrote to Thomas MacGreevy in 1928 of the 'strangely uneven' texture of Proust's writing[41] – he was nevertheless carefully responsive to the French writer's treatment of time and motion. As Beckett observes of Proust: 'We are not merely more weary because of yesterday, we are other, no longer what we were before the calamity of yesterday' (*P*, p. 13), for 'the individual is the seat of a constant process of decantation' (p. 15). 'Attainment' is impossible, since it merely represents the gratification of yesterday's aspirations. That does not make the *idea* of attainment any less attractive: thus, 'love, [Proust] insists, can only coexist with a state of dissatisfaction, whether born of jealousy or its predecessor – desire. It represents our demand for a whole' (*P*, p. 55). Yet the very passage of time not only modifies the conditions of that demand, but also undermines the notion of the hypothesised whole.

Moreover, over-absorption in the goal, to the detriment of the continuum, can lead to the phenomenon described by the philosopher Imlac, in Johnson's *The History of Rasselas* (considered by Beckett, according to Patrick Bowles, to be 'a grand book'[42]): ' "It seems to me", said Imlac, "that while you are making the choice of life you neglect to live" ' (*Rasselas*, p. 98). Beckett was sufficiently impressed by this sentiment to write it, in shorthand form, in his 'Whoroscope' notebook, under the form of: 'making the choice of life, neglecting to live'. The precept might be seen as the antidote to the dilemma-ridden existence described by the narrator in *Molloy*: 'Car en moi il y a toujours eu deux pitres, entre autres, celui qui ne demande qu'à rester là où il se trouve et celui qui s'imagine qu'il serait un peu moins mal plus loin' (*ML*, p. 64).

Later, Imlac develops further the idea of the importance and dynamism of the present moment. Addressing a grieving Nekayah, he advises clinging neither to past nor future, for: 'Distance has the same effect on the mind as on the eye; and while we glide along the stream of time, whatever we leave behind us is always lessening, and that which we approach increasing in magnitude. Do not suffer life to stagnate; it will grow muddy for want of motion; commit yourself again to the current of the world' (pp. 115–6). Nekayah

herself is later heard espousing a very similar sentiment: 'Such [...]
is the state of life that none are happy but by the anticipation of
change: the change itself is nothing; when we have made it, the next
wish is to change again' (p. 157).

Eschewing the notion of an earthly nirvana does not mean,
however, that vision is retracted. On the contrary, as noted earlier in
this chapter, Beckett's strongest responses to writers and artists are
expressed in terms of the degree of lightness and movement which
he discerns in them. It is these qualities which are often char-
acterised by him in quasi-mystical terms. Some caution is, however,
needed here. Just as Beckett takes good care, at the beginning of his
Dante...Bruno.Vico..Joyce to draw attention to a distinction between the 'practical' and the 'mystic' with reference to Vico, he
demonstrates a similar wariness with regard to those spiritual
writers who attempt to extend their insights to the practical circumstances and dilemmas of everyday life. Hence, when writing to
Thomas MacGreevy about Thomas à Kempis's *The Imitation of
Christ*, Beckett rejects the opinion of those who would claim for it
the status of 'a Compendium of Christian behaviour, with *oeuvres
pies*, humility, utility, self-effacement, etc. etc'.[43]

Indeed, what is noticeable about the *Imitation* is its stress upon
the cultivation of good habits. To that extent, many readers over the
centuries who have experienced inner struggles with aspects of
their own behaviour or personality have found such precepts as:
'Habit is by habit overcome' (*IMI*, p. 49) to be salutary and bene-
ficial. For Beckett, however, the value of habit (as has earlier been
explored with reference to Proust) is more ambiguous. In *Proust*,
Beckett demonstrates full cognizance of this complexity: 'Habit is
the ballast that chains the dog to his vomit' (*P*, p. 19). When Vladimir in *Waiting for Godot* states: 'Habit is a great deadener' (*WFG*,
p. 91), he is exploiting that ambiguity to the full. As a 'deadener',
habit can remove pain by numbing the nerves. However, by
'deadening', it also disables all other feeling, thus fostering quiescence and stagnation. Indeed, Beckett's chief grievance against the
Imitation, as he makes clear in that same letter to MacGreevy, is that
it proffers 'an abject self-referring quietism'. As such, it differs
profoundly from that 'humanistic quietism', the 'self-absorption
into light' ('Humanistic Quietism', p. 69) which Beckett promotes as
a positive value in his review of MacGreevy's own work.

If, then, Beckett is to admit of any spiritual vision or illumination,
it must be one which is mobile rather than static, occasional rather

than habitual, and one which emerges in its transparency only when the intervening veils have been parted. The light is not one to be bathed under or luxuriated in, but one to see and walk hesitantly towards, like Dante's Pilgrim. Accordingly, Beckett copies into his 'Whoroscope' notebook lines from the fourth canto of Dante's *Inferno* (lines 103–5) which describe the approach by Virgil and Dante to the glowing light they glimpse from the Limbo which they are presently traversing.

Moreover, this quality of lightness (in both senses: illumination, and lack of weight or solidity) is something which is fundamental to a wide range of Beckett's aesthetic responses. In writing of the painting of the van Velde brothers, he draws attention to their radiant, organic quality: 'Comment parler de ces couleurs qui respirent, qui halètent? De cette stase grouillante? De ce monde sans poids, sans force, sans ombre?' [How can I speak of these colours which breathe and gasp? Of this swarming stasis? Of this world without weight, without strength, without shadow?] ('La Peinture des van Velde', p. 128). He writes in related terms of the painting of Jack Yeats: 'He brings light, as only the great dare to bring light, to the issueless predicament of existence'.[44]

What is notable is that, whether discussing art or writing, Beckett endows the works which appeal most powerfully and illuminatingly to him with a visual quality which is often described in terms derived from, or equally accessed by, the mystical or spiritual. In this respect, one might cite the Notebooks of Leonardo da Vinci, which Beckett refers to more than once in his early critical writing. Although Beckett speaks of a characteristic of 'possessiveness' which he discerns in da Vinci's Notebooks (*TD*, p. 112), the latter are nonetheless suggestive of a visionary conception of art which is not far removed from that of Beckett. Speaking with the assurance of one who has proved himself in both painting and sculpture, da Vinci has no hesitation in maintaining that sculpture is not only less 'intellectual' than painting, but is also deficient in terms of its luminosity. Da Vinci is often at his most fascinating when talking of light and shade, which are portable in a painting but must be applied from without to sculpture, for sculptors 'can neither represent transparent bodies nor luminous bodies nor angles of reflection nor shining bodies such as mirrors and like things of glittering surface, nor mists, nor dull weather, nor an infinite number of things'.[45] Therefore, since painting (as he conceives it) deals with 'nature' – a world, in his view, created and made radiant by a Deity who commanded: 'Let there be light' – da Vinci concludes that painting may be referred to as 'the grandchild of nature and as related to God Himself' (p. 160).

Beckett would, of course, be profoundly antagonistic towards the idea of applying that kind of derivative status to art. This does not prevent him, however, from according a special status to the quality of light in works of art, and from allowing that perception of radiance to carry him, spiritually rather than intellectually, towards the unknowable and unnamable beyond and within himself. Hence, to see Bram van Velde's painting is for Beckett to encounter 'ignorance, silence et l'azur immobile' [ignorance, silence and motionless azure] ('La Peinture des van Velde', p. 125), while before the 'high solitary art [...], with its wellhead in a hiddenmost of spirit' of Jack Yeats, he is content merely to 'bow in wonder'.[46]

This apprehension of inwardness has nothing of the reverential hush about it. Indeed, for Beckett, that 'bowing in wonder' takes place in the presence of works which betray their own anxieties, which make no assertions or symbolic parades, and which disintegrate and reform even while the observer negotiates with them. The art which engages Beckett – and which he himself aspired to write – does not trade in absolutes or universals. As Beckett wrote of the artist Avigdor Arikha: 'Eye and hand fevering after the unself. By the hand it unceasingly changes the eye unceasingly changed. Back and forth the gaze beating against unseeable and unmakable'.[47]

Thus, if all life is in flux, God cannot be an exception; this God is not an eternally unchanging essence, but an exemplification of potentiality, bound up with a changing universe. This, at least, is the insight which process theology affords. In this respect, Pascal might be seen as a process theologian 'avant la lettre'; for him, human beings, 'toujours incertains et flottants' [ever uncertain and floating] (*Pensées*, p. 119) are faced with a God who is 'un point se mouvant partout d'une vitesse infinie' [a point moving everywhere with infinite speed] (*Pensées*, p. 191).

This early writing of Beckett gives little evidence of wanting to track or locate that point, still less to detain it. Yet, if any instinct or nostalgia for a Deity subsists in the mystical space reserved by Beckett, then it seems most likely to engage with a God-in-movement, a Godhead in which 'tout bouge, nage, fuit, revient, se défait, se refait' [everything moves, swims, flees, returns, unmakes itself, remakes itself] ('La Peinture des van Velde', p. 128).

2

The Early Fiction

Prayers will be offered for my soul, as for that of one
dead, as for that of an infant dead in its dead mother,
that it may not go to Limbo, sweet thing theology.
(Samuel Beckett, *Texts for Nothing*).

For Beckett, theology is sweet and sour. In it, he finds ample measures of depth, complexity, abstraction and intellectual challenge. When inhering in a work such as Dante's *The Divine Comedy*, it could even assume for him a kind of beauty, in alliance with the intense imagery and poetry of that work. Yet theology, as 'God-talk', is also deeply problematic for Beckett. It engages with notions of a being who eludes the material grasp, the being whom Camier terms 'Omni-omni, l'inemmerdable' (*MC*, p. 39) (in the English translation, 'Omniomni, the all-unfuckable' [*MAC*, p. 26]). Moreover, in its doctrinal and liturgical outreach, theology aspires to unite emotion and rationality (always a dangerous undertaking in the Beckettian world). Credal formulae, as enshrined in worship, thus encapsulate personal assent and acclamation within collective and orthodox paradigms.

Of course, it is possible for the uncommitted, the agnostic, or the atheist to study theology, just as it is possible for the theist to study post-Renaissance or scientific humanism. Yet it is difficult to ignore the issues of discipleship and belief which radiate outwards from the study of Christian theology. Moreover, many modern political theologians would go so far as to maintain, in common with many Marxian thinkers, that orthodoxy can only be validated by its orthopraxis: that is, that theology cannot be regarded as 'neutral', apolitical, or detached from human affairs. Rather, theology is a continuous dialectic of theory and practice: it cannot thrive independently of its praxis.

It is at this point that Beckett demurs. While preoccupied by many of the same issues with which religious belief grapples – suffering, injustice, survival – he resists the imposition upon them of a religious or devotional template. Thus, in a noteworthy letter to

Thomas MacGreevy in 1935,[1] Beckett writes lengthily of his difficulty in responding to Thomas à Kempis's *The Imitation of Christ*, which he appears to have read in both the original Latin and in an English translation. This religious classic did have some impact upon him. Indeed, he cites (in Latin) three phrases which, he claims, 'seemed to be made for me and which I have never forgotten'. They are[2]: 'Qui melius scit pati, majorem tenebit pacem' [He who knows better how to suffer will hold the greater peace] (Book 2, Chapter 3, p. 87); 'Nolle consolari ab aliqua creatura, magnae puritatis, et internae fiduciae signum est' [It is a sign of great purity and confidence within, not to wish for consolation from any creature] (Book 2, Chapter 6, p. 93; Beckett incidentally misses out the words 'et internae fiduciae' in his transcription); and 'per viam pacis, ad patriam perpetuae claritatis' [along the path of peace to the fatherland of everlasting light] (Book 3, Chapter 59, p. 296).[3] Indeed, the first five words of the second phrase – 'Nolle consolari ab aliqua creatura' – are incorporated into *Dream of Fair to Middling Women* (*DFMW*, pp. 194–5), appropriately, when the Alba is brooding over Belacqua's standoffishness. The third phrase had also found its way into *Dream of Fair to Middling Women*, where it is proposed by the narrator as a fitting destination for the character known as the 'Polar Bear', for: 'He merits peace. *Per viam pacis ad patriam perpetuae claritatis*' (*DFMW*, p. 178).

These three phrases have in common that they all constitute aspirations towards peace and light, through turmoil and darkness: the first points to peace amid and despite suffering, and the second to equanimity achieved by other than human means (poise without a safety net other than God). The third concentrates upon an onward journey towards the light. It is a journey akin to that of Dante the Pilgrim in *The Divine Comedy*: one which could be typified by the phrase 'per ardua ad astra', for, at the close of each testing journey through the zones of Hell, Purgatory, and Heaven, the last word of each canticle is 'stelle', as the Pilgrim turns his attention to the stars.

Beyond phrases such as these, in which Beckett found great resonance, the terms of à Kempis's overall project appear to have held little attraction. To modern ears, *The Imitation of Christ* can seem gratingly negative and nominalist. Nevertheless, what has made it such a powerful text for many people – its constant reversal of material and 'worldly' values in favour of spiritual ones – might, on the face of it, seem likely to appeal to Beckett. After all, in rejecting a 'conventional' career path in academe (for which he was intellectually more than qualified), he was also proclaiming his detachment from long-term material security. Moreover, his subsequent career continued to exhibit an alienation from conspicuous wealth and the trappings of public acclaim. A Kempis's advice to 'keep yourself as a pilgrim and stranger upon earth' (*IMI*, p. 55) seems to be exemplified, on many levels, in the person of Beckett.

Yet, for Beckett, à Kempis's asceticism amounted to an unhelpful path to isolationism. (This issue, as well as Beckett's occasional engagement with the à Kempis text within his own writing, will be explored more fully in the concluding section of this chapter). Although content for long periods with only himself for company, Beckett had recently come to address his own tendency towards isolationism and feelings of superiority, through psychoanalysis with Wilfred Bion. Thus, he goes on in the letter to MacGreevy to explain that this disturbing feeling of 'otherness' now appeared to him as a symptom of a more profound inner malaise, of very long standing. Perceiving that remedies to his own alienation lay within a stripping-down of the layers of his psyche, Beckett could thus see no potential for redemption within what he describes as 'any philosophical or ethical or Christlike imitative sentiments'. In *The Imitation of Christ*, God speaks to the human listener of those who have presumed too much upon their own ambitions and resources: 'They should learn not to fly on their own wings, but hope beneath my feathers' (*IMI*, p. 102). For Beckett, this solution is not a radical act of trust, but a crucial handover of autonomy which is impossible to contemplate. Far from hiding in God's feathers, he has discerned that what he calls 'pleroma' (fullness of being) is 'only to be sought among *my own feathers and entrails*' [my italics].

USES OF THE BIBLE

Beckett often accesses scriptural and devotional literature purely for its evocatory power, its pithiness, or its phonetic appeal, and this must be borne in mind when considering his use of scriptural material. In order to enable the parallels between elements in Beckett's texts and the King James Bible to emerge more clearly, quotations within this section will (contrary to the practice in other sections) be given consistently in English, regardless of the language of original composition.

If Beckett uses both the Old and the New Testaments extensively within his own early writing, it is usually not to enshrine or venerate them, but rather to wring ironic or deviant readings out of them. This is not to say that he consistently undermines or parodies them, for Beckett is too alive to the strength and poetry of many elements within that complex of literatures which constitute the Bible to target them simplistically or homogenously. It does mean, however, that (in contrast to à Kempis's exploitation of the same sources), his use of biblical phrases must not necessarily be seen as signifying his assent to their aspirations. Hence Beckett's well-known statement that his advertence to Christianity stems from the fact that it is 'a mythology which which I am perfectly familiar'.[4]

Being familiar with the writings and practices of Christianity means that Beckett is often reminded of them by specific events or phenomena, just as Walter Draffin, in *More Pricks Than Kicks*, is initially reminded by the formal invitation card to Belacqua's wedding of 'a Church of Ireland Sunday School certificate of good conduct and regular attendance', notwithstanding the fact that his is kept 'in the old home locked up in the family Bible, marking the place where Lamentations ended and Ezekiel began' (*MPTK*, pp. 132–3).

For Walter, that episode from his early career is partly locked away, and partly present. He dismisses the certificate as a comparator in this case, and recalls its inaccessibility within the family home. Yet he can still visualise the certificate, and he can still remember (as the Sunday School would have taught him) that the Book of Ezekiel follows the Book of Lamentations within the running order of the Greek (though not the Hebrew or Vulgate) Bible. Later, too, when proposing the toast to the newly-weds, he will enlist St Paul when alluding to the anticipated glories of marital pleasure: 'Oh may that star, that radiant radical of their desire, not of mine, my friends, nor yet of yours, for no two stars, as Saint Paul tells us, are on a par in the matter of glory, delight them without ceasing with legitimate inflexions!' (*MPTK*, p. 157). The text which has fired Walter is Paul's First Letter to the Corinthians: 'There is one glory of the sun, and another glory of the moon, and another glory of the stars: for one star differeth from another star in glory' (1 Corinthians 15: 41). Paul inserts the image within a discourse on the resurrection of the dead, when 'natural body' is superseded by 'spiritual body' (v. 44). Walter's referent, however, is far from spiritual.

Biblical verses, then, often seem to rise to the surface of Beckett's writing of their own accord, with the Old Testament no less prevalent than the New. When, in *Molloy*, the narrator tells of how a solution to the sucking stones dilemma suddenly dawns upon him, he comments: 'The meaning of this illumination, which suddenly began to sing within me, like a verse of Isaiah, or of Jeremiah, I did not penetrate at once' (*BT*, p. 66). The sound, then, here appears anterior to the meaning. Interestingly, in the handwritten draft of *Molloy* (UTA, Notebook 2), this passage appears in much less specific form. Rather than a passage from the Prophets, it is simply 'un verset de l'Ecriture Sainte' [a verse from Holy Scripture]. On the facing page, Beckett has scribbled down the word 'Kabbala': a reference to a Jewish rabbinic tradition dating from the time of Moses. Moreover, the Kabbala (often spelt 'Cabbala') is essentially an oral tradition, and is thus appropriately cited in the context of perceptions said to 'sing'. Thus, given that Beckett appears to have had in mind the Old Testament when drafting this passage, it is appropriate that the general reference to Scripture should have been amended in the published version to two notably lyrical and poetic components of the Old Testament: the Books of Isaiah and Jeremiah.

The Book of Isaiah is also of relevance to Beckett's earlier novel, *Watt*, in which the 'Addenda' contain the poem beginning: 'who may tell the tale / of the old man? / weigh absence in a scale? / mete want with a span?' (*W*, p. 247). This poem appears, with slight variants, in Beckett's manuscript draft of *Watt* (UTA, Notebook 2). By the side of the draft is written the biblical reference: Isaiah 40: 12. In the King James Bible, that verse appears as: 'Who hath measured the waters in the hollow of his hand, and meted out heaven with the span, and comprehended the dust of the earth in a measure, and weighed the mountains in scales, and the hills in a balance?'.

This passage – part of a sustained contrast between the greatness of God and the weakness of human beings – leads, a few verses later, to the statement: 'All nations before him are as nothing; and they are counted to him less than nothing, and vanity' (v. 17). This corresponds to the final couplet of Beckett's poem: 'nothingness / in words enclose?' Beckett's imaginative handling of these six verses from Isaiah demonstrates not only his familiarity with the original, but also his ability to endow it with a more elliptical flavour. Within Isaiah, the question is a rhetorical one: it is clear that the desired answer is 'God'. Within *Watt*, the question remains in the air, particularly given its semi-detached status within the 'Addenda'.

The main text of the novel *Watt* also contains, however, further subliminal echoes of a hidden, Old Testament Deity. When Watt begins service in the house of Mr Knott, he finds that, though Mr Knott is undoubtedly present, he is always remote, and difficult to catch sight of. Knott is, and is not. He is in some senses akin to Yahweh, He who is, but whose name cannot be uttered. Knott can be pronounced 'not'; Yahweh can be pronounced not. Indeed, within the Old Testament, Yahweh is not a proper name at all: it does not denote an object or quality, but rather a guarantee of presence. It is not to be understood ontologically, but is to be encountered within a process or narrative of salvation. Just as Moses shields his face on being addressed by Yahweh (see Exodus 3: 6), believing that no creature can gaze on God and live, Watt 'abandoned all hope, all fear, of ever seeing Mr Knott face to face, or perhaps this, that Watt, while continuing to believe in the possibility of his seeing one day Mr Knott face to face, came to regard its realization as one to which no importance could be attached' (*W*, pp. 145–6).

Hence, though Watt's curiosity to see the face of Mr Knott aligns him with the psalmist: 'My heart said unto thee, Thy face, Lord, will I seek. Hide not thy face far from me' (Psalm 27: 8–9), he finds eventually that, as his interest in 'what has been called the spirit of Mr Knott increased, his interest in what is commonly known as the body diminished' (*W*, p. 146). What glimpses Watt does manage to catch of Mr Knott are 'as it were in a glass, not a looking-glass, a plain glass, an eastern window at morning, a western window at evening' (*W*, p. 146). Seeing him face to face is an experience constantly deferred, as was the sight of God for St Paul, who compares the spiritual encounter with God on earth with that still to be experienced in heaven: 'For now we see through a glass, darkly; but then face to face' (1 Corinthians 13: 12).

Around the central figure of Mr Knott revolve a number of manservants, among whom is one called Arsene. In the notebook draft of *Watt*, Arsene is a figure like that of the Preacher in the Book of Ecclesiastes. In the well-known words of that speaker: 'Vanity of vanities, saith the Preacher, vanity of vanities; all is vanity' (Ecclesiastes 1: 2). (The narrator of *Dream of Fair to Middling Women* also quotes this passage: 'The dead fart, says the Preacher, vanity of vanities, and the quick whistle' [*DFMW*, p. 146]). Similarly, Arsene is said to be 'a valet vainly knowing that he vainly knew that all was vain' (UTA, Notebook 2). Just as the Preacher, oscillating between resignation and dismay, rehearses the sorry tale of the futility of human effort, Arsene 'rocked himself to and fro, and back and forth. "All error, folly, waste, ruin"'. Within *Watt*, as within the Book of Ecclesiastes, a contrast is drawn between vain comings and goings on the one hand, and stillness and calm on the other. Thus, the narrator states in *Watt* that: 'There is one who neither comes nor goes, I refer I need hardly say to my late employer, but seems to abide in his place, for the time being at any rate, like an oak, an elm, a beech or an ash' (*W*, p. 56). Hence, Mr Knott is like a rooted tree, and the procession of manservants 'nest a little while in his branches' (*W*, p. 56). In like vein, the Preacher in Ecclesiastes observes that: 'One generation passeth away, and another generation cometh: but the earth abideth for ever' (Ecclesiastes 1: 4).

In accordance with this picture of human travail, the narrator in *Watt* recalls his life as having been made up of 'the whacks, the moans, the cracks, the groans, the welts, the squeaks, the belts, the shrieks, the pricks, the prayers, the kicks, the tears, the skelps, and the yelps' (*W*, p. 45). In the manuscript draft of *Watt*, this 'I-voice' is identified as that of Arsene, whose woes are tabulated (with only the substitution of the pair 'growls' and 'howls' to replace, respectively, 'prayers' and 'tears') in such a way as to display the rhyme scheme of [abab, cdcd, efef, gg]. This quasi-sonnet of anguish is followed in the manuscript by a description of Arsene's awareness that, if his life were to be lived over again, it would amount to the same. Despite this, it is observed of Arsene that: 'He would say to the king of ducks, Go! and the duck went, and Come! and the duck came, and Do this! and the duck did that. So extraordinary is the effect of God's image'. This passage is of course a parody of the centurion's speech in Matthew's Gospel (repeated in similar form in Luke 7: 8): 'For I am a man under authority, having soldiers under me: and I say to this man, Go, and he goeth; and to another, Come, and he cometh; and to my servant, Do this, and he doeth it' (Matthew 8: 9). (The humour of the duck parody derives partly from the unlikely image of a subservient duck. It does not match the experience of the narrator of *From an Abandoned Work*, who ruminates: 'Ducks are perhaps the worst, to be suddenly stamping and stumbling in the midst of ducks, or hens, any class of poultry, few things are worse' [*CSPR*, p. 129]).

Thus Arsene, who is earlier described as 'this vulgar little nonentity', gains dignity in the context of the duck world. Just as the centurion is seen as being higher in status than the hundred men who do his bidding, Arsene is distinguished by his status as a human being. Whereas ducks are presumably to be included amongst the 'winged fowl' which God is said in the Book of Genesis to have created on the fifth day, the creation of mankind is reserved until the culminatory sixth day, when God announces: 'Let us make man in our image, after our likeness' (Genesis 1: 26). Moreover, once created, mankind is accorded dominion over all other living creatures. Hence the manuscript's assertion: 'So extraordinary is the effect of God's image'.

Murphy, however, falls victim to a reverse irony, for, in the ascription of Wylie, he is demoted from human status to that of a crawling animal: ' "As an abomination", said Wylie, "the creepy thing that creepeth of the Law. Yet I pursue him" ' (MP, p. 121). The passage Wylie is amusing himself by perverting is from the Book of Leviticus, amongst the listing of unclean foods: 'And every creeping thing that creepeth upon the earth shall be an abomination; it shall not be eaten' (Leviticus 11: 41). Thus Murphy is doubly demeaned: not only is he assigned to the animal kingdom, but he is assigned to those groups of animals which are to be regarded as unclean. In pursuing him, maintains Wylie, he is acting contrary to nature: ' "Even so the beggar mutilates himself", said Wylie, "that he may live, and the beaver bites his off" ' (MP, p. 122). Both these are instances of self-mutilation in the cause of pragmatism: the beggar to elicit more sympathy and thus higher takings, and the beaver to save his life, since art and folklore often depict the beaver, when pursued by hunters for the supposed medicinal qualities of his genitals, biting them off and tossing them to the hunters. Hence, within Christianity, the beaver becomes an image of the soul rooting out sexual excess in the pursuit of virtue. (Indeed, it is in an allied context that Belacqua recalls the legend in Dream of Fair to Middling Women: 'The beaver bites his off, he said, I know, that he may live. That was a very persuasive chapter of Natural History' [DFMW, p. 63]).

Murphy does receive another Old Testament comparator, however: an amalgam of Bildad the Shuhite, and the Devil. Evoking William Blake's series of illustrations for the Book of Job, the narrator relates: 'Murphy on the jobpath was a striking figure. Word went round among the members of the Blake League that the Master's conception of Bildad the Shuhite had come to life and was stalking about London in a green suit, seeking whom he might comfort' (MP, p. 44). A sinister presence is accorded to Bildad by the phrase 'stalking about [...], seeking whom he might comfort', suggestive as it is of the predatory movement ascribed to the Devil in the First Letter of Peter: 'Be sober, be vigilant; because your adversary the devil, as a roaring lion, walketh about, seeking whom he may devour' (1 Peter 5: 8). (Beckett had earlier accessed the same associations in *Dream of Fair to Middling Women*, in the description of the unpleasant wharfinger: 'It was the wharfinger, seeking whom he might devour' [*DFMW*, p. 7]).

Bildad the Shuhite is of course one of Job's three 'comforters'. Having lost everything, Job slumps to the ground, like the narrator's grey hen in *Molloy*, 'which would neither brood nor lay and for the past month and more had done nothing but sit with her arse in the dust, from morning to night', thus prompting the priest to quip: 'Like Job, haha' (*ML*, p. 93). Job's visitors, unrelenting in their rectitude, exhort him to have courage and faith when he is in the depths of misery. (Hence the irony of the phrase 'Job's comforters', and the appropriateness of the association with the Devil, since their 'comforting' is more like 'devouring' than upbuilding).

As a 'Shuhite', Bildad is from the town of Shuah. The conjunction of 'Bildad' and 'Shuah' is itself reminiscent of the earlier figure of Belacqua Shuah in *Dream of Fair to Middling Women* and *More Pricks Than Kicks*. In the Bible, Shuah is the name of a son of Abraham and Keturah (see Genesis 25: 2). More significantly, however, it is also the name of the Canaanite woman who married Judah, and who bore him three sons, Er, Onan, and Shelah (see Genesis 38); in his 1931/32 'Dream' notebook, Beckett jots down this fact, together with the onanistic act in its Latin version: 'semen fundebat in terram'.

In the context of the Book of Job, Shuah is one of the towns east of Palestine, in Arab territory. Bildad's mobility, however, is considered by the narrator to be irrelevant, since: 'What is Bildad but a fragment of Job' (*MP*, p. 44). Bildad it is who utters to Job the chilling words: 'How can he be clean that is born of a woman?' (Job 25: 4). Yet the narrator maintains that Bildad's importance is not to be derived from the erroneous supposition that he was wandering about 'on the *qui vive* for someone wretched enough to be consoled by such maieutic saws as "How can he be clean that is born"' (*MP*, p. 44), but, rather, that the gloomy sentiments of Job and his comforters are to be seen as projections of each other. They rehearse and dramatise them for each other at the theatre of Job's dungheap.

The word 'maieutic' as an epithet for the statement 'how can he be clean that is born of woman' is carefully chosen, and carefully double-edged, since it refers to the act of midwifery. Thus, on the one hand it draws attention to the implications of birth (visualised by Bildad as an entry into the mess of human imperfection). On the other hand, in its metaphorical and now more usual application – that is, the birth of thoughts or ideas – the word brings forth reminders of the multiple connotations which the *idea* of birth has spawned. Within Christian theology, for instance, there is the paradox that the birth process is construed as producing an infant who, while being a sign of hope and new life, is also an individual ready-stamped with original sin.

Within Beckett's work, birth is never a cause for rejoicing, for to give birth is also to give a death sentence. Moreover, within his early work, women are particularly stigmatised, for it is they who are portrayed as engineering predatory incursions upon the solipsistic male, and who are also the more intimately implicated in the process of reproduction. Hence, Pozzo's unforgettable image of women giving birth astride of a grave draws womb and tomb irrevocably together. These two dreads – of the insatiable woman, and of the parturitive act – are drawn together repeatedly in *Murphy* by means of references to the horse leech's two daughters.

The horse leech is said to have two greedy daughters: Sheol and Abaddon. These represent, respectively, that central Beckettian axis of grave and womb. The reference to their insatiability occurs in the Book of Proverbs: 'The horseleach hath two daughters, crying, Give, give. There are three things that are never satisfied, yea, four things say not, It is enough: The grave; and the barren womb; the earth that is not filled with water; and the fire that saith not, It is enough' (Proverbs 30: 15–16). In *Murphy*, it is Wylie who first presents the thought to Neary: 'For every symptom that is eased, another is made worse. The horse leech's daughter is a closed system. Her quantum of wantum cannot vary' (*MP*, p. 36). Wylie's hermeneutics are pragmatic ones. In introducing an element not present in the original text – that of compensatory systems; swings and roundabouts – Wylie forges for himself a comfortable accommodation to life's vagaries: 'While one may not look forward to things getting any better, at least one need not fear their getting any worse. They will always be the same as they always were' (*MP*, p. 36). Later, having internalised the schema, Neary will apply it to his own circumstances. Feeling isolated, and let down by Wylie, Neary decides to upgrade Murphy to the extent that he downgrades Wylie: 'Thus his need for Murphy changed. It could not be more urgent than it was, it had to lose with reference to the rival what it gained with reference to the friend. The horse leech's daughter was a closed system' (*MP*, p. 68). Later in the novel (*MP*, p. 112), he again repeats to himself Wylie's words concerning the horse leech's daughters, when wrestling with the intricate double-crossings operating between himself, Miss Counihan, and Wylie.

In the meantime, the object of the quest, Murphy, is preoccupied with his own conundrums. Pondering on the relationship between the words 'gas' and 'chaos', Murphy muses: 'Gas. Could it turn a neurotic into a psychotic? No. Only God could do that. Let there be Heaven in the midst of the waters, let it divide the waters from the waters. The Chaos and Waters Facilities Act. The Chaos, Light and Coke Co.' (*MP*, p. 100). Thus, God's act of creation is here rather cleverly satirised as an Act of Parliament. Moreover, whereas Genesis accords a positive value to the act – 'And God saw every thing that he had made, and, behold, it was very good' (Genesis 1: 31) – the God portrayed here seems to be no more attached to healing than to aggravating, for, in this ironic rendering, 'only God' could effect the transition of a neurotic to the more serious disorder of psychosis.

In this context, it seems, human beings must survive despite God rather than by means of him. Hence, when the voice in *The Unnamable* appropriates the creative formula of the Book of Genesis, 'Let there be light', the phrase takes on an experimental, experiential function rather than an implemental one: 'Let there then be light, it will not necessarily be disastrous. Or let there be none, we'll manage without it' (*BT*, p. 333). With command reduced to aspiration, outcomes are rendered unpredictable. In such an environment, actions can only be provisional. Thus, even a rolling stone or a piece of wood would be welcome to Worm, provided it could be relied upon to visit him at regular intervals, and thus constitute an event: 'a big stone, and faithful, that would be better than nothing, pending the hearts of flesh' (*BT*, p. 334). These 'hearts of flesh' whose advent is awaited, and their conjunction with the stone, evoke the passage from the Book of Ezekiel, in which God promises: 'And I will give them one heart, and I will put a new spirit within you; and I will take the stony heart out of their flesh, and will give them an heart of flesh' (Ezekiel 11: 19). For the Israelites as for Worm, however, this is a promise for the future, of unspecified date. In the meantime, continues the text, 'we must stick to the facts, for what else is there, to stick to, to cling to, when all founders, but the facts' (*BT*, p. 334).

'Facts', however, have a knack of dissolving into possibilities within Beckett's modificatory discourse. Hence, it can only be irony, or wishful thinking, when the narrator in *Molloy* quotes: 'For all things hang together, by the operation of the Holy Ghost, as the saying is' (*BT*, p. 39). The 'prompt-text' here is the Letter to the Romans, in the chapter dealing with the operation of the Holy Spirit: 'And we know that all things work together for good to them that love God' (Romans 8: 28). It is significant that the words 'as the saying is' are appended here, since the surrounding narrative betrays no sign of the Holy Spirit's bounty. A similar incongruity arises later, when the phrase 'See how all things hang together' is applied to the rain-cloud which appears over the narrator's head just when he had been making for the sunshine (*BT*, p. 58).

Indeed, it can be seen from Beckett's references to the New Testament Epistles, and to the Gospels, that incidents and commentaries are rarely quoted without an ironic context, or without some manipulation of language or scenario. Hence, later in *Molloy*, the narrator at first compares his journeyings to the flight of the Holy Family into Egypt (an episode described by Matthew, but not by the other Gospel writers): 'And the cycle continues, joltingly, of flight and bivouac, in an Egypt without bounds, without infant, without mother' (*BT*, p. 61). With many of the structural elements removed – the motive for the journey, the mother, the child – the comparison dwindles down to one feature alone: a single man (Joseph/Molloy) travelling in an unknown country.

A similar manipulation occurs later in the novel, when Moran, temporarily separated from his son, meets a stranger in the countryside who asks him for bread. The subliminal biblical text here is Matthew 7, where Christ introduces the precept that 'every one that asketh receiveth' by the illustration: 'Or what man is there of you, whom if his son ask bread, will he give him a stone? Or if he ask a fish, will he give him a serpent?' (Matthew 7: 9–10). Beckett amuses himself with a variation on this text in a New Year's Day letter to Thomas MacGreevy in 1935: 'Dublin is as ever only more so. You ask for a fish and they give you a piece of bog oak'.[5] He also experiments with the text in *Watt*. In the manuscript draft, for instance, an exchange is quoted with the valet, Arsene: ' "If you want a stone, ask bread". "And if you want bread?" said Arsene. "Ask cake" we said'. In the published version, a further variant appears, following the mysterious encounter with Mr Ash: 'If you want a stone, ask a turnover. If you want a turnover, ask plum-pudding' (*W*, p. 44). Far from endorsing Christ's description of gratified requests, both these instances destabilise the relationship between want and supply. Developing the technique of substitution, then, Moran in fact offers his menacing visitor fish: 'He asked for bread and I offered him fish. That is me all over. Bread, he said. I went into the shelter and took the piece of bread I was keeping for my son, who would probably be hungry when he came back. I gave it to him' (*BT*, p. 135). The man thus obtains his bread, demonstrating that to ask is to receive (especially if the request is accompanied with 'a fiery look' [*BT*, p. 135]), but at the expense of the son.

Murphy, unencumbered either by son or by money, is particularly adept at finding convenient New Testament phrases to meet his current needs. When goaded by Celia to find work, he falls back on the concept of the tautologous 'Providence will provide' (*MP*, p. 16), following it up with: 'The hireling fleeth because he is an hireling' (*MP*, p. 16). The latter phrase emanates from the Gospel of John, where the hireling functions as a contrast to the Good Shepherd. Motivated only by mercenary concerns, 'the hireling fleeth, because he is an hireling, and careth not for the sheep' (John 10: 13). (Interestingly, in his translation of *Mercier et Camier* into English, Beckett chooses to translate the word 'employé' by 'hireling' in the episode where the barman refuses to allow their bicycles into the pub: 'Perhaps after all he was a mere hireling' [*MAC*, p. 22]. The choice of word hints at the same prejudice: that, just as the hireling has no care for his sheep, the barman has no care for his clients).

No doubt casting Celia in the role of the sheep, Murphy is able to turn the shepherding analogy into a rejoinder: that income is a less worthy consideration than love. For after all, as he goes on to proclaim: 'What shall a man give in exchange for Celia?' (*MP*, p. 16). He thus borrows Christ's formula as reported in Matthew's Gospel: 'What shall a man give in exchange for his soul?' (Matthew 16: 26). Celia will never be interchangeable with Murphy's soul, and nor indeed will she be permitted to fuse with it. (Belacqua exhibits a similar guarded attachment to Ruby Tough in *More Pricks Than Kicks*, where he is said to pay 'pious suit to the hem of her garment' [*MPTK*, p. 94]. In drawing a parallel with the woman who 'touched the hem of [Christ's] garment' in Matthew 9: 20, the narrator makes clear that the encounter will never be one between equals). Murphy is nonetheless able to recruit the phrase concerning the price-lessness of the soul to further his argument. Since Celia cannot be bought – for him, she is not a prostitute – the acquisition of money is not a prime motivation for him.

Later, when it is clear to him that his arguments against finding employment have not convinced Celia, he retorts sarcastically: 'Nothing happens in the world but is specially designed to exalt me into a job. [...] There will be more joy in heaven over Murphy finding a job than over the billions of leatherbums that never had anything else' (*MP*, p. 80). In using this formula, based on that found in Luke's Gospel: 'Joy shall be in heaven over one sinner that repenteth, more than over ninety and nine just persons, which need no repentance' (Luke 15: 7), Murphy is temporarily assuming the mantle of the sinner. Nevertheless, the ironic mode of presentation ensures that he emerges as more sinned against than sinning; moreover, the substitution of the 'billion leatherbums' for the ninety-nine 'just persons' makes clear his contempt for the waged masses.

Even when Murphy does obtain a paid position, in the asylum, his instincts always surge to the quiescent rather than the pro-active mode. Observing the patients, exemplars of various psychiatric disorders, he concludes that: 'Left in peace they would have been as happy as Larry, short for Lazarus, whose raising seemed to Murphy perhaps the one occasion on which the Messiah had overstepped the mark' (*MP*, p. 102). The raising from the dead of Lazarus, brother of Jesus's friends Martha and Mary, indeed constitutes the most dramatic miracle recounted in the Gospels. Related in John's Gospel (Chapter 11), but not in the Synoptic Gospels, the episode functions as a kind of prefiguring of Christ's own resurrection (although differing from it in kind, since Lazarus, remaining mortal, would one day have to die again). Whereas other miracles are primarily a matter of healing from sickness (including the healing of the little girl in Mark 5, who only appeared to be dead), this is a rare instance of a resuscitation from death. By stating that, in this instance, 'the Messiah had overstepped the mark', Murphy acknowledges the special status of this miracle, but at the same time aligns it with what he sees as over-officious therapeutic practice on the part of the asylum's medical personnel. Without such interventions, he maintains, both would rest in peace: Lazarus in his tomb, and the asylum inmates in 'the little world where Murphy presupposed them' (*MP*, p. 102).

In *Dream of Fair to Middling Women* and in *More Pricks Than Kicks*, the bus-riding Jesuit, in conversation with the Polar Bear, takes a very similar view of the raising of Lazarus. The Jesuit's Christology is of a startlingly original kind, for he refers to Christ as 'the first great self-contained man' (*DFMW*, p. 209). In his view, Christ's stubborn individualism prompts him towards both renunciation and self-indulgence. In *More Pricks Than Kicks*, the passage concerning Lazarus runs: 'The cryptic [mis-rendered as 'crytic' in the 1992 and 1993 editions of *Dream*] abasement before the woman taken red-handed is as great a piece of megalomaniacal impertinence as his interference in the affairs of his boy-friend Lazarus' (*MPTK*, p. 61). The 'woman taken red-handed' is another important figure in John's Gospel (again, not in the Synoptic Gospels). Caught in the act of adultery, she is brought to Jesus, who, declining to pronounce on the case, bends down to write on the ground with his finger. He offers only the comment: 'He that is without sin among you, let him first cast a stone at her' (John 8: 7). By this means, the woman's indignant captors are shamed into walking away, as Jesus continues to write on the ground.

The Jesuit's association of the two events is somewhat curious. The raising of Lazarus before a crowd of onlookers certainly constitutes a thaumaturgical and (as screen adaptations have demonstrated) supremely televisual moment. The second incident is very different. On this occasion, Christ is confronted, in the hope that he will betray himself by a careless comment. Thus, there would be two victims (Christ and the woman), instead of one. His posture is well described as one of 'cryptic abasement'. Whereas important pronouncements are often delivered from an elevated position, he lowers himself to the ground. Moreover, what he writes on the ground is 'cryptic': it is secret, indecipherable. It is perhaps the outward signifier of inner tension or debate. Its effect, however, is to defuse a highly charged situation, by deflecting attention from the arrested woman. While deflationary on the one hand, it is devastatingly effective on the other. It is the act of someone with a highly developed psychological insight, for the erosion of violence is achieved not by wonder-working, but by the minimal use of word and gesture. Thus, while the diagnosis of 'megalomaniacal impertinence' can be understood with reference to the raising of Lazarus (an intervention into a passive state), it is only with difficulty extended to the rescue of the accused woman (an essentially defensive or preventive act).

Indeed, when Beckett later returns to the incident, in *Texts for Nothing*, he concentrates upon a different aspect: that of effacement. Paradoxically, Christ creates, by his dust-writing, a *tabula rasa*, for the memory of the woman's act is effaced as her accusers melt away. Accordingly, the labouring subjectivity in *Texts for Nothing VI* experiences 'nostalgia for that slime where the Eternal breathed and his son wrote, long after, with divine idiotic finger, at the feet of the adulteress, wipe it out' (*CSPR*, p. 90). Here, the linked text is no longer one concerning the revival of an individual man (Lazarus), but one concerning the creation of mankind, for 'that slime where the Eternal breathed' refers to the moment when God is said to have 'formed man of the dust of the ground, and breathed into his nostrils the breath of life' (Genesis 2: 7). Hence, the primeval mud both generates and obliterates.

It is to the latter process that the Beckettian organism seems most readily to gravitate: to dispersal rather than consolidation. Hence, in that extended passage in *Dream of Fair to Middling Women* where the narrator pays tribute to a mobile aesthetic in which 'the experience of my reader shall be between the phrases, in the silence, communicated by the intervals, not the terms, of the statement' (*DFMW*, p. 138), St Paul is again pressed into service. Among instances given of this privileged dynamic of disintegration appears 'the Pauline (God forgive him for he knew not what he said) *cupio dissolvi*' (*DFMW*, p. 139). The operative text here is Paul's Letter to the Philippians. However, its truncation leads to a misleading impression, since the phrase (underlined here) is modified by its surrounding context: 'For I am in a strait betwixt two, *having a desire to depart*, and to be with Christ; which is far better: Nevertheless to abide in the flesh is more needful for you. And having this confidence, I know that I shall abide and continue with you all' (Philippians 1: 23–5). Paul is in fact in a state only too familiar to Belacqua: uncomfortably poised between two courses of action. He discerns the importance of his continuing presence, while at the same time aspiring, like Winnie in *Happy Days*, to be in atoms. He opts to remain, while being desirous to depart.

A further dimension is lent to the quotation by the narrator's aside: that Paul 'knew not what he said'. This is presumably a reference to the fact that, in order to dissolve, the process of death must first be endured. Moreover, the words of Christ which are thereby invoked – 'Father, forgive them; for they know not what they do' (Luke 23: 34) – are uttered at the moment of his own crucifixion. Beckett's people are often suffering slower crucifixions of their own. Yet something makes them cling on. Sometimes, it is brittle repartee. Hence, in *Mercier and Camier*, the two men avert Watt's threatened ejection from the pub by claiming he is about to be bereaved. If allowed his 'cry of revolt', claims Camier, Watt will 'clasp his hands and ejaculate, Blessed be the dead that die!' (*MAC*, p. 115). His reference here is to the Book of Revelation: 'And I heard a voice from heaven saying unto me, Write, Blessed are the dead which die in the Lord from henceforth' (Revelation 14: 13). Pursuing his biblical parallels, Camier continues to press for liquid refreshment: 'Pass the sponge, said Camier, according to Saint Matthew' (*MAC*, p. 116). The sponge at issue is that (described by both Matthew and John) on which vinegar was placed for the crucified Christ to drink (see Matthew 27: 48 and John 19: 29).[6]

At other times, Beckett's people resort to a rationing of their moments, an attempt to segment the passage of time into an illusion of manageability. Hence, the voice in *Texts for Nothing V* edits his reeling consciousness with the phrase: 'I haven't been damned for what seems an eternity, yes, but sufficient unto the day, this evening I'm the scribe' (*CSPR*, p. 87), thus echoing the sentiments in Matthew's Gospel: 'Take therefore no thought for the morrow [...]. Sufficient unto the day is the evil thereof' (Matthew 6: 34). One suspects that this is one of the few instances in Beckett's early writing in which a biblical sentiment is evoked at its face value, complete with the speaker's (at least temporary) endorsement.

PRIESTS, PRAYERS AND POPULAR PIETY

Once, tongue in cheek, Beckett described himself in a letter to his Catholic friend Thomas MacGreevy as 'a dirty low-church P[rotestant]'.[7] Indeed, he uses the phrase to describe Belacqua in an identical phrase in both *Dream of Fair to Middling Women* and *More Pricks Than Kicks*: 'Distant lights on a dirty night, how he loved them, the dirty low-church Protestant!' (*DFMW*, p. 227; *MPTK*, p. 78). Further, a similar phrase recurs in both *Dream of Fair to Middling Women*, when 'the Mandarin' accuses Belacqua to his face of being 'a penny maneen of a low-down low-church Protestant high-brow' (*DFMW*, p. 100), and in *More Pricks Than Kicks*, when Belacqua laughs heartily at a joke involving the accidental shooting of a parson: 'It was a mercy that Belacqua was a dirty low-down Low Church

Protestant high-brow and able to laugh at this sottish jest' (*MPTK*, p. 184).

That Beckett should have recourse to a sectarian label such as this (however satirically) is not without psychological interest. For one who, as the preceding chapter has explored, had by now evolved a strategy of doctrinal scepticism, the matter of religious 'identity' may have lost some of its ideological definition, but could not so easily shed its cultural reality, or even some residue of its nostalgic backwash. Examples of similarly self-directed satire can often be found where identity groupings – be they religious, ethnic, political, or cultural – have experienced opposition from without. To appropriate the label (albeit, or perhaps especially, in humorous vein) is in a sense to undermine or control it.

Nevertheless, many of the religious and devotional references to be found in Beckett's early writing are grounded in the Catholic rather than the Protestant tradition. An attempt at an 'explanation' of this, on the part of one who has not replicated Beckett's cultural context, is probably doomed to fall wide of the mark. Nevertheless, a few tentative observations may at this point not go amiss. On a biographical level, the fact that Beckett's family worshipped in a Protestant church clearly does not imply that they were oblivious to the practices of Catholicism. Moreover, as James Knowlson's biography of Beckett points out, Beckett's preparatory school of Earlsfort House was 'deliberately multidenominational',[8] and, for him, denomination would never have been a criterion of friendship. Of course, many of the Catholic-flavoured references within Beckett's early work are highly satirical, and this is consonant with the long tradition of clerical and religious satire among writers with whom Beckett was familiar, not least of whom was Joyce. It is unlikely that Beckett would have deflected his religious barbs away from Protestantism and towards Catholicism in order to avoid offending his family; after all, this consideration did not lead him to clamp down on other scandal-giving possibilities, in fields such as biblical (mis)quotation and sex. Moreover, the devastating satire of his early article on censorship, 'Censorship on the Saorstat'[9] makes clear his opposition towards writerly restraint on grounds of what is deemed to be 'unwholesome'.

Added complexity is lent to the matter when one considers that Beckett's move towards writing in French was acknowledged by him to have been prompted partly by his desire to feel the strangeness or otherness of language. Could this pull towards the linguistic other have embraced other 'othernesses', including the religious? Further, if it can be inferred that, by writing in French, Beckett was also writing for a French audience, then a satirical context based upon Catholicism would have taken on additional significance: and, moreover, a variant one, for French Catholicism differs from English or Irish Catholicism, just as Irish Protestantism differs from its English, French, or German counterparts.

Priests

Mention has already been made of the Jesuit who boards the bus and enters into theological dialogue with a waspish Polar Bear in *Dream of Fair to Middling Women* and *More Pricks Than Kicks*. This Jesuit is no ordinary theologian. Addressing the matter of Christ's 'interference' in the affairs (temporarily terminated) of his friend Lazarus, and of the 'woman taken red-handed', he attributes to Christ a 'megalomaniacal impertinence' (*DFMW*, p. 209). However, for him, this is not necessarily a matter for censure, for he conceives of Christ as the possessor of a very muscular kind of humility: as he tells the Polar Bear, it is 'beyond masochism'. This radical humility does not need the goad or stimulus of self-flagellation, for it is a symptom of 'a love too great for skivvying and too real for the tonic of urtication' (*DFMW*, p. 210). The Jesuit cannot subscribe to a cost-accounting Christianity. He believes because he considers unbelief to be 'a bore', and because he does not wish 'to count our change'. Claiming, in the face of the Polar Bear's challenge, to be 'strictly orthodox' (*DFMW*, p. 211), the Jesuit nevertheless demonstrates that his orthodoxy is the antithesis of conventionality. He is a stylish and provocative thinker. Moreover, like the Christ he professes to follow, his provocation is probably underpinned by a greater sense of humour than might appear.

It is not inconceivable that the nameless Jesuit has in him something of the Reverend Francis Mahony, who wrote under the pseudonym of 'Father Prout'. Mahony (1804–66), who was born in Cork, was an excellent scholar, well-versed in Latin, and fluent in French and Italian. He did in fact join the Jesuit novitiate in France, and spent some time in Rome. However, it seems likely that the brilliant, mischievous and gregarious Mahony – a man considered by Blanchard Jerrold to be 'a combination of Voltaire and Rabelais'[10] – was not temperamentally suited to long-term commitment to a religious community. As with Beckett's Jesuit on the bus, his wit and intellect went along with a contempt for superficial politeness. Hence, even those who paid tribute to Mahony's gifts often acknowledged that he could be rude and over-assertive in discussion. Moreover, his sense of the ridiculous ensured that 'the humourist chuckled audibly under the soutane' (*Final Reliques*, p. 5). Leaving the Jesuits (presumably by mutual consent), Mahony was eventually ordained as a secular priest, by an Italian bishop, and thereafter lived a cosmopolitan life, undertaking parochial duties in various countries but also producing copious quantities of humorous poems and articles. His manner and attributes reminded many of Dr Johnson, especially when, during periods in London, he was spotted slouching towards the Fleet Street tavern where Johnson's chair still stood.

Beckett was undoubtedly familiar with Mahony's work and/or reputation. In *Murphy*, Miss Counihan gives Neary 'a forenoon appointment at the grave of Father Prout (F.S. Mahony) in Shandon Churchyard, the one place in Cork she knew of where fresh air, privacy and immunity from assault were reconciled' (*MP*, p. 32). (Nowadays, since its opening to the public, the site is not quite so quiet; moreover, the once-Catholic church is now Protestant and would presumably be no longer the burial-place of a Catholic priest[11]). Later, the location is re-evoked when Wylie is said to be 'mindful of Neary's blunder by the grave of Father Prout (F.S. Mahony)' (*MP*, p. 72). That blunder, appropriately made over the grave of one who was himself noted for ruffling feathers, was 'to disparage Murphy' (*MP*, p. 34).

That the location was known to Beckett is apparent from the series of journals which he wrote during his travels in Germany in 1936-37.[12] Beginning his journey via Cork, he visited Mahony's grave on 28 September 1936. Indeed, his journal entry for that day includes a diagram of the church (St Anne's) as it stands in relation to the grave. Under it, Beckett wrote: 'Shandon. Grave of Father Prout (Rev. Francis Mahony). Buried with 19 of same name'. By the side of the diagram, Beckett has drawn a simple sketch of the church steeple. St Anne's Church steeple houses the famous chiming bells which inspired Mahony's best-known song, 'The Bells of Shandon'. This song became popular in both Ireland and England, partly because of the rendering of it by one Mr Morgan D'Arcy. Despite D'Arcy's distinguished performances of the song, Mahony is said to have preferred to sing or shout it himself, such that, on one social occasion in 1851, 'one or two ladies [...] endeavoured at first to stop their ears out of regard for their tympanums; but after the first stanza they got used to the fun, and joined in it most heartily' (*Final Reliques*, pp. 90–1).

Whatever anecdotes are told of 'Fr Prout' (and there are many), the fact remains that he eluded all classification. If he did appeal to Beckett, this may be the reason why. Mahony was an individualist and yet a convivialist, a serious scholar with a taste for the ridiculous (who was not above teasing Thackeray about his broken nose by alleging that he must have fallen down and trodden on it [see *Reliques*, p. 151]), and a keen observer of humanity who could nevertheless exasperate acquaintances with his obliviousness. Further, he was a Jesuit *manqué*, and yet not a parish priest in any conventional sense. Just as the Jesuit of *Dream of Fair to Middling Women* dissociates himself from parish priests, maintaining that, though 'excellent men', they are 'a shade on the assiduous side. A shade too anxious to balance accounts' (*DFMW*, p. 211), Mahony's assiduity was of the self-chosen kind. Not for him a life of disciplined routine, for: 'He wove his Parnassian wreaths instead of composing his homilies, and changed the smoke of the incense and the sacerdotal chalice for the fumes of the Virginian weed and "the cup that cheers"' (*Final Reliques*, p. 170).

The Jesuit of *Dream of Fair to Middling Women* is perhaps the most striking amongst the company of priests who appear in Beckett's work. Most are identified merely *en passant*. The exception to this is Father Ambrose, of *Molloy*, whose role emerges when Moran realises that he has missed Sunday Mass on the very August Sunday on which he is due to set out on his mission. Notwithstanding his omission, Moran resolves to request a private communion from the priest, for 'avec le bon père Ambroise il y avait toujours moyen de s'arranger' (*ML*, p. 129). There are, however, obstacles to be overcome. One is Moran's scrupulosity concerning the eucharistic discipline (a scrupulosity which he does not extend to his treatment of his son). Moran has broken the eucharistic fast with a pint of Wallenstein lager; hypocritically, he decides to disguise the evidence of it on his breath by sucking peppermints.

A further obstacle is that Father Ambrose is asleep when Moran arrives at the presbytery. Once awoken, however, the priest turns out to be less legalistic than Moran had feared: 'Tout le monde disait de lui qu'il était très large' (*ML*, p. 136). Moreover, he appears to comprehend that, for Moran, Mass-going is largely a matter of habit rather than commitment. After all, Moran has previously divulged that his devotion extends no further than the midday Mass of Sunday, for he has 'personnellement aucune expérience des autres offices, où je ne mettais jamais les pieds' (ML, p. 130). Nevertheless, Moran maintains that a Sunday without communion is for him incomplete. Although urged by the priest to desist from making 'comparaisons profanes', Moran cannot help but conjecture: 'Peut-être pensait-il au baiser sans moustaches ou au rosbif sans moutarde' (ML, p. 136). Heavenly viaticum or not, the ingested wafer does not rest easily on the stomach of the departing Moran, who finds that the spiritual food 'ne passait pas' (ML, p. 138). As such, it prefigures the bodily food which Moran is about to receive. Like the Eucharist, the Irish Stew disappoints its resentful consumer. Suspicious of priest and housekeeper alike, he wonders whether the former has dealt him unconsecrated bread, and the latter has removed the onions, to spite him.

The portrait of Fr Ambrose is not an unsympathetic one. Indeed, in the post-communion chat he has with Moran, he exclaims: 'Que cela fait du bien de rire, de temps en temps' (ML, p. 138). Laughter (prompted here by his own comparison of Moran's hen to the figure of Job on his dungheap) is, he avers, mankind's prerogative, since 'les animaux ne rient jamais'. For the few moments of their interchange, Moran and the priest begin to seem reminiscent of Mercier and Camier, or Vladimir and Estragon. After reflection, the priest observes: 'Le Christ n'a jamais ri non plus, [...] qu'on sache'. To assert that Christ never laughed (since he is not recorded in the Gospels as having done so) is to force affirmation onto absence. On those grounds, one could also assert that Christ never coughed or sneezed. Recognising this, the priest adds the rider: 'qu'on sache'. Moran's rejoinder is, however, matter-of-fact: 'Que voulez-vous'. Both men smile at the grim irony. Its subtext – the shadow of crucifixion – is very similar to that suggested by a phrase which Beckett had copied into his 'Whoroscope' notebook in the 1930s (RUL MS 3000): 'Christ had his ups and downs'.

If Fr Ambrose is made the butt of satire, it is of only the gentlest kind. In the end, however, his ministry vis-à-vis his parishioner is shown to be unavailing. Moran emerges into the rain in poor temper, conscious of having glimpsed what he construes as 'un manque de noblesse' (ML, p. 138) in the priest's face. His sacramental offices, like the non-sacramental ones of Marthe, have done nothing to transform Moran. Fr Ambrose reappears at the very end of the novel. By now, however, he has become even more superfluous.

While acknowledging his regard – 'Je crois qu'il m'aimait vraiment, à sa façon' (*ML*, p. 237) – the narrator recounts his dismissal of the priest: 'Je lui dis de ne plus compter sur moi'.

No other priest receives the extended narrative treatment accorded to Fr Ambrose. Indeed, few are identified by name, although the historical figure of Pope Celestine the Fifth is cited in *More Pricks Than Kicks*, when Thelma bboggs's mother is said to be 'almost as non-partisan as Pope Celestine the fifth. Dante would probably have disliked her on this account' (*MPTK*, p. 136). The chief notoriety of Celestine the Fifth was the fact that he was the first pontiff to resign. Elected at a time of crisis, when the papacy had been vacant for two years, the simple and unassuming Celestine was already in his mid-eighties when he was consecrated, in 1294. His chief recommendation appears to have been precisely that 'non-partisan' quality of which Beckett's narrator speaks. An ascetic, and founder of the Celestine order, Celestine was untainted by association with either of the rival Orsini and Colonna factions. Nevertheless, his administrative inexperience soon revealed itself in seemingly contradictory policies. Recognising his own incompetence, he drew up a constitution declaring a pope's right to resign, and promptly did so, less than five months after his election. Imprisoned, though apparently well treated, he died just over a year later.

To modern eyes, Celestine can be seen as a deeply honourable man, who had the courage to resign when he realised his inefficacy. Indeed, Petrarch had great admiration for Celestine. Dante, however, seems to have taken a different view. In canto 3 of *Inferno* (line 60), he places at the entrance of hell 'the coward who had made the great refusal' (*INF*, p. 91), and many critics have supposed this sufferer to be Pope Celestine. Beckett's narrator does not adopt a stance on the matter, but simply cites Dante's probable dislike, thus achieving the double object of footnoting his own reference, and of suggesting to the reader unfamiliar with papal history a wariness towards Mrs bboggs.

A further example of a named priestly (though presumably fictional) character is one 'Father Fitt of Ballinclashet', who is said in *Murphy* to be 'bound to acknowledge a certain vocation for a Mrs West of Passage, who loved Neary' (*MP*, p. 7), but he is merely mentioned by report. The insinuated threat to Fr Fitt's vow of celibacy is paralleled by the reference in *Watt* to the product called 'Bando'. Recommended for its efficaciousness in energising the body (including, seemingly, its sexual performance[13]), Arthur tells the ailing Mr Graves of its circulation on the black market. He includes in his description of its secret traffic the presence of Bando in 'ladies' underclothing', or in 'the hollow missal of a broad-minded priest' (*W*, p. 169). Nevertheless, broad-mindedness apart, Watt later distinguishes priests and nuns very firmly from men and women in his attempted taxonomy of the figure approaching along the road: 'Watt was unable to say whether this figure was that of a man, or that of a woman, or that of a priest, or that of a nun' (*W*, p. 224). Moreover, his judgement of the figure is not furthered by the fact that 'on the head there sat, asexual, the likeness of a depressed inverted chamber-pot, yellow with age' (*W*, p. 225).

There are also instances in Beckett's early work where priests are referred to anonymously, in terms of their ministries and functions. Thus, when Mercier and Camier at one point sit in a field, filled with thorns, thistles, and nettles, they imagine that 'on finirait bien par comprendre' (*MC*, p. 88). When the waste land was reclaimed, houses would be built on it, or 'un prêtre viendrait, avec son goupillon, et ce serait un cimetière'. A more sinister image, of rampaging priests, is evoked by the narrator in *Dream of Fair to Middling Women*: 'Beyond Cobh across the harbour fireflies are moving in Hy-Brasil's low hills, the priests are abroad there with bludgeons' (*DFMW*, p. 140).

In both these cases, priests are viewed in an interventionist or coercive role. By the same token, however, reverends are allocated a fair share of accidents within Beckett's writing. In *More Pricks Than Kicks*, as cited above, a parson is asked to play a role in amateur dramatics which involves his being shot. Baulking at the prospect of blaspheming by shouting 'By God!', he negotiates an alternative: 'Oh my!' (*MPTK*, p. 184). On the night of the performance, the revolver accidentally discharges a live bullet and shoots the parson. This hyper-realistic incident elicits from him an even stronger exclamation than the one he had earlier repugned: 'By Christ! I am shot!'. Belacqua always finds this story 'very funny indeed', no doubt because of its blackly comic exposure of hypocrisy.

Even more imaginative mishaps are recounted in *Watt*, where Watt hears the 'little voice' telling him of accidents befalling priests supposedly known to Mr Knott, who 'once frequented a canon who was kicked by a horse, in the crotch'. In addition, 'he once knew a missionary who was trampled to death by an ostrich, in the stomach, and he once knew a priest who, on leaving with a sigh of relief the chapel where he had served mass [sic. Presumably, 'communion'], with his own hands, to more than a hundred persons, was shat on, from above, by a dove, in the eye' (*W*, p. 88). The latter case takes on an added irony when one considers that the dove is the symbol of the Holy Spirit.

Prayers

There are many instances in Beckett's early writing of what can only be called 'prayer'. Usually emitted in adversity, this is not the prayer of worship, thanksgiving, or intercession, but the prayer of petition: an entreaty, or an appeal to a putative listener beyond. Often, these 'misereres' emanate from a psychical environment in which punishment and expiation are key notions. These will be considered in a separate chapter.

This section, however, deals with prayers in their more formal and specific sense: 'set' prayers, or liturgies. Again, many of these references take their significance from a Catholic setting, including Marian devotion. Thus, in a reference to the rosary, Belacqua is said in *Dream of Fair to Middling Women* to have 'told the beads of his spleen' (*DFMW*, p. 61), thus transforming the emotions denoting the three 'decades' of the rosary – the Joyful, the Sorrowful, and the Glorious – into the splenetic. A similar transference is effected by the narrator in *Molloy*, who tells of waking to hear the ring of the angelus. For him, this is not a mere chronological reference, for he elaborates upon it, adding an explanatory clause: 'l'angélus, rappelant l'incarnation' (*ML*, p. 19). The angelus does indeed recall the incarnation of Christ, but the narrator's mind does not rest there, for one conception merely provides a mental bridge to another: his own. Hence, 'je résolus d'aller voir ma mère'.

At the end of the novel, a Marian frame of reference again intervenes, this time in much more satirical vein. Accosted by a farmer as he walks home, and asked his business, Moran improvises the riposte that he is on a pilgrimage to 'la madone de Shit' (*ML*, p. 235) (in the English translation, 'the Turdy Madonna' [*BT*, p. 159]). Appropriately, given the scatalogical association, the farmer enquires as to whether this is the black Madonna, but is told: 'Elle n'est pas noire que je sache'. Her distinctive property, maintains Moran, is that she is 'la madone des femmes enceintes', and he is going to give thanks that his infant boy died while his wife survived. It is only with difficulty that Moran succeeds in extricating himself from the confrontation, by means of this cock-and-bull story. There are, of course, a number of black Madonnas around the world, and it is tempting in this context, given Moran's travelling difficulties, to think of the famous Black Madonna of Rocamadour, the hilltop pilgrimage village in southern France. Indeed, the English translation of the passage renders Moran's state ('un pélerin en marmelade' [*ML*, p. 235] in French) as 'a pilgrim on the rocks' (*BT*, p. 160), which is exactly the situation of those approaching that shrine. Nevertheless, such stray associations apart, Moran is also 'on the rocks' in the metaphorical sense. Once again he is vulnerable to a stranger in his path, and it is probably the florin he passes the farmer which is the decisive factor in getting rid of him.

Just as, in the passage cited above, the Madonna is drawn into association with the excremental, she is also evoked in the context of excretion in *Textes pour rien XI*. Once again, as with *Molloy*, a mother closer to home again participates in the scenario. Thus, the narrator recalls standing in a urinal which makes a pleasing gurgle, reminiscent of 'maman qui siffle' (*NTPR*, p. 192). While 'poussant de la prostate', the narrator is said to be 'graillonnant des ave'. This alignment of urination with the Hail Mary, the principal prayer to Mary – the building block of both the rosary and the angelus – is paralleled a few lines later, when the narrator is 'secoué d'éjaculations, Jésus, Jésus' (*NTPR*, pp. 192–3). An 'ejaculation' is the term, in currency until recent times, to describe a short exclamatory prayer from the heart, which can be uttered at any time. 'Jésus, Jésus' would be a good example. However, Beckett exploits here and elsewhere the other (and now much more common) use of the word – namely, the emission of semen – and then places it in apposition with the figure of Christ. (A similar juxtaposition occurs in the manuscript draft of *Watt* [UTA, Notebook 2], where a pious young man is humorously accredited with having, 'in the space of 3 summer months, on the Pigeon House wall alone', made 'the Sign of the Cross, with accompanying ejaculations, prior to casting himself feet foremost on the face of the waters, 937 times'.)

By thus appending spiritual outflow to bodily outflow, these texts deny the spiritual a separate or privileged field of operation. The corollary of this is that, satirised or not, the spiritual is rendered more immediate by virtue of its bodily realisation. This is, for instance, the case with that devotion known as 'The Stations of the Cross', or 'The Way of the Cross', which invites the faithful to consider fourteen distinct stages of Christ's passion, from his condemnation to his being placed in the tomb. In the form devised by St Alphonsus, these draw the imagination quite vividly into the bodily reality of crucifixion. Insofar as crucifixion deals with extreme physical suffering, it is not in itself subjected to ridicule within Beckett's writing. Nevertheless, when it is used as a parallel to the suffering described within the text, a contrast is sometimes drawn between an acute and finite crucifixion – one which can be divided into fourteen stations and which has a beginning, a middle, and an end – and one which is chronic and endless. Hence, Estragon's observation that 'on crucifiait vite' (*EAG*, p. 47) – with its subtext that his own crucifixion is, by contrast, infinitely long drawn out – is also reflected in the narrator's bitter preview in *Molloy* of his own protracted passion: 'la passion sans forme ni stations m'aura mangé jusqu'aux chairs putrides' (*ML*, pp. 32–3).

Later, the same idea returns in more elaborated form: 'Ma progression s'en ressentait, de cet état de choses, et de lente et pénible qu'elle avait toujours été, quoi que j'aie pu en dire, se transformait, sauf votre respect, en véritable calvaire, sans limite de stations ni espoir de crucifixion, je le dis sans fausse modestie, et sans Simon, et m'astreignait à des haltes fréquentes' (*ML*, p. 105). On this occasion, the narrator insists further upon the disparity between his own passion experience and that of Christ, for not only has he no 'hope' of crucifixion (and thus an end to his sufferings), but also he is 'sans Simon'. In other words, he does not have the equivalent of a Simon of Cyrene, the man who, as the Synoptic Gospels are unanimous in relating (see Matthew 27: 32; Mark 15: 21; Luke 23: 26), was recruited to help Christ carry his cross to Golgotha. Simon's recruitment constitutes the Fifth Station of the Cross. As such, it represents for Christ a palliative (though only a meagre one), as does the following Station, which recounts the pious tradition attaching to the woman, Veronica, who is said to have wiped Christ's face with a towel as he passed. In contrast, *Molloy*'s narrator claims familiarity only with a Sisyphean ascent to Golgotha, with no prospect of finitude.

There are many occasions in Beckett's early work when fragments of prayers drift through the consciousness for no apparent reason, as is the case with Belacqua: '*God bless dear Daddy*, he prayed vaguely that night **for no particular reason** before getting into bed, *Mummy Johnny Bibby* (quondam Nanny, now mother of thousands by a gardener) *and all that I love and make me a good boy for Jesus Christ sake Armen*' (*DFMW*, p. 8: my emphasis). (This formula also appears in a letter from Beckett to MacGreevy, probably dating from 1931, in which 'Frank' takes the place of 'Johnny'[14]. This is not, however, flotsam whose provenance is unknown, for: 'That was the catastasis their Mammy had taught them, first John, then Bel, at her knee, when they were tiny. That was their prayer. What came after that was the Lord's. Their prayer was a nice little box and the Lord's was a dull big box. You went down in a lift and your only stomach rose up into your craw. Oooaaah' (*DFMW*, pp. 8–9). Despite the association with the mother figure, this prayer has not, then, been jettisoned for good; neither does it appear to have been irrevocably tainted by feelings of irrelevance. It is simply there, buried where it was laid, somewhere within Belacqua's mental glory-hole.

What stands out from the recollection of the prayer is the fact that it has not been updated. It remains in a time-warp: that time when two small boys, deferring to a grown woman, prayed to one almighty male. Further, the emotional charge of the prayer attaches much more strongly to its personal voicing (however stylised) than to its collective manifestation. The intercession for significant others ('all that I love'), combined with the modest petition for oneself ('make me a good boy'), thus constitutes 'a nice little box', whereas the respectful address from humanity-on-earth to God-in-his-heaven ('Our Father') represents only 'a dull big box'. Belacqua's metaphor is that of the elevator: after the agreeable slump-down of inwardness and finality (the 'catastasis') comes the disagreeable jerking back, upwards and outwards. The perceived imbalance can still induce nausea in his mind: 'Oooaaah'.

At other times, old prayer-fragments are put to work in new manifestations. One example of this is Murphy's act of saying grace before consuming his twopenny packet of assorted biscuits 'with reverence, because as an adherent (on and off) of the extreme theophanism of William of Champeaux he could not but feel humble before such sacrifices to his small but implacable appetite, nor omit the silent grace: On this part of himself that I am about to ingest may the Lord have mercy' (*MP*, p. 49). It can be seen from this formula that Murphy scorns to use a standard form of grace; neither does he address the prayer directly, in the vocative case, to God. On one level, his version of the grace is nonsensical, for he is asking God to have mercy on a packet of biscuits he intends immediately to consume.

Moreover, Murphy innovatively links the biscuits – product of modern industrial processes – with the concept of 'theophany'.

Within the Old Testament, theophanies describe manifestations of God to mankind, either in direct encounter (as with Adam, Abraham, etc.), or indirectly (in the burning bush, in dreams, storms, etc.). Theophanies are few in the New Testament (since Christ is presented as the Father's self-revelation *par excellence*) but episodes such as the annunciation and the transfiguration can be elicited as examples, and the future *parousia* (the 'second coming', at the consummation of the age) is perhaps to be seen as the ultimate theophany.

The mention of William of Champeaux (1070–1122) is more obscure. William is remembered as the bishop who ordained St Bernard of Clairvaux. However, he reached eminence several years earlier, as head of the cathedral school of Paris, at the time when Peter Abelard was a pupil. Indeed, a theological dispute arose between Abelard and William concerning the doctrine of universals. Insofar as William was 'extreme' (Beckett's word), he held the more platonic, 'realist' view of universals, seeing them as essences which were prior to individuals; hence, a species was fully present in each individual, while also being common to very different individuals. Thus, it is possible to affirm within language that 'men and horses are animals'. Abelard, on the other hand, took the 'nominalist' position, maintaining that universals were mental constructs, such that, within epistemological discourse, they could describe several individuals. Thus, although to say that 'Man is a horse' is grammatically possible, it is logically absurd, since one would need an additional ideal form: that of 'horsehood'.

Although his reference is elliptical in the extreme, Beckett's reference to what were important and virulent debates in the Middle Ages is presumably a condensation of a spiralling parody of which Abelard himself would have been proud. It would run, I think, along these lines: 'God is to be perceived [theophany] infused in creation and therefore in matter. Biscuit is matter. Therefore God is in biscuit (biscuit is theophanous). Therefore to eat biscuit is to eat God'. On one level, parody reigns. On another level, interestingly, Murphy has identified what is seen by many modern Christian theologians as an inappropriateness in saying grace at all. If incarnation (God taking material substance in Jesus) is to be taken seriously, then matter is already grace-filled, and 'saying grace' before food is a redundant action. (Ironically, of course, it will not be Murphy who consumes the biscuits, in any case, but Miss Dew's dachshund in the park: a creature whose appetite Murphy considers to be one of 'depravity' [*MP*, p. 60]).

The prayer of grace is here moulded to suit unusual circumstances, however incongruous. Moreover, the same phenomenon
can be seen no less in the case of personal prayers than in that of
liturgical words and formulae, for Beckett's early work demonstrates more than a passing familiarity with the Latin Mass. Hence,
in *More Pricks Than Kicks*, Belacqua uses the response 'Sursum corda' ('Lift up your hearts') – which is one of the responses which
precede the Preface to the Canon of the Mass – as his private
shorthand to denote an uplifting experience (preferably indulged in
on his own). Thus, one place where he experiences this 'sursum
corda' is within the square tower in a field beside the asylum. His
girlfriend Winnie cannot participate in his enthusiasm: ' "Then
hadn't we better be getting on" said Winnie, quick as lightning'
(*MPTK*, p. 30). A later girlfriend, Lucy, will be similarly un-
comprehending of 'all his fugues into "sursum corda" and "private
experience", from the inception of their romance' (*MPTK*, p. 116).

Just before his marriage to Thelma, Belacqua confesses his solipsistic nostalgia to Capper: 'If what I love [...] were only in
Australia' (*MPTK*, p. 146). What he is seeking is, he maintains,
'nowhere as far as I can see'. Capper, however, economically signals
his understanding by using another formula from the Ordinary of
the Mass: 'Vobiscum' ([With you], used in the phrase 'Dominus
Vobiscum' [The Lord be with you]). The appointment Belacqua is
seeking is indeed not with Thelma but with himself. This assign-
ment with self does not always, however, provide a comfortable
experience. In *Dream of Fair to Middling Women*, Belacqua finds that
'going back into one's heart' (*DFMW*, p. 44) is initially exhilarating,
but then leads into a tunnel in which the experience of interiority
must be deepened. This can require a considerable investment of
effort, in which he is aware of 'his soul at stool, per faecula faecu-
lorum' (*DFMW*, p. 45). Again, the remnant of a Latin doxology
surfaces, ripe for conversion, for 'per omnia saecula saeculorum'
[for ever and ever] is a frequent conclusion to the prayers of the
Mass. In this context, however, the simple substitution of a consonant transforms the phrase into the much more subversive
'through the dreg of dregs', thus according neatly with the preceding image of the 'soul at stool'.

A much more extended engagement with the prayers of the Latin
Mass occurs in the manuscript draft of *Watt* (UTA, Notebook 2).
Here, the theological poser concerning the fate of the rat who has
eaten a consecrated wafer receives considerably more detailed (and

often riotously funny) treatment than it receives in the published version. In the latter, Mr Spiro, the editor of a Catholic monthly called *Crux*, addresses the question himself, quoting a multitude of authorities. In the draft manuscript, however, the question is treated not within the magazine, but within the dissertation of a young seminarian called Matthew McGilligan. This young man seems to have been marked from his youth by a special distinction, since 'at the age of 17 his urine floated', and 'rainwater stagnated on his cranial vault'.

Moreover, McGilligan 'had been heard to recite the entire Canon from the *Te Igitur* to the *Per Omnia* without omission of a syllable and with only one pause for breath (before the *Unde et memores*) in 48¼ seconds'. This is indeed an impressive achievement, for the *Te Igitur* constitutes the opening words of the Canon, or Eucharistic Prayer – 'Te igitur, clementissime Pater, per Jesum Christum Filium tuum Dominum nostrum, supplices rogamus...' [We humbly pray and beseech thee, therefore, most merciful Father, through Jesus Christ thy son our Lord...] – while the *Per Omnia* refers to the closing doxology of the Canon – 'Per omnia saecula saeculorum' – just before the recitation of the Lord's Prayer. The *Unde et memores* is the memorial prayer, or anamnesis, which follows on immediately after the Consecration. This liturgical segment of the Roman Canon – the very kernel of the Mass – could be expected to last at least ten minutes. Therefore, for McGilligan to complete it in $48\frac{1}{4}$ seconds, with only one pause for breath just over half-way through, is indeed little short of miraculous.

Earlier in the manuscript draft of *Watt* (UTA, Notebook 1) appears another passage reminiscent of the Roman Canon. His wife and children having died, 'Mr Alexander Quin' is described as leaving a deathbed note in which he expresses the hope of rejoining, in the next life, 'Willy, Willy, little Leda, Willy, Agnes, Laurence, Prisca, Zoe, Perpetua, Willy and their unfortunate mother'. As the litany proceeds, its rhythms begin to draw it into affiliation with the lists of proper names of apostles and martyrs which appear at two junctures in the Canon of the Mass. Indeed, two of the names – Perpetua and Lucy – are also to be found in Beckett's list: 'Peter, Felicitas, Perpetua, Agatha, Lucy, Agnes, Cecily, Anastasia, and with all thy saints: into whose company we beseech thee to admit us'. Any possibly poignancy arising from Quin's litany is, however, removed by its humorous context, and by the multiple replacement 'Willies' who pepper the list.

The same notebook also contains an expanded section relating to the exchange between the old man and Arthur (here, 'Quin'). In the published version, the almsgiving proceeds straightforwardly into the reminiscences of boyhood: 'God bless your honour, said the old man. Amen, said Arthur. Good day' (*W*, p. 253). In the draft version, however, so many prolongations are added to the doxology that the conversation begins to take on in words the exaggerated impetus which Vladimir and Estragon's hat-swopping routine will later achieve in gesture: 'God bless your honour, said the toucher. Amen, said Quin. And so be it, said the beggar. As it was in the beginning, said Quin. Is now and ever will be, said the mendicant. World without end, said Quin. Amen, said the vagabond. Good-day, said Quin'. Farcical as the exchange is, it does establish a rapport which momentarily transcends the disparity between the two men.

Popular Piety

In the early 1930s, Beckett cut out from a French newspaper an item relating to St Labre. Sellotaping it into his 'Whoroscope' notebook, he jotted beside it a note of Labre's feastday: 16 April. The article is a diverting one, for it chiefly recalls St Labre as a kind of patron saint of the unwashed. Born in France in 1748, Labre eventually moved to Rome, where he took up nightly residence in a niche of the Coliseum. In his pursuit of asceticism, he wore only rags, and had recourse to neither blanket nor pillow. Neglecting his body, which was covered with sores, he is said to have died in 1783, in the odour of sanctity. His personal odour was, however, reportedly less fragrant. Indeed, 'elle était même insoutenable, à l'avis de ceux qui ont visité le Saint' [it was even unbearable, in the opinion of those who visited the Saint].

That Beckett excised this item from the newspaper, and took the trouble to stick it into a valued notebook, is no doubt attributable to its incongruous humour and curiosity value rather than to any benevolence on his part towards the canonised elect. Nevertheless, Beckett elsewhere demonstrates his familiarity with a number of other saints. Hence, in *Dream of Fair to Middling Women*, Belacqua refers enthusiastically in a conversation of a flagellatory tenor to 'blissful Saint-Bridget the Rose without the white goat and the bunch of keys and the besom' (*DFMW*, p. 98) (presumably a reference to St Bridget of Sweden, who was noted for her penitential practices).

Later, a much less overt saintly linkage occurs when the narrator comments ironically of women that 'they have such winning little ways. [...] Even the Syra-Cusa, though we think she might have sent him at least *one* of her eyes in a dish' (*DFMW*, p. 179). It is argued convincingly by James Knowlson in his biography of Beckett that the Syra-Cusa is in fact based upon the figure of Lucia Joyce (Knowlson, pp. 150–1). Amongst other evidence adduced, Knowlson points out that the bodily description of the Syra-Cusa, together with her personality, accord with what is known of Lucia at the time that she knew Beckett. Moreover, in Dante's *Divine Comedy*, Lucia (a fourth-century martyr) comes from Syracuse.

Interestingly, further corroboration can be added to Knowlson's suggestion by the narrator's reference to the 'eyes in a dish'. Popular legend has it that a nobleman pressed his suit upon St Lucy on account of the beauty of her eyes; being determined not to marry, she tore them out and presented them to her suitor, declaring: 'Now let me live to God'. However, the symbol of the eyes on a platter may also have arisen because the name Lucy is suggestive of light. Whatever the reason, Lucy is regarded as the patron saint of diseases of the eyes, and the nod of Beckett's narrator towards this tradition seems to establish the Lucy/Lucia connection on an even surer footing.

Given the difficulties with his eyes which Beckett undoubtedly experienced, St Lucy's brief, as patron saint of the eyes, may have struck a chord with him. Perhaps this was also the case with St Jude, who until recent times featured largely on the citation index of *The Times* personal columns. St Jude is said to be the patron saint of hopeless causes, and is appropriately cited in *L'Innommable* in the context of hope: 'Ils n'espèrent rien, ils espèrent que ça durera, c'est un bon fromage, ils ont l'esprit ailleurs, hommes-rats, en appelant Jude, tout ça c'est des prières, ils prient pour Worm, ils prient Worm, pour qu'il ait pitié, pitié d'eux, pitié de Worm' (*LI*, p. 125).

A little later in the same text, the narrator imagines how welcome a face would be, passing before him now and then: 'Un visage, comme ce serait encourageant, si ça pouvait être un visage, de loin en loin, toujours le même, changeant méthodiquement d'expression' (*LI*, p. 126). At the occasional prospect of such a face, it would be a case of: 'Enfoncé le cul de cochon d'Antoine'. Indeed, the symbols of Saint Antony the Great are a pig and a bell, for Antony, the hermit of Egypt, is the patron saint of herdsmen. Accordingly, the pet pig, the runt of the litter, is known as the 'tantony pig'. By referring to 'le cul de cochon', Beckett is presumably making somewhat frank reference to sensual temptations (from which the hermit Antony notoriously suffered and which his contemporary St Athanasius described).

Another saint often depicted with an animal companion is St Roch. In this case, the animal is a dog, in acknowledgement of the legend that a hound brought Roch food every day when he was dying of plague in a forest. (Thus, 'St Roch et son chien' is a kind of French equivalent of 'Darby and Joan'). Since St Roch developed a reputation as a healer from the plague, various legends began to attach to his life, and, in *Molloy*, Beckett poses one of the more fanciful of the genre: 'Serait-il exact que saint Roch enfant ne voulait têter ni les mercredis ni les vendredis?' (*ML*, p. 227).

In addition to the saints themselves, there are several references in Beckett's early writing to saints' days or other feastdays of the Roman calendar. In *More Pricks Than Kicks*, for example, as Belacqua is wandering at Christmastide through the streets of Dublin, he is put in mind of 'the Feast of St. John, when they lit the torches of resin on the towers and the children, while the rockets at nightfall above the Cascine were still flagrant in their memory, opened the little cages to the glutted cicadae after their long confinement and stayed out with their young parents long after their usual bedtime' (*MPTK*, pp. 54–5). Among the many St Johns, the one in question here is St John the Baptist, whose feastday of 24 June is celebrated in several Italian cities. Beckett's description, however, appertains to Florence, the city he had visited in the summer of 1927. St John the Baptist is the patron saint of Florence, and the festival is therefore celebrated there with particular vigour, with fireworks and other revelries.

Beckett refers to St John the Baptist's Day again in the opening few lines of *Malone meurt*: 'Il se peut que je me trompe et que je dépasse la Saint-Jean et même le Quatorze Juillet, fête de la liberté. Que dis-je, je suis capable d'aller jusqu'à la Transfiguration, tel que je me connais, ou l'Assomption' (*MM*, p. 7). Thus, by using the signposts of the succeeding festivals (three religious, and one secular), the narrator is able to string out into the future his putative life-span. Hence, by surviving 24 June, 14 July, and 6 August, the narrator may manage to 'pant on' (as the English translation has it [*BT*, p. 165]) to 15 August.

Amongst references to churches in Beckett's early writing are the two parishes mentioned in connection with Belacqua's marriage to

Thelma bboggs. The ceremony itself is said to take place at the 'Church of Saint Tamar' (*MPTK*, p. 147). Tamar is not, in fact, a saint, but the daughter-in-law, appropriately, of Shuah (that namesake of Belacqua) and Judah (see Genesis 38). As daughter-in-law of Shuah and Judah, she is also sister-in-law of Onan. (The name Tamar also attaches to a daughter of David who was raped by Amnon).

Earlier, however, it is the genuine Church of St Nicholas in Galway (though spelt, in the French way, as 'Saint Nicolas') which is envisaged by Thelma and Belacqua as a place, 'if it were not closed when they arrived, to repair without delay and kneel, [...] and invoke, in pursuance of a vow of long standing, the spirits of Crusoe and Columbus, who had knelt there before him' (*MPTK*, pp. 135–6). Beckett had made a trip to Galway in 1932 with his brother Frank, and the reference to entering the church 'if it were not closed' may stem from the memory of having been disappointed to find that access to the mosaics of the Dominican and Franciscan churches was denied to them, as he told Thomas Mac-Greevy, because of 'some damn retreat'.[15] They had, however, been able to enter the Church of St Nicholas, 'which is charming and where they say Cristoforo C. had a dish of mass before committing his indiscretion'. There is indeed a tradition that Christopher Columbus received communion in the Church of St Nicholas before setting out to the New World. As a 1948 guide to Connemara states: 'It is believed that Christopher Columbus heard Mass in this Church before setting out to discover the New World. It is not improbable that this was the case, for during the Middle Ages the tales of the voyages of St Brendan the Navigator were part of the cultural heritage of Europe, and Columbus could hardly fail to have heard of his great precursor, and came to obtain more information regarding the country discovered by the Irish Saint'.[16]

Unfortunately, as the final story in *More Pricks Than Kicks*, 'Draff', reveals: 'Thelma née bboggs perished of sunset and honeymoon that time in Connemara' (*MPTK*, p. 189). If the newly weds' prayer, and invocation of Columbus, did indeed take place, then it hardly provided an auspicious start to their marriage.

Other features of what might be called popular piety find their way into the early writing from time to time. Thus, Belacqua is accosted in the bar by a woman taking it upon herself to sell 'seats in heaven' (*MPTK*, p. 47). Resisting Belacqua's enquiry – 'Have you got them on you?' – she succeeds in selling him four.

Before hearing of her doubtful wares, Belacqua had noticed that the approaching woman not only had no hat, but also was wearing shoes which are described as 'the cruel strait outsizes of the suffragette or welfare worker' (*MPTK*, p. 47). Women with missions motivated by social or religious concerns do not receive sympathetic treatment in Beckett's early writing. In *Molloy*, for instance, the narrator describes some unappetising tea and bread pressed upon him at the police station by a woman. He comments ruefully: 'Quand les assistantes sociales vous offrent de quoi ne pas tourner de l'oeil, à titre gracieux, ce qui pour elles est une obsession, on a beau reculer, elles vous poursuivraient jusqu'aux confins de la terre, le vomitif à la main. Les salutistes ne valent guère mieux. Non, contre le geste charitable il n'existe pas de parade, à ma connaissance' (*ML*, p. 30). Nevertheless, Molloy does manage to fling the offering away from him, 'aussi loin de moi que mes forces le permettaient'.

Belacqua demonstrates a similar wariness at the approach of the paradise ticket agent, who is described as a 'mysterious pedlar' (*MPTK*, p. 46). Her self-awarded licence to peddle draws her into more than phonetic affiliation with 'Lady Pedal', of *Malone meurt*, notwithstanding the fact that this lady, far from being hatless, sports a large straw hat betrimmed with artificial daisies. Mme Pédale 'adorait faire le bien et apporter un peu de joie aux moins fortunés qu'elle' (*MM*, p. 178). Unfortunately, she does so with more than a little regimentation. As she leads the party of inmates from the asylum, the outing starts to take on the character of an enforced pilgrimage. Indeed, the community singing which she attempts to lead – a song celebrating spring in the French original – is rendered in the English translation as a kind of evangelical hymn: 'Oh the jolly jolly spring / Blue and sun and nests and flowers / Alleluiah Christ is King' (*BT*, p. 261).

Mme Pédale's philanthropy is, however, undermined by Lemuel, who, having killed two members of the party, leaves her swooning on a rock. In a sense, Lemuel has usurped the role of his namesake in the Old Testament, where Chapter 31 (verses 1–9) of the Book of Proverbs professes to consist of 'the sayings of Lemuel'. Yet Lemuel, king of Massa, remains entirely silent in the passage, for the sayings appear in the form of a direct address to him by his mother: 'What, the son of my vows? Give not thy strength unto women, nor thy ways to that which destroyeth kings' (verses 2–3). Beckett's Lemuel is also a man of few words. Yet his actions with the hatchet demonstrate that, if any connection with the Old Testament Lemuel is to be established, it can only be in terms of a rebellion against his mother's injunction to 'plead the cause of the poor and needy' (v. 9).

Another casualty of a benefactress is Watt, who falls victim to one Lady McCann. The latter, said to be a product of 'her traditions, catholic and military' (*W*, p. 30), throws a stone at Watt which narrowly misses him. He, however, is equipped with another reminder of religious tradition: a 'little red sudarium', which he uses to mop any passing flow of blood. By presenting Watt as a victim of violence, and by using the esoteric word 'sudarium' (a term which Beckett entered into his 'Whoroscope' notebook, most commonly denoting the 'veronica cloth', with which, according to pious belief, Veronica wiped the face of Christ), Beckett draws Watt into momentary association with the figure of Christ. Indeed, this association is made explicit later in the novel, when Watt, walking through the garden, is said to resemble a painting of Christ by Bosch (*W*, p. 157). In the latter episode, Watt is also heard to request a handkerchief with which to wipe away the blood on his face. Later, in *Fin de partie*, a similar veronica cloth (referred to in the English translation as 'old stancher' [*EG*, pp. 12 and 53]) will be seen on the face of Hamm.

THEOLOGY AND SPIRITUALITY

The foregoing section has explored what might be regarded as visible or audible aspects of religious practice as they occur within Beckett's early writing. In some cases they arise simply as part of a cultural background to which Beckett finds it convenient to allude. It is clear, however, both from the early writing and from private notebooks which Beckett kept, that, despite much scepticism about religious practice, his reading of theology and spirituality was careful and wide-ranging. Much of the doctrine referred to would, of course, have been imparted to him in the course of his religious upbringing. However, his reading, both then and subsequently, stimulated further reflection upon those doctrines. Where Beckett stood in relation to particular theological and doctrinal questions at any given moment is impossible to ascertain. Nevertheless, it is probably true to say that the most effective satire issues from those who have a thorough knowledge of what they are satirising, and, if much of the theological speculation in Beckett's early writing is parodic, even exuberantly so, it is carefully and knowledgeably so.

An example of Beckett's engagement with theological controversies occurs in his poem 'Whoroscope', where eucharistic debate is evoked by the lines:

> So we drink Him and eat Him
> and the watery Beaune and the stale cubes of Hovis
> because He can jig
> as near or as far from His Jigging Self
> and as sad or lively as the chalice or the tray asks.
> How's that, Antonio?
>
> (*CP*, p. 3).

Since even the clue of 'Antonio' is insufficient to render this passage immediately identifiable, Beckett adds the footnote: '[Descartes's] Eucharistic sophistry, in reply to the Jansenist Antoine Arnauld, who challenged him to reconcile his doctrine of matter with the doctrine of transubstantiation' (*CP*, p. 5).

The objections which Arnauld launched in 1640, when still preparing his doctoral dissertation, take their foundation from the eucharistic dogma promulgated by the Council of Trent in 1551. The terms of this dogma were that, when the bread and wine are consecrated in the course of Mass, the substances of bread and wine are changed into the body and blood of Christ, while the 'species' (that is, their qualities as bread and wine) remain. In other words, it is only the deeper reality of the bread and wine which is transformed by God's power: the 'accidents' (the perceptible characteristics) retain their customary appearance.

Arnauld maintained that Descartes was unorthodox in holding that the 'accidents' were only modes of being rather than permanent and simultaneous realities, since Descartes could not conceive of an accident remaining constant when its habitual substance had been removed. Descartes's response to Arnauld maintains that he had not denied the 'reality' of accidents, since he must allow for the fact that 'Dieu peut faire une infinité de choses que nous ne sommes pas capables d'entendre'.[17] It is probably this argument – that of God's omnipotence – which Beckett is parodying in the lines referring to 'His Jigging Self' being present in the elements represented by 'the watery Beaune and the stale cubes of Hovis'. In this connection, the use of the word 'jigging' takes on an interesting complexity. While clearly used contemptuously in the phrase 'His Jigging Self' (where a rhyming overlay of 'frigging' is presumably being suggested), the verb 'jig' can mean not only to dance, but also (in mining) to separate ore or coal from waste material. Hence, while Christ (the 'Lord of the Dance') is perceived as dancing within, around and beyond the rather disreputable-looking ('watery' and 'stale') elements, the concept of differentiation (between substance and species) is also proposed by the mining term.

In fact, Beckett's rather pejorative characterisation of Descartes's argument (including his footnote reference to 'sophistry') deals rather rough justice to Descartes's intellectually rigorous discourse. Descartes is certainly demonstrating sophistication in his response to Arnauld, but he does so with style and a certain amount of humour. For Descartes, the only logical explanation of transubstantiation is that, if the Body and Blood have appropriated the substance of the bread and wine, then the accidents cannot be 'real' in the same sense as before; they can only be perceived as real. God, he maintains, does not need a double miracle: that is, first the transubstantiation, and secondly the preservation as before of the accidents. He therefore concludes his essay by a head-on collision with Aquinas, for, in Descartes's amused rendering, the Thomist argument amounts to a double-layered miracle, in which the sole purpose of the second miracle is to hide the evidence of the first. This is, despite the panache of its presentation, heavy-weight material. In debating with such assurance a subject of central importance to the Church's sacramental theology, Descartes is clarifying his previous argument rather than moderating it. Beckett's dismissal of it as legerdemain is uncharacteristically lazy, even if it suits the purpose of the poem's elliptical dynamic.

Beckett's use of the uncommon word 'pleroma' has already been quoted with reference to his letter to Thomas MacGreevy (Letter 73) concerning à Kempis's *The Imitation of Christ*. He also jots it down in his 'Dream' notebook, with the definition 'Totality of divine attributes'. Indeed, he uses the word in *Dream of Fair to Middling Women*, when Belacqua is considering the question of fidelity versus the brothel: 'He plastered the poor girl with the complete pleroma' (*DFMW*, p. 42). Although St Paul uses the word with reference to Christ (see, for example, Colossians 1: 19; 2: 9, where it is normally translated as 'fullness'), it is probably borrowed (with reservations, in Paul's case) from Gnosticism, where the word represents that concept of fullness of being to which all believers must aspire. For Gnostics, the pleroma, or Place of Fullness, is associated with an anticipated transcendence of all distinctions, including that of gender, a place where all material manifestations would be submerged into the spiritual. Since Beckett was undoubtedly interested in the early 1930s in Gnosticism and Manichaeanism (where the dualism of mind and body is a central concept), it is appropriate that he should introduce the term 'pleroma' into a discussion about what relation there could be (if any) between 'carnal frivolity' and 'real spirit' (*DFMW*, p. 42).

'Pleroma' is, however, a very *un*Beckettian word. For Beckett, any 'place of fullness' would have to contain moveable spiritual and psychological furniture. Moreover, it would have to be convertible enough to accommodate what he described to MacGreevy as that 'pleroma only to be sought among my own feathers and entrails' (Letter 73). After all, ponders the narrator in *Molloy*, even paradise itself might seem unduly static eventually: 'La vision béatique ne serait-elle pas une source d'ennui, à la longue?' (*ML*, p. 227). A similar suggestion arises in *Dream of Fair to Middling Women* with regard to the Real Presence (the Catholic belief that Christ's body and blood are fully present in the bread and wine of the Eucharist): 'The real presence was a pest because it did not give the imagination a break' (*DFMW*, p. 12). In other words, permanence induces insignificance. Accordingly, 'the object that becomes invisible before your eyes is, so to speak, the brightest and best'.

This distrust for the idea of completion finds many forms in Beckett's writing. Sometimes, a mere hiatus in the reproduction of a doctrinal formula is enough to allow Beckett an ironic detachment. Such is the case, for example, in *More Pricks Than Kicks*, where the lolling Belacqua ponders the three 'Theological Virtues': 'But it was useless. Faith, Hope and – what was it? – Love [...]. What would he not give now to get on the move again! Away from ideas!' (*MPTK*, p. 42). The third virtue (usually translated as 'love' or 'charity') is, according to St Paul, the greatest: 'And now abideth faith, hope, charity, these three; but the greatest of these is charity' (1 Corinthians 13: 13). This virtue, however, is the one before which Belacqua has paused. It hangs, separated from the rest, seemingly subjected thereby to an element of doubt or irony. Indeed, in his 'Dream' notebook, Beckett turns the same formula on its head by jotting it down, in humorous mode, in antithetical form: 'And now abideth these 3: Doubt, Despair & Scrounging, but etc...'.

In some respects, Beckett's creatures appear at times to be tormented by the thorny theological question of the relationship between free will and God's will, but again there is no degree of conclusiveness to be found. In the short story *La Fin*, for example, the narrator recounts receiving a visit from a priest: 'Un jour je reçus la visite d'un prêtre. Je lui appris que j'appartenais à une branche de l'Eglise réformée. Il me demanda quel genre de pasteur j'aurais plaisir à voir. On s'y perd, dans l'Eglise réformée, c'est forcé' (*NTPR*, p. 85). The comment: 'on s'y perd' is here ambiguous, referring possibly to the difficulty of navigating through the diverse branches of the Reformed Church. Beckett's English translation, however – 'you're lost, it's unavoidable' (*CSPR*, p. 57) – suggests a possible linkage with the idea of predestination: the idea (sometimes attributed to Calvin, although he did not consider himself the originator of it) that the soul's eternal destiny is pre-ordained.

Molloy, on the other hand, seems to work back from an initial assumption of free will at one point: 'Toutes les choses qu'on ferait volontiers, oh sans enthousiasme mais volontiers, qu'il n'y a aucune raison apparemment pour ne pas faire, et qu'on ne fait pas! Ne serait-on pas libre? C'est à examiner' (*ML*, p. 47). Of course, the whole issue of human freedom extends, beyond theology, to the fields of anthropology, philosophy, and psychology. Nevertheless, given Beckett's familiarity with St Paul, the structure of this passage suggests that he had in mind the well-known text by St Paul in which he anatomises the failed operations of the will: 'For that which I do I allow not: for what I would, that do I not; but what I hate, that do I. [...] For the good that I would I do not: but the evil which I would not, that I do' (Romans 7: 15 & 19).

For Paul, the 'reason' for these inconsistencies is mankind's tendency to sin, inherent since the fall of Adam. (Indeed, the narrator borrows Paul's argument in *Dream of Fair to Middling Women* when he describes Belacqua as being in 'distress at being a son of Adam and afflicted in consequence with a mind that would not obey its own behests' [*DFMW*, p. 6]). Molloy finds the matter to be more mysterious: 'C'est à examiner'. It is unlikely, however, that Molloy's examination of the matter would result in a proclamation akin to that of Paul in his following chapter: that 'all things work together for good to them that love God' (Romans 8: 28). For Molloy, the image of creation as a watch in the hands of the Divine Watchmaker – intricate, and full of carefully regulated components – is not meaningful. Rather, using his own life as the model, he tends towards the image of a failed or decomposing creation, a decreation: 'Elle est finie et elle dure à la fois, mais par quel temps du verbe exprimer cela? Horloge qu'ayant remontée l'horloger enterre, avant de mourir, et dont les rouages tordus parleront un jour de Dieu, aux vers' (*ML*, p. 47). It is a vision akin to that of the tailor within Nagg's story in *Fin de partie*, for whom God's creation can be compared unfavourably with a botched pair of trousers.

Yet, if the concept of creation as a lovingly constructed mechanism fails at the first hurdle, this does not mean that arguments for the existence of God are not aired, even if satirically. Indeed, Moran reveals at one point that: 'Moi j'aimais les végétaux, tout simplement. J'y voyais même quelquefois une preuve superfétatoire de l'existence de Dieu' (*ML*, p. 135). The assumption here is that this is a luxury argument, a spare one, since it is 'superfetatory' (i.e. it supplies an 'add-on' fertilisation). Nevertheless, perhaps such 'natural' intuitions are more meaningful than the implanted ones. Belacqua experiences a similar feeling in *More Pricks Than Kicks*, where the opening paragraph of 'Walking Out' consists of a finely judged description of an evening walk across the 'bright green grass' (*MPTK*, p. 109). One feels in the writing the familiar tug towards irony. Yet the sardonic is by a whisker evaded, allowing lyricism a brief sway. On this particular evening, nature has furnished every required element except the cuckoo, and even the cliché of 'the sky was Mary's cloak' seems grudgingly welcome. 'It was one of those Spring evenings' reports the narrator, 'when it is a matter of some difficulty to keep God out of one's meditations'.

Of course, to say that the Deity was in these circumstances more resistant to suppression than in others, is far from placing a vote of confidence in God. Yet in some ways this sentence is eloquent of a great deal of the para-theological activity which can be witnessed in Beckett's writing: attitudes of indifference, blame or incomprehension towards God are repeatedly struck, and yet it seems that to exclude such position-seeking altogether 'is a matter of some difficulty'. For one thing, there is the occasional onset of little surges of hope. These are, admittedly, limited in scope. Thus, the voice in *L'Innommable* is resigned to the fact that hope for the future is inevitably short-lived, for he talks of 'juste le temps qu'il faut pour que l'espoir puisse naître, grandir, languir, mourir, mettons cinq minutes' (*LI*, p. 126). Even these brief attacks of hope could, he suspects, be deliberately arranged by the anonymous forces which seem to govern his life: 'Ils s'arrangeraient pour que je puisse avoir des poussées d'espoir' (*LI*, p. 185). Yet the fact remains that the consciousness, despite periods of denial, continues to allow for the presence of God and for his possible attentiveness. It is as if a God who were always in the shadows, always chary of self-revelation, is one who is more difficult to eradicate from the consciousness. Conversely, as the narrator in *L'Innommable* suggests, a God who zooms into direct and intense encounter may just as quickly fade away: 'De même la croyance en Dieu, soit dit en toute modestie, se perd quelquefois à la suite d'un redoublement de zèle et d'observance, paraît-il' (*LI*, p. 95).

Even when theological issues are explicitly introduced, however, there is a recurrent uneasiness with regard to their implications. However preoccupied Beckett's people may be, from time to time, with concepts of infinity, eternity, and even destiny, they are beset by feelings of puzzlement, ill-adjustment, and irritation. If they conceive of a God at all, they nevertheless apprehend simultaneously that they are always in the wrong place, at the wrong time, or on the wrong footing. Faith would require a response; yet they are never in a position to feel assured that such a response would be heard.

Hence, in *L'Innommable* (arguably Beckett's most God-ridden text of all), the voice, pondering on its own beginnings, has recourse to the chronology of hell in order to try to situate itself: 'Car je dois supposer un commencement à mon séjour ici, ne serait-ce que pour la commodité du récit. L'enfer lui-même, quoique éternel, date de la révolte de Lucifer. Il m'est donc loisible, à la lumière de cette lointaine analogie, de me croire ici pour toujours, mais non pas depuis toujours' (*LI*, pp. 14–15). A few pages later, he peels back further layers of theological and biblical landmarks in an effort to retrieve a base from which to write: 'C'est moi qui pense, juste assez pour écrire, moi dont la tête est loin. Je suis Mathieu et je suis l'ange, moi venu avant la croix, avant la faute, venu au monde, venu ici' (*LI*, p. 24). By means of this device, the voice is enabled to multiply itself and to extend its versatility and portability. He is both Matthew and the angel: that is, both the teller (the evangelist) and that which is told (the angel's message to Joseph is told in Matthew, Chapter 1). He is both the past and the future, for Matthew retrojects the post-Resurrection faith in the light of the Old Testament expectations, while the angel's role is that of herald of the future. Predating both Cross and Fall, the voice experiments with liberation. From the trammelled body comes a spinning mind.

It is as if all specifications must be removed before any journey towards identity can be embarked upon. As with the narrator of *Textes pour rien X*, space must be cleared in order to think: 'Non, pas d'âmes, pas de corps, ni de naissance, ni de vie, ni de mort, il faut continuer sans rien de tout cela' (*NTPR*, p. 186). In theological terms, the overriding characteristic of these journeyings is the apophatic: that which resides in the negative. Whereas cataphatic theology proceeds by affirming, and by applying names to God – Being, Good, Life – the apophatic tradition recognises that such names can only be provisional, for God is beyond the nameable: he is the Unnamable. Of course, these two traditions are not necessarily hermetic, for positive theology can serve as an introduction to negative theology.

L'Innommable is full of interfaces of this kind; indeed, its dynamic is admirably summed up in the voice's own formula: 'Worm ne peut rien noter. Voilà en tout cas une première affirmation, je veux dire négation, sur laquelle bâtir' (*LI*, p. 88). Molloy, too, recalls his attachment to the splintering away of names from things, and vice versa: 'Oui, même à cette époque, où tout s'estompait déjà, ondes et particules, la condition de l'objet était d'être sans nom, et inversement' (*ML*, pp. 40–1). There is in some ways a circularity about this process, within the Beckettian world, in that the negations often lead back to the muddy psychical waters from which they set out. Hence, in Molloy's humorous diagnosis, mankind can end up being subjected to the same processes of negation to which God is subjected, with results which are little more than satisfactory: 'Ce que j'aimais dans l'anthropologie, c'était sa puissance de négation, son acharnement à définir l'homme, à l'instar de Dieu, en termes de ce qu'il n'est pas. Mais je n'ai jamais eu à ce propos que des idées fort confuses, connaissant mal les hommes et ne sachant pas très bien ce que cela veut dire, être' (*ML*, pp. 51–2).

Even amid the layers of negation, however, a kind of groping out is taking place. The 'innommable' is both within and beyond, as described in *Textes pour rien XI*: 'Et je suis encore en route, par oui et par non, vers un encore à nommer, pour qu'il me laisse la paix, pour qu'il ait la paix, pour qu'il ne soit plus, pour qu'il n'ait jamais été' (*NTPR*, pp. 189–90). Moreover, the passage which is perhaps the most beautiful of all in *L'Innommable* is also the one which is most markedly swathed in terms of negation, a grammatical negation which seems to coexist with a semantic affirmation: 'Ne sentant rien, ne sachant rien, il existe pourtant, mais pas pour lui, pour les hommes [...]. Un seul tourné vers le tout-impuissant, le tout-ignorant, qui le hante, puis d'autres. Vers celui dont il se veut l'aliment, lui l'affamé, et qui, n'ayant rien de l'homme, n'a rien d'autre, n'a rien, n'est rien. Venu au monde sans naître, sans vivre y demeurant, n'espérant pas mourir, épicentre des joies, des peines, du calme. Ce qu'ayant de moins changeant on croit avoir de plus réel' (*LI*, pp. 100–01).

With so much at stake, it is perhaps not surprising that the intensive search for identity within language is often abandoned in favour of a less debilitating path of sarcasm and reservation. Much of this is directed at those who make it their business to promulgate God's message, including theologians and catechists. Hence, the voice in *L'Innommable* speaks ruefully of those who speak with 'cette langue de catéchiste, mielleuse, fielleuse, c'est la seule qu'ils sachent parler' (*LI*, p. 116). These nameless people presume to enlighten him about his dependence on God: 'Ils m'ont également affranchi sur Dieu. Ils m'ont dit que c'est de lui que je relève en dernière analyse' (*LI*, p. 18). Such diagnostic statements are always undermined by the surveying consciousness of Beckett's early writing. In this respect, the conventional exactitudes of scholastic discourse, which to modern ears often resemble pointless pedantry, are a sitting target. Beckett is perfectly familiar with the lexis: indeed, he uses the word 'quodlibet' (a scholastic argument) early in *More Pricks Than Kicks* to describe Beatrice's exposition, within *The Divine Comedy*, of the spots on the moon. He is also familiar with that penchant for fine distinctions and relentless logic which renders the 'schoolmen' so easy to parody: a skill he shows off to best advantage in *Molloy* and *Watt*.

In the former, Moran capitalises on those shades of misogyny which are often to be found in patristic (and later) theological discourse: 'Je me rappelle à ce propos une vieille blague sur l'âme des femmes. Question, Les femmes ont-elles une âme? Réponse, Oui. Question, Pourquoi? Réponse, Afin qu'elles puissent être damnées. Très amusant' (*ML*, p. 186). The fact that Moran enjoys this joke so much is arguably more significant than is the joke itself, especially since no argument based upon the putative absence of a soul in women has ever held sway within mainstream theological debate.

Yet, if the detail is phoney, the structure is plausible, and it is upon this principle that many of Beckett's cod-theological queries rely for their effect. Hence, in the long list comprising 'certaines questions d'ordre théologique' (*ML*, pp. 226–7) with which Moran preoccupies himself, there are one or two of potential profundity, such as: 'Que foutait Dieu avant la création?' and 'L'antéchrist combien de temps va-t-il nous faire poireauter encore?' Interestingly, with reference to the former question, Beckett notes down in his 'Dream' notebook St Augustine's dismissive handling of the same old chestnut, in Book 11 of the *Confessions*: 'I answer him that asketh, "What did God before He made heaven and earth?" I answer not as one is said to have done merrily, [...] "He was preparing hell (saith he) for pryers into mysteries". It is one thing to answer inquiries, another to make sport of inquirers. So I answer not' (*CONF*, pp. 260–1).

Alongside these questions are many which range in tone from the legalistic to the hilariously improbable. These include the attempt to pronounce upon matters not open to verification: 'Le serpent rampait-il ou, comme l'affirme Comestor, marchait-il debout?'; the implications of misapplications of procedure: 'Si l'on disait la messe des morts pour les vivants?', and the deconstruction of prescribed gesture: 'Cela a-t-il vraiment de l'importance de quelle main on s'absterge le podex?'. This latter query – relating to which hand should be used to wipe one's bottom – also appears in *Watt*, where it is briskly dismissed by the editor of *Crux*: 'I personally am a neo-John-Thomist. I make no bones about that. But I do not allow it to stand in the way of my promiscuities. *Podex non destra sed sinistra* – what pettiness. Our columns are open to suckers of every persuasion and freethinkers figure in our roll of honour' (*W*, p. 26). In designating the editor as a 'neo-John-Thomist', the narrator enjoys a joke at the narratee's expense. While the term 'neo-Thomism' is commonly used to denote the revival of interest in the medieval scholastic method during the nineteenth and early twentieth centuries, the insertion of 'John' entrains other connotations, for a 'John-Thomas' is a euphemism for the penis. Even if taken individually, the terms have an earthy frame of reference, for a 'john' is a slang term for the toilet, and 'le Thomas' in French is a chamber-pot.

In *Molloy*, the litany of questioning gradually gives way to dilemmas of a more personal nature before erupting in one further robust visual image of do-it-yourself sacraments: 'Quel était le nom du martyr qui, étant en prison, chargé de chaînes, couvert de vermine et de blessures, ne pouvant se remuer, célébra la consécration sur son estomac et se donna l'absolution?' (*ML*, p. 228).

This combination of the picturesque, the grotesque, the exaggerated and the satirical is also found in the episode in *Watt* (briefly referred to above), when Watt meets the editor of *Crux*, a Catholic monthly. Mr Spiro (whose name can be translated as 'I breathe', or 'I am inspired') says of his organisation: 'We keep our tonsure above water' (*W*, p. 25), and this is apparently achieved mainly by means of selling advertising space. The prize competitions are also popular, and Mr Spiro quotes a typical poser: 'What do you know of the adjuration, excommunication, malediction and fulminating anathematisation of the eels of Como, the hurebers of Beaune, the rats of Lyon, the slugs of Mâcon, the worms of Como, the leeches of Lausanne and the caterpillars of Valence?' (*W*, p. 26). Mr Spiro does not enlarge further upon the responses elicited from readers, although his subsequent disquisition upon the correct manner of dealing with a rat who consumes a host clearly has a bearing on the subject, insofar as it relates to the notion of sin or blasphemy in animals.

In fact, Beckett is not indulging in invention here, since criminal trials and excommunications of animals in the Middle Ages and subsequently are known to have taken place in many parts of Europe.[18] Indeed, one of Racine's plays, *Les Plaideurs*, features the trial of a dog for the theft of a capon. These dealings with animals took two forms, according to whether they were conducted by the secular or the religious authorities. In the case of the former, an individual animal accused of a crime might have to undergo a public trial and punishment on the same basis as a human being. Thus, for instance, a man and a cow implicated in bestiality were both condemned by the parliament of Paris in 1546 to death by hanging (Evans, p. 147). Often, however, animals were executed on their own, as with the cock of Bâle who was sentenced to be burned at the stake in 1474 for having laid an egg (Evans, p. 162). In the case of religious proceedings, whole groups of animals could be accused of being pests or thieves, and then dealt with by some form of malediction. Strictly speaking, animals cannot be 'excommunicated', since they are not legitimate communicants in the first place, but this term does seem to have been used alongside that of anathematisation.

However far-fetched it may sound, then, Beckett's unlikely animal defendants certainly find their historical precedents. Hence, in 1225, the eels of Lausanne were anathematised, as were the leeches of Lake Geneva in 1451, the slugs of Autun in 1487, the rats of

Nîmes in 1479, the caterpillars of Mâcon in 1481, and the worms of Lausanne in 1541 (Evans, Appendix). The mention of the 'hurebers of Beaune' is also genuine, since in the fifteenth century the inhabitants of Beaune successfully applied to the ecclesiastical court of Autun for a decree of excommunication against the hurebers, who were probably a kind of harvest-fly or locust. Against this background, Moran's theological question 11 in *Molloy* – 'Que penser de l'excommunication de la vermine au seizième siècle?' (*ML*, p. 227) – turns out (unlike many of the neighbouring questions) to be only superficially outlandish. It is, in fact, perfectly authenticated, for there are, for example, cases involving vermin in Lausanne in 1509, and rats and insects in Langres in 1512–13. Moreover, the question of what to think of this – 'Que penser?' – is a legitimate one, for under what heading of sociology, cultural history, theology, or psychology are modern thinkers to consider such curious phenomena?

After citing this esoteric competition question, Mr Spiro goes on to quote from a letter he has received from a reader in Lourdes concerning the prickly problem of what to do with a rat which has consumed a consecrated host. Again, this is not a red herring on the part of Beckett. In 1394, for example, a pig was tried and hanged at Mortaign for precisely the same offence: that of having consumed a eucharistic wafer (Evans, p. 156). The three questions posed by the reader concerning the rat are: '1. Does he ingest the Real Body, or does he not? 2. If he does not, what has become of it? 3. If he does, what is to be done with him?' (*W*, pp. 26–7). Questions 2 and 3 are, of course, mutually exclusive, and it is therefore significant that Mr Spiro replies to only questions 1 and 3, thus indicating his opinion that the transubstantiated host indeed remains unchanged. Moreover, in addressing the questions, he quotes from a large number of theological sources: 'Saint Bonaventura, Peter Lombard, Alexander of Hales, Sanchez, Suarez, Henno, Soto, Diana, Concina and Dens'.

Despite appearances, it is a well-authenticated list of theologians, among whom are many prolific writers. The first three writers are from the Middle Ages: Bonaventure (c. 1217–74); Lombard, the 'Master of the Sentences' (c. 1095–1160); and Alexander of Hales, the 'Doctor Irrefragabilis' (c. 1185–1245). Franciscus Henno (died 1720) was a Franciscan theologian[19], while Sanchez, Suarez, and Soto are all Spanish contemporaries: Thomas Sanchez (1550–1610), a Jesuit moralist and canonist; Francisco Suarez (1548–1617), a philosopher and theologian; and the theologian Pedro de Soto (1500–63). Of the last three names in the list, Antonino Diana (1585–1663) was a moral theologian skilled in casuistry, Daniel Concina (1687–1756) was a Dominican preacher and theologian, and Pierre Dens (1690–1775) was the author of a major fourteen-volume work of theology.

Acknowledging the extent of Spiro's learning, the narrator declares (as if in explanation) that he is 'a man of leisure' (*W*, p. 27). The list in the corresponding manuscript draft (UTA, Notebook 2) contains still more names, however: 'St Thomas Aquinas, Saint Bonaventura, Peter Lombard, Alexander of Hales, the 4 great doctors of the west, the 4 great doctors of the east, St Stanislas Kostka, etc. etc'. (The last-named is an incongruous addition, since Kostka was a Polish boy who died at the age of eighteen, after only ten months as a Jesuit novice, and who therefore had no opportunity to establish himself as a theologian).

In the manuscript draft, the tri-pronged dilemma concerning the rat is inserted into a quite different context, for it forms the matter of a dissertation composed by one Matthew McGilligan (previously mentioned in the preceding section, with reference to his uncommon speed in uttering the Canon of the Roman Mass). McGilligan, like Spiro, devotes most of his attention to the third question, although he does briefly deal with the second question by stating that 'the body being consubstantial with the wafer, as much of the body was in the rat as the rat had eaten of the wafer'.

The third question, concerning the fate of the rat, forms a lengthy passage of uproarious comedy in the draft material for *Watt*. Declaring in answer to the third question that 'the rat, when caught, should be pursued with all the vigour of the Canon Laws and pontifical decrees', McGilligan adds that a feeling of delicacy forbids him from spelling out in detail what the procedure should be. Pressed by his superiors to elucidate, McGilligan emerges from seclusion to present his conclusions, which in the text are rendered in an attempt at phonetic spelling of his broad Irish dialect. Emphasising that he has only overcome his feelings of reluctance in 'obayjence tew me higherarsical sewpayriers', McGilligan begins his disquisition by considering the main difficulties to be grappled with. The first concerns catching the rat, and being sure that it is the right rat. The second considers the desirability of adoring the host which the rat has swallowed. In the third point, McGilligan states that the rat's body cannot be buried, since one would then be burying the Real Body as well. He therefore considers removing the wafer from the rat's body, followed by the ticklish question of whether to consume it on the spot, or whether to replace it in the ciborium. In the fourth point, McGilligan examines what should be done if one cannot catch 'd'ould rat unthil afther what he's bane an [...] done his doolies'.

At this stage – the stage which delicacy had earlier prevented him from describing – McGilligan is clearly on the point of suggesting that, if the rat has already excreted by the time he is caught, then the faeces must be consumed. Mercifully, he is cut short by his superiors and sent on holiday to Rome. It is here that he enters an art gallery with the intention of meditating upon the anathematisation of 'the flies of Lyon, the slugs of Mâcon, the worms of Como, the hurebers of Beaune and the eels of Lake Leman, as recorded by the egregious jurisconsult Barthélemy de Chassanée, in the fifth part of his first consultation, Lyon, in-folio, 1531'. This, then, is the passage corresponding to Mr Spiro's listing in *Watt*.

At the draft stage, however, Beckett has not yet suppressed his source, which is once again one with impeccable credentials. Bartholomée de Chassanée (also spelt Chassenée and Chasseneux) was indeed a sixteenth-century French lawyer of considerable distinction (see Evans, p. 21 ff). Chassanée established himself at the bar by acting as defence counsel to some rats, who had been put on trial at Autun for the crime of having eaten up the entire crop of barley in that region. Chassanée brought great legal dexterity to bear on the case, arguing that, since the defendants were very widely dispersed, they could not all be covered by a single summons. When, after expiration of the extended summons, the rats still did not present themselves, he argued that, given the serious difficulties attendant upon their journey to court (including the constant vigilance of local cats), they should be granted the right to appeal against the order.

It appears that Chassanée's legal defence of the rats was conducted with full seriousness, and its success even established a precedent which was cited later in a case involving human beings. Moreover, Chassanée himself wrote a long and learned treatise on various legal questions, including the anathematisation of animals. Beckett's dating of the treatise – 1531 – is indeed correct, and, since the treatise was reprinted in 1581, he may well had had access to the original work or to a facsimile. (There would, for instance, have been a copy of it in the Royal Court and State Library of Munich when Beckett visited Munich in 1937). It is likely that the mixture of erudition and quaintness in content in Chassanée's work would have appealed to Beckett.

In the draft, however, Beckett's young McGilligan is prevented from embarking upon his consideration of Chassanée's material in the cool of the art gallery, since his eyes fall upon a painting of 'a girl in a nightdress catching a flea by candlelight'.[20] From then on, his life takes a different course. Far from proceeding comfortably to ordination, McGilligan embarks on a life which is one long litany of struggle, culminating in: 'recovery of faith, last rites, deathrattle, loss of faith, annihilation, funeral with friends and flowers, oblivion'.

The theological discourse is cut off even more abruptly in the published version of *Watt*, where, after Spiro's citation of the theologians, it is stated that 'Watt heard nothing of this, because of other voices, singing, crying, stating, murmuring, things unintelligible, in his ear' (*W*, p. 27). Thus, Watt, like McGilligan, retires from the courts of scholasticism to take counsel with his own psyche.

These disjunctures from theological and religious impulses are very frequent in Beckett's early writing, where any potential current of divine communion tends to be rapidly short-circuited or unplugged. In *Molloy*, Moran (despite his observance of Sunday Mass) simply includes God in the list of targets of his antipathy: 'Je n'aime pas les bêtes. C'est curieux, je n'aime pas les hommes et je n'aime pas les bêtes. Quant à Dieu, il commence à me dégoûter' (*ML*, p. 143). His attitude to God has not moderated by the end of the novel, when he states: 'Il y a les hommes et les choses, ne me parlez pas des animaux. Ni de Dieu' (*ML*, p. 225).

This feeling of disgust leads on occasion beyond dissociative impulses to active hostility to God. In *Mercier et Camier*, the two men are suddenly caught in a shower of rain. Moreover, neither is able to put up the umbrella. For Mercier, it is the last straw, and he blames the only power he can hold responsible for their misfortune: 'Il ajouta, en présentant au ciel une face convulsée et ruisselante, et en levant et serrant les poings, Quant à toi, je t'emmerde' (*MC*, p. 38). Later in the novel, the episode is recalled when the umbrella again fails to work. On this occasion, Mercier resists the temptation to curse God. But perhaps it is too late, for Camier suspects that God the magistrate has remembered the previous offence: 'Qu'avons-nous fait à Dieu? dit-il. Nous l'avons renié, dit Camier. Tu ne me feras pas croire qu'il est rancunier à ce point, dit Mercier' (*MC*, p. 125).

The image of God the Father, then, tends to be one of implacability, unresponsiveness, and even cruelty. Indeed, the voice in *L'Innommable* thinks of himself as a squirming fish being baited by God the fisherman: 'L'essentiel est de gigoter jusqu'au bout au bout de son catgut, tant qu'il y aura des eaux, des rives et déchaîné au ciel un Dieu sportif, pour taquiner la créature' (*LI*, p. 86). There is an interesting parallel here with the figure of Jesus, who, on the whole, is not seen as part of a Trinity of conspirators. On the contrary, in his crucified manifestation, Jesus can sometimes evoke a feeling of empathy within the Beckettian consciousness. Far from representing the incarnation, or human face, of God, as Christian theologians would maintain, the Jesus who emerges from Beckett's work is often one who is also a helpless victim of God; the one who died calling to his father may be seen, like the voice of *L'Innommable*, as a fellow fish impaled on the end of God the Father's line. Indeed, that voice at one point envisages himself as being subjected by his tormentors, as was Christ, to a crown of thorns: 'Ensuite ils mettront l'accent sur les épines. Quelle prodigieuse variété. Celles-ci, il va falloir qu'on vienne me les enfoncer, comme à ce pauvre Jésus' (*LI*, p. 105).

The fishing imagery is also meaningful in relation to the fish as an ancient symbol of Christ. The Greek word for fish was used as an acrostic by the early Christian community, since each of its five letters represent the initial Greek letter of the formula 'Jesus Christ, Son of God, Saviour'. There are abundant references thereafter to the fish, to symbolise both Christ and those who profess him. Tertullian, for example, speaks of Christians as 'little fishes' in his *De Baptismo*. In his 'Dream' notebook, in which he makes many notes from St Augustine's *Confessions*, Beckett jots down the phrase 'Christ the fish', since, in Book 13 of that work, Augustine adverts to the acrostic in stating that 'therefore was He taken out of the deep, that He might feed the dry land' (*CONF*, p. 331). Moreover, Beckett uses the formula in his poem 'Serena III', in the line 'Jesus Christ Son of God Saviour His Finger' (*CP*, p. 25), and also in *More Pricks Than Kicks*, when the question of naming the lobster arises: 'He did not know the French for lobster. Fish would do very well. Fish had been good enough for Jesus Christ, Son of God, Saviour' (*MPTK*, p. 19). The 'fish' – 'Christ!' he said 'it's alive!' (*MPTK*, p. 20) – will be victim no less than Christ, for 'it was going alive into scalding water' (*MPTK*, p. 21). God will not help the tortured lobster, for, contradicting Belacqua's 'It's a quick death, God help us all', the narrator adds tersely: 'It is not'.

What Beckett's people find hard to forgive, it seems, is that they can sense no space for negotiation between God in Heaven and life-forms on earth, including the human. Hence, like Joyce's Stephen Dedalus, they find the concept of 'serving God' difficult to stomach. This is a God whose omnipotence they constantly begrudge and disparage. 'C'est à notre petit omni-omni que tu tiens ce langage?' asks Camier when Mercier is cursing God. 'Tu as tort', he continues, 'C'est lui au contraire qui t'emmerde toi' (*MC*, p. 39). This God is experienced as being accountable to nobody, as described in *Malone meurt*: 'Il le fallait, pour des raisons obscures et connues qui sait de Dieu seul, quoique à vrai dire Dieu ne semble pas avoir besoin de raisons pour faire ce qu'il fait et pour omettre ce qu'il omet, au même degré que ses créatures' (*MM*, p. 118).

The diverse descriptions of God's will with which Beckett was familiar, from the scriptures and from his wide reading of theology and spirituality, would probably have in common that, however actively they portray human beings as cooperators with God and formulators of their own destiny, they in the last analysis acknowledge deference to God's will rather than the individual's, believing the former to be working for the good of the latter. For Thomas à Kempis, whose book *The Imitation of Christ* was well known to Beckett, the renunciation of human will in favour of God's will is a central goal, constantly to be pursued. He articulates it particularly clearly in Chapter 15 of Book 3: 'Lord, you know what way is better; let this or that be done as you shall will. Give what you will, as much as you will, and when you will. [...] Put me where you will, and deal freely with me in all things. I am in your hand, turn me this way or that in my course' (*IMI*, p. 113). When the narrator in *Dream of Fair to Middling Women* uses the formula of '[God's] will, never ours', however, it is in decidedly satirical mode: 'Thus little by little Belacqua may be described, but not circumscribed; his terms stated, but not summed. And of course God's will be done should one description happen to cancel the next, or the terms appear crazily spaced. His will, never ours' (*DFMW*, p. 125).

Mention was made in the introduction to this chapter of Beckett's mixed response to *The Imitation of Christ*. While subject to reservations about many of à Kempis's assumptions, he could react favourably to selected passages which either chimed with his own experience or seemed to him to be endowed with linguistic beauty. Indeed, as that earlier section noted, he does pick out three such phrases for mention in a letter to Thomas MacGreevy.

Nevertheless, in contrast with these three approved phrases –
which might be seen as incarnating positive states or attributes –
Beckett also cites in the same letter[21] three phrases of a more
negative and penitential kidney: 'What is one to make of "seldom
we come home without hurting of conscience", and "the glad going
out and sorrowful coming home" and "be ye sorry in your cham-
bers" but a quietism of the sparrow alone upon the housetop and
the solitary bird under the eaves? An abject self-referring quietism
indeed'. These three phrases in fact all occur within a few pages of
one another in *The Imitation of Christ*, in the first of the four books
which make up the whole. (The third phrase, which Beckett copies
side by side with the Latin original in the 'Dream' notebook – 'In
cubilibus vestris compungimini' – cannot, in fact, be attributed to à
Kempis, since it is taken word for word from Psalm 4: 5. Nevertheless, the words are clearly quoted with à Kempis's endorsement). This first book of the *Imitation*, 'Counsels Useful for Spiritual
Living', aims to lay down the guidelines for a spiritual disposition:
cultivation of solitude and recollection, defeating temptation, living
at peace with others. It sets great store by rooting out the vice of
pride by its countervailing virtue, humility. This is to be seen not as
a creeping, Uriah Heep-like abasement, but as a clear-sighted
knowledge of oneself, resulting in the abjuration of any kind of
posturing or vociferous self-assertion. Nonetheless, what Beckett
appears to take exception to – as his selection of phrases indicates –
is what he sees as an underlying assumption that virtue is more
easily acquired in solitude than in society, and that an individual's
room should be a kind of courtroom of the soul, in which conscience is racked and the soul embarks upon exercises of self-
reproach. Such a process is for à Kempis a precondition of spiritual
equilibrium, since 'no one is worthy of heavenly consolation who
has not diligently exercised himself in holy self-reproach' (*IMI*,
p. 47).

Of course, à Kempis's text is steeped in the Bible, and phrases
from the Old and New Testaments often hum beneath the surface of
his writing, just as they do (in often more satirical mode) within
Beckett's own writing. Moreover, it is not difficult to affiliate the
sensitivities of both writers to those passages in scripture which
consist of awareness of human wretchedness, or of the transience of
life. The origin of the phrase 'sic transit gloria mundi' cannot be
definitively known, but it may well originate with à Kempis's 'O
quam cito transit gloria mundi!' (Book 1, Chapter 3, p. 10). In

voicing this observation, à Kempis is undoubtedly mindful of the many references, in the Book of Psalms and elsewhere, to the passing nature of human affairs, in contrast with the infinity of God. (See, for example, Psalm 90: 'a thousand years in thy sight are but as yesterday when it is past, and as a watch in the night. [...] The days of our years are threescore years and ten; [...] it is soon cut off, and we fly away').

However, if both writers are imprinted with a recognition of life's ephemerality, the use they make of this recognition is markedly different. For à Kempis, the observation that 'the life of man like a shadow suddenly passes away' (*IMI*, p. 55) is an echo of 1 Chronicles 29: 15: 'For we are strangers before thee, and sojourners, as were all our fathers: our days on the earth are as a shadow, and there is none abiding', or of Psalm 102: 11: 'My days are like a shadow that declineth'. Within à Kempis's presentation, this knowledge should be salutary; it should lead to a redoubling of fervour. 'While you have time', enjoins à Kempis, 'gather for yourself wealth that does not perish' (*IMI*, p. 55). Thus prepared, 'in death's hour you may be able rather to rejoice than fear'.

Beckett's writing is also suffused with a perception of the brief passage from womb to tomb, summed up notably by Pozzo in *En attendant Godot*: 'Elles accouchent à cheval sur une tombe, le jour brille un instant, puis c'est la nuit à nouveau' (*EAG*, p. 83). This baleful and recurrent insight remains, however, an insight. It does not translate into spiritual action plans. Within à Kempis's economy of salvation, adversity may be recruited in the service of good. Hence: 'It is good for us that at times we have sorrows and adversities, because they often make a man realise in heart that he is an exile' (*IMI*, p. 35). Such a transformation of negative into positive is quite alien in the Beckettian world, for, while intensely aware of present circumstances, the Beckettian organism can discern no way of converting loss (current or impending) into profit. Beckett thus rejects any posited linkage between suffering and salvation. As he asks in his letter to MacGreevy: 'Is one to insist on a crucifixion for which there is no demand?'

Despite grave reservations about its matter, however, Beckett was still able to enjoy the linguistic resonances of à Kempis's text, and even to exploit some of them in his own writing. For instance, à Kempis's phrase 'Amator Jesus et veritatis, et verus internus' (Book 2, Chapter 1, p. 82) is jotted down in condensed form in Beckett's 'Dream' notebook as 'Amator Jesus et verus internus'. This is then, in *Dream of Fair to Middling Women*, applied to Belacqua: 'He is a great, big, inward man [...] versus [sic] internus' (*DFMW*, p. 46; 'versus' is here presumably a misprint, since the pun would here be inefficacious). Moreover, although Beckett's letter to MacGreevy singles out for disapprobation the phrase 'the glad going out and sorrowful coming home', it appears both in *Dream of Fair to Middling Women* and in *More Pricks Than Kicks*. In the case of the former, the context is that of the donning by Belacqua of some new hobnail boots: 'But laetus exitus etc., we all know that, the joyful going forth and sorrowful coming home' (*DFMW*, p. 129). The unfinished phrase runs: 'Laetus exitus tristem saepe reditum parit: et laeta vigilia serotina triste mane facit' [Often glad departure brings a sad return, and late evenings a sad morning] (*De Imitatione*, Book 1, Chapter 20, p. 49). Transposed into comic vein, the phrase (supposed by the narrator to be known to all) no longer refers to the chafing of conscience, but rather to the chafing of unweathered leather. A similar adaptation is effected by the narrator of *More Pricks Than Kicks*, who reports having observed Belacqua returning home 'transfigured and transformed. It was very nearly the reverse of the author of the Imitation's "glad going out and sad coming in"' (*MPTK*, p. 40).

Similarly, in his 'Dream' notebook, Beckett jots down other phrases from *The Imitation of Christ* which he has found striking. They include: 'Read: meekly simply and truly: humiliter, simpliciter, fideliter' (from Book 1, Chapter 5, in which à Kempis recommends the search for usefulness rather than subtlety in the scriptures: 'Si vis profectum haurire, lege humiliter, simpliciter, et fideliter' [*De Imitatione*, p. 13]). Beckett appends it in *Dream of Fair to Middling Women* (and in the corresponding passage in *More Pricks Than Kicks*), to the description of the Alba's careful dressing for the party: 'gladly, gravely and carefully, humiliter, simpliciter, fideliter, and not merely because she might just as well' (*DFMW*, pp. 208–9; *MPTK*, p. 60). Beckett also notes down the phrase: '*Neither* is *no* order so holy *nor no* place so sure ... *but*'. The latter phrase (in which I have reproduced Beckett's own underlinings) is from Book 1, Chapter 13, in which à Kempis deals with the defeat of temptations: 'Non est aliquis Ordo tam sanctus, nec locus tam secretus, ubi non sint tentationes vel adversitates' (*De Imitatione*, p. 27) [There is no order so sacred, no place so set apart, that there are no temptations and adversities there]. The sentence is constructed upon the basic tenet that, since temptations originate within the self, there is no place on earth, however sacred, which can be considered immune from them. However, it seems clear from Beckett's own treatment of the quotation within the notebook that his primary interest lay in the phrase's complex network of negative and modificatory signifiers rather than in its theological aptness.

The combination which one finds in Beckett's early work, of a strong will and a sifting intellect, beset with periods of doubt and irresolution, is a striking and distinctive one. It finds a kind of parallel, however, in the early life of a theologian with whose writing Beckett was familiar: namely, St Augustine. Indeed, if the young Augustine and the young Sam had been contemporaries, they might have got on very well (with Augustine probably being the more ferociously energetic and pro-active of the two).

St Augustine's *Confessions* is one of the great autobiographies of all time. What is so remarkable about it is not only its variety – its range of tone, its poetic qualities, visual immediacy, and intellectual rigour – but also its relentless honesty and frankness. This latter quality achieves something which Augustine could hardly have foreseen or provided for: since the author is so hard on himself, and so consistently intent on showing himself in a bad light, the reader tends to supplement and compensate for the portrait, so that Augustine's fundamental integrity and kindness begin to emerge.

It is known that Beckett read the *Confessions*, since he copied out selected extracts from the work in his 'Dream' notebook. Occasionally his jottings are from the Latin original, but most of them are in English, and appear to be from the E.B. Pusey translation. Pusey's translation was a revision of the 1631 translation by William Watts. It was published in 1838, was frequently reprinted, and was for many years the standard translation. The irregularity of the interspersed Latin quotations in the notebook suggests that Beckett was relying mainly on the Pusey translation, and supplementing it either from footnotes in a scholarly edition, or from a separate Latin edition. Some of the extracts are then incorporated (often in slightly adapted form) into his *Dream of Fair to Middling Women*. Beckett seems to have been strongly drawn, for example, to Augustine's descriptions of natural phenomena. Thus, Belacqua at one point looks up and sees that 'the night sky was stretched like a skin' (*DFMW*, p. 27). In the corresponding passage in *Confessions* (which Beckett copied into his notebook), Augustine states: 'For heaven shall be folded up like a scroll; and now is it stretched over us like a skin' (*CONF*, Book 13, p. 321). Given his knowledge of the scriptures, Beckett would also have been alive to the many biblical quotations and resonances which underpin the *Confessions*. In this case, the cross-textual echoes are with the Books of Isaiah – 'The heavens shall be rolled together as a scroll' (Isaiah 34: 4) – and Revelation: 'And the heavens departed as a scroll when it is rolled together' (Revelation 6: 14).

Just as Augustine frequently applies his own spin to passages from scripture, by omitting sections or by adding phrases of his own, Beckett also finds it convenient to modify some Augustinian passages for his own purposes, as in a parallel drawn towards the end of the novel: 'It was strange how this expression of themselves at odds, the surface ruffled, if they had known (she may have), of the profound antagonism latent in the neutral space that between victims of real needs is as irreducible as the zone of evaporation between damp and incandescence (We stole that one. Guess where.)' (*DFMW*, pp. 191–2).

It is apposite to mention here that Beckett's parenthetical admission at the close of the quotation demonstrates that these early borrowings and adaptations are not so much plagiarism as pastiche or even tribute. It might reasonably be maintained that the difference between a plagiarist and a pasticheur is that the former conceals borrowings while the latter hopes that they will be recognised. It is true that there are examples of practically undetectable appropriations in Beckett's early writing (which may of course be unconscious). A good example of this is one narratorial interjection in *Dream of Fair to Middling Women* – 'This may be premature. We have set it down too soon, perhaps. Still, let it stand' (*DFMW*, p. 216) – which mirrors almost exactly a similar intervention in Dickens's *David Copperfield*: 'This may be premature. I have set it down too soon, perhaps. But let it stand' (Chapter 3).[22] On the whole, however, Beckett's manipulations and incorporations have a self-advertising quality about them which tease and intrigue rather than deceive.

In the case of the 'zone of evaporation' reference mentioned above, Beckett even demonstrates his honesty by using the word 'stole': fittingly, since the term 'borrowing' is clearly a euphemism. (An author who annexes ideas or expressions and publishes them has no intention of giving them back). The narrating magpie has probably 'stolen' this from Augustine, who writes in Book 13 of the zone between the upper part of the material world (the firmament) and the lower part (the sea and dry land). Augustine regarded this zone as being one in which vapour arose from the water, and descended again on the earth in the form of dew. Thus, birds could fly in this intermediate zone of evaporation, since 'the grossness of the air, which bears up the flights of birds, thickeneth itself by the exhalation of the waters' (*CONF*, Book 13, p. 345). Moreover, just as Augustine suggests that the polarities of this division (heaven and earth) may be seen as representing the spiritual and the material creations, Beckett uses the parallel within a passage which explores incompatibilities between bodily and spiritual expectations within a human relationship. The detail of Beckett's differentiation of zones is different – it is doubtful, for instance, that Augustine would have understood or sympathised with Belacqua's assertion that 'my mind goes blank' (*DFMW*, p. 191) any more than does the Alba – but Belacqua's instinct for spatial and intellectual detachment finds affiliation with that of Augustine.

Earlier in the novel, Beckett at one point stitches together a whole embroidery of para-quotations from *Confessions*, in his description of Belacqua, who 'dared to go off the deep end with his shadowy love and he daily watered by daily littles the ground under his face and beerbibbing did not lay siege to his spirit and he was continent though not in the least sustenant and many of his months have since run out with him the pestilent person to take him from behind his crooked back and set him before his ulcerous gob in the boiling over of his neckings and in chambering and wantonness and in bitter and blind bawling against the honey what honey bloody well you know the honey and in canvassing and getting and weltering in filth and scratching off the scabs of lust' (*DFMW*, p. 73).

The first part of the passage relates to the opening passage of Book 2: 'I dared to grow wild again, with these various and shadowy loves' (*CONF*, p. 21), where Augustine describes the sensual turmoils of his adolescent years. The weeping on the ground, however, was the preserve of Augustine's mother, Monica, whose tears 'watered the ground under her eyes in every place where she prayed' (*CONF*, Book 3, p. 47), at the time when her son's erratic behaviour distressed her. (One could also compare here the description of Watt, whose 'tears fell, a slow minute rain, to the ground' [*W*, p. 208]). Perhaps significantly, Augustine, like Beckett, grew up in a household where the mother represented the strong model of Christianity (in the case of Augustine, his father did not become a Christian until just before his death). Both mothers seem to have despaired at times at the waywardness and unpredictability of their sons.

It is also Monica, however, who is implicated in the reference to 'beerbibbing', for Monica had the endearing foible of having developed a fancy for wine which dated from girlhood, when she was sent to draw wine from the cask for her parents: 'And thus by adding to that little, daily littles, [...] she had fallen into such a habit, as greedily to drink off her little cup brim-full almost of wine' (*CONF*, Book 9, p. 190). However, the subsequent section of Beckett's collage echoes Augustine's emphasis that this liking for wine was never a dependency, for 'wine-bibbing did not lay siege to her spirit' (*CONF*, Book 6, p. 96). In the corresponding passage relating to Belacqua, it is claimed that 'beerbibbing did not lay siege to his spirit'.

The subsequent reference, to Belacqua being 'continent though not in the least sustenant', relates rather complicatedly to the experiences of Augustine immediately before his final conversion. In Book 8, Augustine describes how he aspires to continence but is pulled back at the same time by the habits of his youth. While on the brink of renouncing his way of life, he nevertheless prays that classic and very human prayer: 'Give me chastity and continency, only not yet' (*CONF*, p. 163). Beckett, of course, places this aspiration in the mouth of Belacqua in *Dream of Fair to Middling Women* (*DFMW*, p. 186). The Alba, on the other hand, is proof against such tugs-of-war between two wills. Augustine asks in Book 8: 'What then if one of us should deliberate, and amid the strife of his two wills be in a strait [...]?' (*CONF*, p. 167). For a long time, Augustine remained in that strait, for it 'held me in suspense' (*CONF*, p. 169). When such questions are asked of the Alba, however – 'Shall she founder in a strait of two wills?' and 'by hanging in suspense be the more killed?' (*DFMW*, p. 209) – the implied negative answer is fulfilled as she immediately busies herself with a series of actions.

In this context, Beckett writes in his 'Dream' notebook that continency is 'not to trust in the happiness of the world', whereas sustenancy is 'not to give way to the unhappiness of the world'. These are not so much definitions as signs, or allied conditions. Continence is not synonymous with detachment, but its practice may be one result (among others) of not placing reliance upon worldly pleasures. To translate this into Belacqua's terms, then, is to suggest that he is at this stage theoretically resigned to the hollowness of pleasure, while at the same time being flooded with unhappiness.

At that stage immediately preceding his conversion, Augustine states that 'many of my years (some twelve) had now run out with me since my nineteenth' (*CONF*, Book 8, pp. 162–3), and it is this simple affirmation which Beckett modifies in this passage to 'many of his months have since run out with him'. In the following words, however, Beckett flashes back and forth between Augustine's pre- and post-conversion. Looking back on his previous life, Augustine refers to himself in Book 9 as 'a pestilent person, a bitter and a blind bawler against those writings, which are honied with the honey of heaven' (*CONF*, p. 183). Beckett's version, however, interleaves a section condensed from Book 8, as Augustine describes the sudden insight into himself which he was afforded: 'setting me before my face, that I might see how foul I was, how crooked and defiled, bespotted and ulcerous' (*CONF*, p. 162). Compounding this self-lambasting, Beckett also borrows from Book 2 – 'I boiled over in my fornications' (*CONF*, pp. 21–2) – and then from the passage towards the close of Book 8: 'Not in rioting and drunkenness, not in chambering and wantonness' (*CONF*, p. 171).

The final part of the long chain of quotations retains almost unchanged that opening part of Book 9 where Augustine writes of the change he notes in himself after deciding to devote his life to God: 'Now was my soul free from the biting cares of canvassing and getting, and weltering in filth, and scratching off the itch of lust' (*CONF*, p. 174). The phrase which is not allowed to pass unmolested, interestingly, is 'the honey of heaven', for Beckett inserts an irritable interjection: 'against the honey what honey bloody well you know the honey'. Moreover, he re-uses the phrase later, with reference to the Alba: 'A fizz of scampering birds, it would lead her to the honey. What honey? [...] The fizz of their endeavour leads her forward to the court of honey. What honey?' (*DFMW*, p. 155). For Augustine, the honey is the word of God, as he describes in the closing pages of the *Confessions*: 'And I heard, O Lord my God, and drank up a drop of sweetness out of Thy truth' (*CONF*, Book 13, p. 343). Beckett/Belacqua cannot, however, swallow that same honey, however much their journey to it may appear to them to resemble that of Augustine.

Hence, although Beckett seems to gravitate repeatedly to Book 8 of the *Confessions*, where Augustine approaches the climactic moment of his conversion and at last grasps hold of what he has until then been evading, there is no comparable apex in his own novel. The moment of no return for Augustine is described in Book 8, when, out in the garden, he hears the voice of a child from a neighbouring house repeating the words 'Take up and read; Take up and read' (*CONF*, p. 170). He thereupon takes up the Bible and opens it at random, and finds that the text upon which his eyes fall seems to be made for him. At that point, all his remaining doubts are dispelled. No such definitive moment of illumination or turning-point occurs for Belacqua, who retains the perception – now (and probably always) alien to Augustine – that the borderlands can be a kind of home, rather than a place of transit or unwelcome exile. In his 'Whoroscope' poem, Beckett does cite that crucial Augustinian phrase in its Latin original – 'Tolle, lege; tolle, lege' – but he does so with ironic detachment: 'He tolle'd and legge'd / and he buttoned on his redemptorist waistcoat' (*CP*, p. 4).

If that sense of detachment differs between Augustine and Belacqua in terms of both its motivation and its long-term application, it nevertheless results in rather similar outcomes with regard to the significant women in their lives. Augustine gives up longing for marriage, and Belacqua stubbornly clings to his solipsism. It is, however, a messy solipsism, because of its often half-hearted of recidivist quality. Hence, although Augustine prays that his soul be not 'rivetted' with 'the glue of love, through the senses of the body' (*CONF*, Book 4, pp. 60–1), he does finally manage to dispel the instinct to postponement, summed up in 'those dull and drowsy words, "Anon, anon"' (*CONF*, Book 8, p. 158). The result is that, in the following Book, he is able to refer to the kindling of anger against himself, and to the concept of having put off 'the old man' and put on the new. This is a recurrent image within the Pauline Letters when used in the context of conversion, or 'metanoia' (see, for example, the Letter to the Romans: 'Our old man is crucified with [Christ], that the body of sin might be destroyed' [Romans 6: 6]). Having embraced a new way of life, Augustine recalls: 'I was angry within myself in my chamber, where I was inwardly pricked, where I had sacrificed, slaying my old man and commencing the purpose of a new life' (*CONF*, Book 9, p. 182).

These elements – the 'glue', the drowsy postponement, the inward anger, and the 'old man', which originate in three different Books of the *Confessions* – are skilfully sewn together by Beckett in a passage referring to Belacqua: 'This was the moment if ever, now that he was alone in his chamber and pricked into anger, to slay his old man, to give, there and then, this love the slip. But the moment passed with the dull and drowsy formula. Anon, he said, anon, take your hurry, and he opened wide the lids of his mind and let in the glare' (*DFMW*, p. 63). Thus, though drawn to Augustine's decisiveness, Belacqua lets the moment pass as 'the libido sentiendi flared up'.

Nevertheless, in between more or less debilitating encounters, Belacqua retains his attachment to love at a remove, so that he is able to say to the Smeraldina: 'I leave you now in a day or two in order that I may have you, in three days or four or even next month, according to my God' (*DFMW*, p. 25). Perhaps *this* 'god' is not after all so dissimilar to that of Augustine. Beckett's narrator uses the phrase 'the heavy gloom of carnal custom' (*DFMW*, p. 166) with reference to the Alba, just as Augustine writes of 'mine own weight [...]. This weight was carnal custom' (*CONF*, Book 7, p. 138). The alternative to carnal custom, however, appears to be carnal visualisation. When parted from the Smeraldina, Belacqua experiences difficulty in accommodating to what he sees as the two separate spheres of the spirit and the flesh. While drawn to the brothel, he nevertheless cherishes ('by fraud', he admits [*DFMW*, p. 42]) the spirit of her as 'incorruptible, uninjurable, unchangeable'. This is the precise phrase which Augustine uses at the beginning of Book 7 to describe the dilemma he experienced in conceiving of God, as both a being in space, and as a being beyond spatialisation: 'Yet was I constrained to conceive of Thee (that incorruptible, uninjurable, and unchangeable, which I preferred before the corruptible, and injurable, and changeable) as being in space' (*CONF*, p. 119).

Both Augustine and Belacqua find that remedies for their malaise lie within themselves, and not from conventional external sources. When Belacqua is feeling both physically ill and emotionally ill at ease, the narrator quotes the phrase: 'The Greek bath drives sadness from the mind' (*DFMW*, p. 86). This remark is taken directly from Augustine, in Book 9, who takes a bath while grieving after the death of his mother, as he has heard that 'it drives sadness from the mind' (*CONF*, p. 199). It fails, however, to have any such effect, 'for the bitterness of sorrow could not exsude out of my heart' (*CONF*, pp. 199–200). Both could claim to be what the narrator in *Dream of Fair to Middling Women* (after à Kempis, as noted earlier) calls 'a great, big, inward man' (*DFMW*, p. 46). Indeed, in the passage immediately preceding this statement, Belacqua is judged to be the antithesis of Augustine's description of the proud. In Book 5, Augustine compares the proud to high-flying birds, or diving birds: such people, he maintains, cannot 'slay their own soaring imaginations, as fowls of the air, nor their own diving curiosities, (wherewith, like the fishes of the sea, they wander over the unknown paths of the abyss)' (*CONF*, p. 75). In clear acknowledgement of this passage, it is said that Belacqua 'was not proud, he was not a bird of the air, passing off into outermost things, casting out his innermost parts [...]. He was not curious, he was not a fish of the sea, prowling through the paths of the sea' (*DFMW*, pp. 46–7).

These are not the only Augustinian references within *Dream of Fair to Middling Women*. The central point of interest, however, is Beckett's careful response to the *Confessions*. He has clearly been drawn to many of Augustine's images and ideas, and to the sheer energy of the writing. Like many readers, he has been drawn to the spiritual suspense of the text, for the most absorbing aspect of the *Confessions* is not so much its closing 'Te Deum' as its depiction and dramatisation of an inner conflict working painfully towards its resolution. As the foregoing analysis has examined, however, Belacqua is only fitfully and temporarily to be allied with the young Augustine. In the end, their paths diverge. Augustine painstakingly reconstructs his developing perceptions of 'willing and nilling': 'When then I did will or nill any thing, I was most sure, that no other than myself did will and nill: and I all but saw that there was the cause of my sin' (*CONF*, Book 7, p. 122). At that stage, he 'all but saw'; later, he saw, and acted to conform his will. Belacqua experiences the same symptoms, but cannot resolve them in the same way: 'The will and nill cannot suicide, they are not free to suicide. That is where the wretched Belacqua jumps the rails. And that is his wretchedness, that he seeks a means whereby the will and nill may be enabled to suicide and refuses to understand that they cannot do it, that they are not free to do it' (*DFMW*, pp. 123–4).

What emerges from this passage is that side of Belacqua which his customary sarcasm should not be allowed to obscure: namely, the struggles he undertakes as he 'seeks a means'. This dichotomy between ironic detachment and anxious questing is a characteristic not only of Belacqua but also of many of the other labouring subjectivities of Beckett's early fiction. The Belacqua who, like his Dantean namesake, is only too content to slump in indolence, is also the one who, in *More Pricks Than Kicks*, wrestles with his inability to catch Beatrice's drift in her explanation of the spots on the moon (in

Canto 2 of *Paradise*): 'Still he pored over the enigma, he would not concede himself conquered, he would understand at least the meanings of the words, the order in which they were spoken and the nature of the satisfaction that they conferred on the misinformed poet' (*MPTK*, p. 9).

Belacqua in *Dream of Fair to Middling Women* approaches a variation upon Augustine's treatment of memory with equal doggedness. It is in Book 10 that Augustine ponders lengthily upon the mysterious properties of the memory, and its relationship with the feelings: 'How is it, that when with joy I remember my past sorrow, the mind hath joy, the memory hath sorrow; the mind upon the joyfulness which is in it, is joyful, yet the memory upon the sadness which is in it, is not sad?' (*CONF*, p. 216). Belacqua, appropriately substituting 'indifference' for 'joy', presents to the Alba the 'absurd dilemma' which is his paraphrase of Augustine: 'When with indifference I remember my past sorrow, my mind has indifference, my memory has sorrow. The mind, upon the indifference which is in it, is indifferent; yet the memory, upon the sadness which is in it, is not sad' (*DFMW*, p. 236). A further iteration of the dilemma is cut short by the Alba with a curt 'Basta'. Yet the episode has served not only to illustrate Beckett's internalisation of the complex mix of philosophy, theology and psychology which Augustine offers to his readers, but also to reveal that Augustine's wrestling intellect, and his scorn for superficial readings, were fully matched by the same qualities in Beckett.

What emerges from Beckett's engagement with Augustine is both a profundity of response and a self-differentiation. Beckett may have admired or been preoccupied with the *Confessions*, but he exploits the work for his own purposes, and clearly demurs from some of the text's 'givens'. This is also the case with Beckett's handling of other spiritual writers. In his 'Dream' notebook, he copies an extract from Julian of Norwich, the fourteenth-century anchorite. Her *Revelations of Divine Love* tells, in its vivid, imaged prose, of her insights into the primacy of love in the relationship between God (referred to as both Father and Mother) and humankind. Hers is a positive, joyous mysticism, and the extract which Beckett seizes upon is perhaps her best-known observation: 'Sin is behovable, but all shall be well and all shall be well and all manner of thing shall be well'.[23] This passage, attributed by Julian to Jesus, in the course of her thirteenth revelation, duly appears in its entirety in *Dream of Fair to Middling Women*, at a point where

Belacqua has spent the night 'crowned in gloom' at the absence of the Smeraldina-Rima (*DFMW*, p. 9).

Later in the novel, Beckett again borrows from Julian. In the 'Dream' notebook, he had already jotted down the phrase 'dearworthy death'. The phrase's rhythm and alliteration presumably appealed to him, as well as the adjective 'dearworthy' itself. Julian uses it several times, in various descriptions relating to Jesus or to his mother. The entire phrase 'dearworthy death' in fact occurs in Chapter 6, where Julian writes of 'His holy Passion, His dearworthy death and wounds: and all the blessed kindness, the endless life that we have of all this' (*Revelations*, pp. 12–13).[24] Only the adjective is used by Beckett. Now archaic, it is normally replaced in modern translations of the *Revelations* by such synonyms as 'precious', 'beloved', or 'honoured'. However, rescued and contextually reassigned by Beckett, the word lives on in the narrator's description of the Alba: 'Thenceforward we keep our hands off her, we let her speak for herself, we state her dearworthy cuticle and hair if we state her at all, and leave it at that' (*DFMW*, p. 193). In applying the intimate adjective only to elements of the external shell of the Alba's body, the narrator underlines his aspiration towards detachment.

Picturesque phrases apart, however, Beckett appears to be little enthused by the figure of Julian, and, in *More Pricks Than Kicks*, he enjoys himself by mixing and moulding her image into a more grotesque one: 'The elder daughter was very dull. Think of holy Juliana of Norwich, to her aspect add a dash of souring, to her tissue half a hundredweight of adipose, abstract the charity and prayers, spray in vain with opopanax and assafoetida, and behold a radiant Una' (*MPTK*, p. 131). Hence, the ethereal Julian is rendered corpulent, and sprayed with two kinds of gum-resin, bogging her down to fuse with Una (the one and only) bboggs.

A rather more sustained engagement with a spiritual writer in Beckett's early work is found with reference to St John of the Cross, the sixteenth-century mystic. John's meeting with Teresa of Avila, in his mid-twenties, was to prove one of the most important events of his life. Sharing a desire to root out laxities in the Carmelite order of friars and nuns, they both spearheaded a return to the primitive rule in their respective communities, often amid opposition. Both left extensive writings (extended poems and commentaries in the case of John, works on prayer and an autobiography in the case of Teresa), and both were eventually proclaimed Doctors of the Church (John in 1926 and Teresa in 1970).

There is passing reference to Teresa of Avila in the 'Dream' note-book, but the more interesting use of her reputation is in the phrase 'dauntless daughter of desires', which is applied to the Alba in *Dream of Fair to Middling Women* (*DFMW*, p. 222), and in the corresponding passage in *More Pricks Than Kicks* (*MPTK*, p. 73). It also appears in the poem 'Sanies I' (*CP*, p. 18). This noteworthy description – aptly used of the doughty Teresa – is to be found in the seventeenth-century poet Richard Crashaw's poem, 'The Flaming Heart upon the Book and Picture of the Seraphicall Saint Teresa',[25] where the poet exclaims: 'O thou undanted daughter of desires!'.[26] (Two lines later, Crashaw writes of 'all the eagle in thee, all the dove', a phrase used by Vita Sackville-West, respectively to contrast Teresa of Avila with Teresa of Lisieux, in her dual-biography of those saints, *The Eagle and the Dove*).[27] Although the note in Beckett's jotted version runs: 'St. Teresa – undaunted daughter of desires' (replacing the earlier form 'undanted' with its modern spelling), the word is further adjusted in the two novels, and in the poem, to its synonym 'dauntless', thus endowing the phrase with a more emphatic alliterative quality. There are indeed parallels between the Teresa who crackles through Crashaw's poem, and the fire-raising Alba. Crashaw addresses Teresa as 'O sweet incendiary!', and constantly aligns her with images of fire and love (as he does throughout the complementary poem 'A Hymn to the Name and Honor of the Admirable St Teresa'). Similarly, the envisioned Alba elicits from the narrator in *More Pricks Than Kicks* the exclamation: 'O Love! O Fire!' (*MPTK*, p. 58), and, entering the party in her scarlet gown, she is described as having 'fired the thorns under every pot' (*MPTK*, p. 73).

Teresa's coadjutor John of the Cross attracts an altogether different frame of reference in Beckett's early work. In his *Ascent of Mount Carmel* and *Dark Night of the Soul* (properly speaking, a single un-finished treatise), John presents the journey of the soul to the Union of Light as being necessarily undertaken through the Dark Night, which is a series of purifications. These, he maintains, take the form of active purifications (by which the soul can prepare itself), and passive ones (which only God can accomplish in the soul), and, in his 'Dream' notebook, Beckett notes down under the phrase 'Dark Night of the Soul' a three-stage schema: 'Dark Night of the Senses', 'Dark Night of the Mind', and 'Dark Night of the Will and Mem-ory'. In the 'Dark Night of the Senses', the soul renounces its desires and appetites; in the 'Dark Night of the Spirit' (or 'Mind', as Beckett has it, even though the original Spanish word is 'espíritu'), the soul opens itself to faith rather than to knowledge, and in the 'Dark Night of the Will and Memory', the soul withdraws from memory of knowledge, and suspends the power of imagination.

Unfortunately, since the treatise remained unfinished at the time of John's death, the emergence of the soul from the dark tunnel of purgation into the light of God remains undescribed. Hence, there is in the extant manuscript a weightier emphasis than there would have been, proportionately, upon what is known as 'The Great Dereliction' (a phrase which Beckett jots down in his 'Dream' notebook prior to using it in his novel). This refers to the suffering consequent upon the emptying of self, as the soul painstakingly releases its grasp upon its 'natural' desires and inclinations.

Interestingly, Beckett's early fiction takes a different view of the blindness and renunciation of will implied by the condition of dereliction. Instead of being something necessarily endured for the sake of a greater potential good, it is viewed as an elusive state, to be sought as an antidote to other, more unpredictable pangs. Hence, for Belacqua in *Dream of Fair to Middling Women*, 'the Great Dereliction was the silver lining and its impertinent interventions. For the mind to pore over a woe or in deference to a woe be blacked out was all right' (*DFMW*, p. 6). What he cannot tolerate is the dismantling of his 'machinery of despond', such that it develops in directions his psyche has not foreseen.

To that extent, there is in Beckett's early male protagonists a (nonreligious) attraction to aspects of that darkness of abandonment and detachment advocated by John of the Cross. In other words, it is often found convenient in the early fiction to use the terms of that theology without displaying a corresponding conviction of their Godward bent. Accordingly, it is stated of Belacqua in *More Pricks Than Kicks* that 'the objects in which he was used to find such recreation and repose lost gradually their hold upon him, he became insensible to them little by little' (*MPTK*, p. 45). This sounds like a perfect realisation of the 'Dark Night of the Senses'. Moreover, in a context where many of Beckett's males look with alarm upon the prospect of an apparent engulfment in a sensual domain controlled by women, there are ready-made affiliations with that economy of desire which is described in the *Ascent of Mount Carmel*: 'Even as one that digs because he covets a treasure is wearied and fatigued, even so is the soul wearied and fatigued in order to attain that which its desires demand of it; and although in the end it may attain it, it is still weary, because it is never satisfied'.[28] Moreover, the impulses generating much of Beckett's writing do seem to co-resonate with some of those enunciated by John: 'In order to arrive at that which thou knowest not, Thou must go by a way that thou knowest not. In order to arrive at that which thou possessest not, Thou must go by a way that thou possessest not. In order to arrive at that which thou art not, Thou must go through that which thou art not' (*Ascent*, p. 63).

Beyond this point, however, the paths diverge. There is no question of the narratee not being conversant with the theoretical destination. Indeed, Belacqua is perfectly capable of enlisting spiritual arguments in support of material ones, as he does with Ruby Tough: 'He was able to pelt her there and then with the best that diligent enquiry could provide: Greek and Roman reasons, [...] and John of the Cross reasons, in short all but the true reasons' (*MPTK*, p. 95). Moreover, he is able to ironise the mystical experience so as to apply it to other frames of reference. Thus, in *Dream of Fair to Middling Women*, Belacqua is said to liken the self-emptying which accompanies the Dark Night of the Soul and the Great Dereliction to the context of defecation, 'coinciding with the period of post-evacuative depression' (*DFMW*, p. 185).

The comparison is appropriate, for Belacqua's efforts to void his racing mind do seem to result in blockage, a kind of spiritual constipation. In a sustained passage earlier in the novel, he strains in every way known to him to suspend his will in the desired manner: 'He trained his little brain to hold its breath, he made covenants of all kinds with his senses, he forced the lids of the little brain down against the flaring bric-à-brac [...] until he would begin and all things to descend, ponderously and softly to lapse downwards through darkness' (*DFMW*, p. 123). However, all is to no avail, for 'it was impossible to switch off the inward glare'. Thus, he lingers always between two states. He is, the text continues, 'a horrible border-creature'. Later, in an agreeable pun, he perverts the John of the Cross patronage for his own more janiform positioning: ' "John" he said "of the Crossroads, Mr Beckett. A borderman" ' (*DFMW*, p. 186). He is, he asserts, 'a dud mystic'.

The narrative voice destabilises this conclusion somewhat: 'From the live-and-let-live anchorite on leave, to *dud mystic* was a longer call than we cared immediately to undertake' (*DFMW*, p. 186). Some of Beckett's later work indeed suggests that certain kinds of mystical impulse are not so easily aborted. Nevertheless, there is no doubt that any journey to a still centre can only be accomplished within the writer's own criteria, and with the imagination remaining fully in play: 'Imagination Dead Imagine'. Without it, dud mysticism would surely be compounded by dud writing.

3

Drama and Later Prose

The previous chapter focused, within Beckett's early fiction, mainly upon references to the Bible; to priests, prayers, and popular piety; and to theology and spirituality. This chapter, based upon evidence from Beckett's drama and from his later prose, will be similarly divided, but differently weighted. This reflects the fact that religious references are still recurrently present in this later work, but are glancing, often less explicit, and rarely dwelt upon.

USES OF THE BIBLE

Whereas citations of religious practice are fewer in Beckett's later writing, the Bible continues to provide inter-textual pulses throughout the oeuvre. Biblical references are not, of course, discernible in every work. Moreover, some of the subtextual scriptural resonances are so muted and integrated that they do not necessarily detach themselves from the texture of Beckett's own writing. At other times they are more self-advertising. In addition, as with the early fiction, the allusions originate both in the Old and in the New Testaments, with the Old Testament now slightly predominant. In all cases, it is the King James translation which provides the template. Hence, as with the corresponding section of the previous chapter, textual citations within this section will be given in English, regardless of the language in which the work was originally written, so that the parallels with the King James Bible may emerge more clearly.

Among the Old Testament references, there is a noticeable concentration upon passages dealing with the transience of human life and of the material world. Perhaps the ultimate among these is that reminder of cyclical decay which is addressed by God to Adam and Eve in the Book of Genesis, after they have eaten the forbidden fruit: 'Dust thou art, and unto dust shalt thou return' (Genesis 3:

19). An allied recognition of deterioration and death as an inevitable corollary of life lies at the heart of Beckett's writing. The provenance of this recognition is, however, dim and unexplicated. To be preoccupied with the great curses of humankind – pain, death, and sorrow – does not imply a subscription to the idea of their linkage with 'Fall' as causal agent. For Beckett, the terms in which the author of Genesis (adapting material from an ancient poem) presents the grim outcome of rebellion against God are resonant linguistically and symbolically, but not theologically or historically. In literary terms, original sin engenders originative images.

The phrase 'Dust thou art, and unto dust shalt thou return' is a somehow satisfying stylistic formula. In the King James translation, its rhythm seems to incarnate its air of finality. Semantically, however, it sounds the death knell. It is designed to be experienced as chilling and punitive by its human listeners. Even by substituting lexical variants, Beckett can evoke the power of the phrase. Hence, in *Eh Joe*, the quietly menacing voice can suggest to Joe that there is retribution ahead for him merely by projecting the words ' "Mud thou art" ', the phrase which 'His Nibs' (presumably God) will address to Joe 'one dirty winter night' (*CSPL*, p. 205). Here, 'mud' is appropriately substituted for 'dust'. Earlier in Genesis, God is said to have 'formed man of the dust of the ground' (Genesis 2: 7), after it had been watered by 'a mist from the earth' (v. 2). This moist dust is the generative material for human life, like the warm mud evoked in *How It Is*: 'warmth of primeval mud impenetrable dark' (*HI*, p. 16). Indeed, within that work, the phrase lends its structure to yet another variant, that of the cyclical oblivion which fringes the mess of human life: 'From sleep I come to sleep return between the two there is all all the doing suffering failing bungling achieving until the mud yawns again' (*HI*, p. 25). Moreover, in the retributive context of *Eh Joe*, the substitution of 'mud' for 'dust' draws in an extra textual echo: that of the mire of the Styx, in which condemned sinners flounder in Dante's *Inferno*.

Other Old Testament images of human fragility are taken from the Book of Psalms. Thus, in *How It Is*, the narrator's mother, a sombre 'column of jade' with a bible in her hand, is glimpsed with her 'black finger inside psalm one hundred and something oh God man his days as grass flowers of the field wind above in the clouds' (*HI*, p. 86). The 'psalm one hundred and something', with its vibrant images of grass, flowers, and wind, is in fact Psalm 103: 'As for man, his days are as grass: as a flower of the field, so he flourisheth. For the wind passeth over it, and it is gone' (Psalm 103: 15–16). The same source is also accessed in *From an Abandoned Work*, although to a slightly different purpose. Whereas Psalm 103 presents the 'flowers of the field' as a vision of vigour and beauty soon to fade, Beckett halts the onward progression of time so as to celebrate flowers in their rootedness, as opposed to cut flowers condemned to an even shorter lifespan: 'Great love in my heart too for all things still and rooted, [...] even the flowers of the field, not for the world when in my right senses would I ever touch one, to pluck it' (*CSPR*, p. 129).

Shortly after the citing of Psalm 103 in *How It Is*, a similarly pointed advertence to the brevity of human life, also from the Book of Psalms, is quoted: 'I remembered my days an handbreadth[1] my life as nothing man a vapour' (*HI*, p. 88). The relevant psalm here is Psalm 39, but it is stitched together with a complementary passage from the Letter of James. In an address to God, imploring him to vouchsafe a knowledge of mankind's frailty, the psalmist states: 'Behold, thou has made my days as an handbreadth; and mine age is as nothing before thee' (Psalm 39: 5). Reinforcing the theme further is the quotation from a resonant passage in James: 'For what is your life? It is even a vapour, that appeareth for a little time, and then vanisheth away' (James 4: 14).

In the above example, the second source illustrates further the message of the first. In an earlier passage in *How It Is*, however, the second source undermines, rather than underlines, the first. Again evoking the mother, gazing down 'with severe love' in her eyes, the narrator relates: 'I offer her mine pale upcast to the sky whence cometh our help and which I know perhaps even then with time shall pass away' (*HI*, p. 17). The first source is the opening words of Psalm 121: 'I will lift up mine eyes unto the hills, from whence cometh my help'. This is a short psalm of praise and reassurance, proclaiming that 'the Lord shall preserve thee from all evil' (v. 7). Moreover, this security is not interpreted as short-lived; it is, in the closing words of the psalm, 'even for evermore' (v. 8). However, in the Beckettian rendering, this vision of long-term security in God is abruptly blotted out by the subordinate clause: 'which I know perhaps even then with time shall pass away'.

This is the reverse side of God's image: not as a haven in which to find repose, but as a source of disruption and disquiet. It is described in the eschatological perspective in the closing chapter of the Second Letter of Peter: 'The day of the Lord will come as a thief in the night; in the which the heavens shall pass away with a great noise' (2 Peter 3: 10). In this moment of verbena-scented stillness, then, as the prone narrator gazes upward at his mother's face against the sky, there is a dual awareness of severity and security, of permanence and temporality: an awareness which seems, moreover, to unite motherhood and God-the-fatherhood. Indeed, the narrator seems only to operate within the religious domain via the channel of his mother: 'I pray according to her instructions' (*HI*, p. 17). He watches her as she 'drones a snatch of the so-called Apostles' Creed'. Her droned assent seems dutiful rather than heartfelt; as for the narrator, the credo – or a 'snatch' of it – is experienced only second-hand, through the lips of his mother. Moreover, the status of the credo is further undermined by the attachment of the term 'so-called' (implying that the speaker does not so call it).

An aspiration very similar to that voiced in Psalm 121 occurs in *Happy Days*, when Winnie cranes round and addresses Willie: 'Lift up your eyes to me, Willie' (*HD*, p. 40). Willie does not, in fact, comply, and Winnie's exhortation remains unanswered. Turning painfully back, she observes: 'The earth is very tight today [. . .]. The great heat possibly'. Winnie is, of course, at a point of detention between heaven and earth, and, oppressed as she is by encroaching heat and engulfment, she wishes at least to feel the gaze of another upon her. This conjunction of elements – of eyes lifted in her direction, and of elemental unpredictability with its inevitably human casualties – recalls the Book of Isaiah: 'Lift up your eyes to the heavens, and look upon the earth beneath: for the heavens shall vanish away like smoke, and the earth shall wax old like a garment, and they that dwell therein shall die in like manner' (Isaiah 51: 6). The Isaiah verse ends on a note of confidence: 'but my salvation shall be for ever'. For all her dogged optimism, Winnie is never enabled to attain this level of assurance.

A further echo of the Book of Isaiah is to be found in *For to End Yet Again*, where the viewing eye ranges through panoramas of bone-strewn bareness and desolation. Early in the text, the 'grey timeless air' is established as being 'of those nor for God nor for his enemies' (*CSPR*, p. 180). Yet Beckett's vision of the dusty ruins under a for-saken sky suddenly chimes in his consciousness with allied pan-oramas invoked in the Old Testament. On the last page of his handwritten draft of the English translation (RUL MS 1552/2), near the phrase 'sky forsaken of its vultures', Beckett writes in the mar-gin a biblical reference: 'Isa. vii. 16'. This verse reads: 'For before the child shall know to refuse the evil, and choose the good, the land that thou abhorrest shall be forsaken of both her kings'. The child referred to is the one mentioned two verses earlier in that well-known passage which so often forms part of Advent and Christmas liturgies: 'A virgin shall conceive, and bear a son, and shall call his name Immanuel'. These verses form part of the succession of so-called Emmanuel oracles delivered by the prophet Isaiah, and here addressed to King Ahaz, threatened by the invading forces of the Kings of Israel and Syria. The prophet's tragic monotone – alternately stern and tender, and elegantly sustained throughout the Book of Isaiah – is perhaps perceived most resonantly in the King James translation, and it is here that the word 'forsaken' appears.

Even while immersed in the minutiae of translation, then, Beckett could interact with the biblical intertext deep within his memory. What is open to conjecture is whether Isaiah's visions of parched lands and fallen empires was present in Beckett's conception of the piece from the outset, even at a subliminal level, or whether they were elicited by the trigger-word 'forsaken'. The latter scenario is quite feasible, given that 'forsaken' is not a common verb in English, and that the verb used in the French original is 'déserté'. The corresponding verb in the most commonly used French translations of Isaiah would be 'dévasté' or 'abandonné'. Whatever the case may be, it seems that, as with the *Happy Days* instance, Beckett's text does not move on beyond the intermediate, purgatorial stage, and Isaiah's vision of the desert a-flower with God's future bounty remains sealed off.

Another powerful Old Testament image of human beings threatened by outside events is that of the Flood (Genesis 6–8). In a manuscript draft (OSU, Act 1 only) on the way to *Fin de partie*, the character 'B' staggers in with a large bible (at 'A'''s request) and first suggests reading a psalm, and then 'un peu de Pentatuque'. He is corrected by A: 'Tatuque! Tat*euque*. Pentateuque'. The Pentateuch (being the first five books of the Old Testament) affords a wide range of reading options – narratives, laws, sermons, genealogies, poetry, etc. – from the call of Abraham to the death of Moses. A finally selects the Flood narrative (although, properly speaking, this early part of the Book of Genesis is a prologue to the Pentateuch). B then proceeds to read out Genesis 7: 21–2, which details the death of every living creature left on dry land, until abruptly halted by A, whereupon he jumps forward to Genesis 11: 14 ff, where he embarks on the genealogical succession emanating from Shem, son of Noah.

The published *Endgame* retains a remnant of the Flood narrative, when Hamm suggests to Clov the creation of an Ark-like conveyance on which they could make their escape: 'You can make a raft and the currents will carry us away, far away, to other... mammals!' (*EG*, p. 28). Unlike Noah's project, Hamm's is never realised or even realisable. His escape fantasy will never get off the ground.

This, and the many other Old Testament resonances in *Endgame*, have already been well documented elsewhere. What is notable about them, however, is their variety, and their overwhelmingly negative bent. Hamm's first rhetorical question – 'Can there be misery [...] loftier than mine?' (*EG*, p. 12) – sets early the tone of foreboding, with its evocation of the Book of Lamentations; 'Behold, and see if there be any sorrow like unto my sorrow' (Lamentations 1: 12). Later, Hamm perverts an incident from the Book of Exodus when he relates in his story an address to the famished man: 'But what in God's name do you imagine? That the earth will awake in spring? [...] That there's manna in heaven still for imbeciles like you?' (*EG*, p. 37). In the Book of Exodus, the message of God to Moses is: 'At even ye shall eat flesh, and in the morning ye shall be filled with bread' (Exodus 16: 12), thus anticipating the provision of quails and manna to save the people from starvation. The quails and the manna duly arrive, heaven-sent, gratuitous.

The narrator in *How It Is* no doubt has this model in mind when he imagines with contempt 'a celestial tin miraculous sardines sent down by God at the news of my mishap wherewith to spew him out another week' (*HI*, p. 53). The phrase 'spew him out' adds to the disparagement of God, reminiscent as it is of the passage in the Book of Revelation in which God talks of spewing out those who are merely tepid in their commitment: 'I know thy works, that thou art neither cold nor hot: I would thou wert cold or hot. So then because thou art lukewarm, and neither cold nor hot, I will spue thee out of my mouth' (Revelation 3: 15–16). Beckett's narrator here implements a neat reversal, since, in his rendering, the prolongation of his life will afford him further time in which to spew God out. There is, then, no heavenly succour to be had in either *How It Is* or *Endgame*, and, in the latter, Hamm's story luxuriates in the wordy and callous confirmation of this fact.

Hamm's quotation from the Book of Daniel also participates in the theme of dissolution. When he asks of Clov: 'And what do you see on your wall? Mene, mene?' (*FP*, p. 17), he is echoing Daniel's interpretation of the word written on King Belshazzar's wall: 'MENE; God hath numbered thy kingdom, and finished it' (Daniel 5: 26). Interestingly, in typescript 2 of the *Fin de partie* drafts held at Ohio State University, the Hamm-figure 'A' imagines that B views on his wall not the 'Mene, mene' inscription, but 'les lettres de Ninive'. Although the Old Testament referent is different, its association with apocalypse is very similar, since Nineveh (the city which became the capital of Assyria in Sennacherib's reign) eventually fell to the Babylonians in about 612 BC. Accordingly, the prophet Nahum, predicting the destruction of the great city, proclaims; 'And it shall come to pass, that all they that look upon thee shall flee from thee, and say, Nineveh is laid waste: who will bemoan her?' (Nahum 3: 7).

Overwhelmingly, then, the Old Testament references in Beckett's later writing are chosen for their enunciation of the ephemerality of human beings and of their material endeavours. Moreover, wherever passages of doom and destruction are followed or counterpointed in the original by messages of hope, these latter palliatives are never allowed to intrude. In *All That Fall*, Mrs Rooney informs her husband that the preacher's text for the following Sunday is to be: 'The Lord upholdeth all that fall and raiseth up all those that be bowed down' (Psalm 145: 14). The quotation occurs close to the end of a play which has been riddled with near-falls and with straining locomotion. It is not surprising that the bowed couple break into 'wild laughter' (*CSPL*, p. 38) at the mismatch between the assured sentiments of the psalm and their own experience of its unfulfilled promise.

Turning to the New Testament resonances, which are fewer in number, one finds little mitigation of the bleak tenor of the scriptural allusions. One example of this seamless transition between bleaknesses is the above quotation from *All That Fall*. It is that same image of God's awareness of all that fall which Christ uses in his commission to the apostles, as rendered by Matthew: 'Are not two sparrows sold for a farthing? and one of them shall not fall on the ground without your Father. But the very hairs of your head are all numbered. Fear ye not therefore, ye are of more value than many sparrows' (Matthew 10: 29–31). However, when Mrs Rooney cites 'the sparrows, than many of which we are of more value' (*CSPL*, p. 37), Mr Rooney immediately disputes this affirmation of the status of humankind relative to smaller creatures: 'Than many of which! ... You exaggerate, Maddy'. His ironic conclusion must be that, if two sparrows are worth a farthing, a human being, not being worth more than many of them, is not worth a penny. Indeed, he has just witnessed to that perception, in begrudging the penny tip given to Tommy.

Mrs Rooney is, however, concerned not with computing God's munificence, but in pointing out that 'they weren't sparrows at all' (*CSPL*, p. 37). Similarly, she has just maintained that the animal on which Christ rode into Jerusalem 'wasn't an ass's colt at all', but a hinny. Her concern with exegesis appears to have more to do with her fascination with parts and properties of animals (cp. her 'life-long preoccupation with horses' buttocks' [*CSPL*, p. 35]) than with religious devotion. In both cases, the argument is humorously specious. Within the context of the English language translation, the word 'sparrow' is here being used not to denote a particular species found in most parts of Britain and Ireland, but whatever is the most common (and therefore, arguably, the least valuable) native bird. Similarly, the argument concerning the ass is a phoney one, since the range of Greek words used in the four Gospels for the Christ-bearing animal simply denote 'ass', 'young foal', or 'little ass'. The Greek word for 'hinny', 'ginnos', is not amongst them.[2]

The more important 'meaning' of each passage is a symbolic one, which is overlooked by Mrs Rooney's historico-literalist reading. In the first case, the sparrow's role is to demonstrate that, if such a tiny part of the ecosystem is the focus of God's loving concern, how much more is a human being, who has, according to the Book of Genesis, been accorded dominion over other living creatures. In the second case, the fact of Christ riding into Jerusalem on an ass carries significance within the biblical tradition as a whole, for to enter a city on a mule is to enter peaceably and humbly. Biblical precedents include the procession of Solomon, upon King David's mule (1 Kings: 38), and the prophecy of Zechariah: 'Behold, thy King cometh unto thee: he is just, and having salvation; lowly, and riding upon an ass, and upon a colt the foal of an ass' (Zechariah 9: 9). Mrs Rooney's synecdochal focus, in which she fastens upon a part or a detail, rather than upon the whole, not only provides humour, but also reinforces the impression that the Rooneys' relationship to religion is a somewhat oblique one: any centrality it ever had in their lives has given way to a more distanced or detached perspective.

Nevertheless, the variety of asinine nouns used in the four Gospels, and the reported discussion Mrs Rooney has had with 'the

Regius Professor' (*CSPL*, p. 37), does highlight the important issue of interpretation. As human, subjective accounts, and not photographic records, the Gospels have to be read within the cultural contexts of their respective writers and target readerships. If not all the product of eye witnesses, they are nevertheless based upon oral traditions emanating from eye witnesses. However, since eye witnesses are themselves multiple and possibly selective in their memories, there are inevitable discrepancies between the Gospels in terms of their inclusion of incidents, or their locating or ordering of events. It is within this perspective that Vladimir's puzzlement with the story of the good thief and the bad thief must be viewed in *Waiting for Godot*.

When Vladimir maintains that 'of the four Evangelists only one speaks of a thief being saved' (*WFG*, p. 12), he is quite correct, since only Luke mentions the conversation in which Christ, hanging between two thieves, assures only one of them of salvation (Luke 23: 39–43). Vladimir goes on to elaborate: 'Of the other three two don't mention any thieves at all and the third says that both of them abused him' (*WFG*, p. 13). 'The third' here denotes Matthew, who relates that 'the thieves also, which were crucified with him, cast the same in his teeth' (Matthew 27: 44). It is not correct, however, to maintain that the remaining two 'don't mention any thieves at all', since Mark's Gospel reads: 'And with him they crucify two thieves; the one on his right hand, and the other on his left' (Mark 15: 27). John's Gospel does mention two others crucified with Christ (John 19: 18), although they are not identified as thieves.

When Vladimir ponders: 'Why believe [Luke] rather than the others?' (*WFG*, p. 13), he is posing a false dilemma. The only real problem would have arisen if the other Gospel writers had flatly contradicted any such account of a conversation. As it is, they simply do not include it amongst their selection of events. Nevertheless, Vladimir's comments do have a double function. First, they draw attention to the fact that visual and linguistic presence is always more powerful than absence. A described event will always outweigh the absence of such an event in the composite memories of Gospel readers. To give a further example, the appearance of the angel Gabriel to Mary is described only in Luke. Yet, generations of readers and artists (believers or not) have nevertheless made this visitation central to their visualisation of the incarnation, regardless of whether or not they have been aware of its exclusive status within one Gospel.

Secondly, however, Vladimir's inability to interest Estragon in his conundrum indicates an important incompatibility between the two men. In a sense, they might be seen as haphazardly representing historical controversies in which an emphasis upon the manhood of Christ is opposed to an emphasis upon his divinity. Impatient with what he sees as an irrelevant debate, Estragon kills the discussion with a definitive punchline: 'People are bloody ignorant apes' (*WFG*, p. 13). For him, biblical hermeneutics will always be secondary to immediate, bodily needs. This does not mean that he discounts the Bible. He simply relates to it on a different plane. A physical being, he appreciates its appearance and physicality: 'I remember the maps of the Holy Land. Coloured they were. Very pretty. The Dead Sea was pale blue. The very look of it made me thirsty' (*WFG*, p. 12). Moreover, the Jesus he can relate to is not the one who is mediated through the accounts of writers and theologians, but Jesus the man, the one who suffered in his body, and who went barefoot. Thus, when Vladimir (imprinted with the concept of Christ primarily as divine saviour) expostulates: 'You're not going to compare yourself to Christ!' (*WFG*, p. 52), Estragon can quietly admit: 'All my life I've compared myself to him'.

Beyond the image of Jesus as suffering servant, however, there is the image of him as pantocrator and divine judge, and this concept serves to produce some waves of disquiet in Beckett's later writing. Hence, although Hamm in *Endgame* satirises Christ's repeated injunction 'Thou shalt love thy neighbour as thyself' by converting the formula to: 'Lick your neighbour as yourself!' (*EG*, p. 44), there seems at times to be a momentarily genuine recognition of his own deficiencies. At one point, he ruminates on 'all those I might have helped' (*EG*, p. 44), as if sharing the rueful realisation of those whom Christ condemns: 'For I was an hungred, and ye gave me no meat: I was thirsty, and ye gave me no drink' (Matthew 25: 42).

This anticipation of a final reckoning also occurs in *Eh Joe*, where the woman's voice grinds on: 'Till one night . . . ."Thou fool thy soul" . . . .Put your thugs on that' (*CSPL*, p. 204). This is a sinister shorthand for that chilling parable in Luke 12, where a rich man plans to build larger barns in which to amass all his produce, telling himself: 'Take thine ease, eat, drink, and be merry'. However, he receives a rude awakening: 'God said unto him, Thou fool, this night thy soul shall be required of thee' (Luke 12: 19–20). In repeating the incisive address: 'Thou fool thy soul', the woman tries to induce Joe to contemplate an even worse impending fate than that envisaged in the parable: not that his stockpiled produce will go to waste, but that there will be retribution for his own brutalities, and that there will be no escape from it: 'Put your thugs on that'.

PRIESTS, PRAYERS AND POPULAR PIETY

Priests

It is perhaps to be expected that, in the undefined and indefinable settings of Beckett's drama and late prose – that space which is no space – the citing of outward observance, and of particular cultural or religious contexts, is much reduced. There are no priests to be found here, although there are a few humorous or satirical references to them. For example, Dr Piouk in the early play *Eleutheria* mentions that his recent marriage to Mme Piouk was 'bénie par Sa Sainteté' (*E*, p. 52). Papally blessed or not, however, the marriage seems unlikely to prosper for long, given that much of the honeymoon has been spent wrestling with the dilemma of whether or not they should kill any child they might have, in accordance with Dr Piouk's recipe for utopia: 'Je noyerais les nouveau-nés' (*E*, p. 50).

Another evocation of priestly ministry in the context of married couples can be found in *All That Fall*, where Mrs Rooney informs her husband that the preacher for the following Sunday is to be a visiting minister called Hardy. For a moment, Mr Rooney assumes this Hardy to be the author of the amusingly-titled *How to be Happy Though Married*, until reminded by his wife that this is not the case. As R.E.R Madelaine related in an interesting article in 1982,[3] this work was indeed written by one Reverend Edward John Hardy. The book, *How to be Happy Though Married: Being a Handbook to Marriage*, was published in 1885, and became a bestseller. Amongst other works, Hardy produced (in 1914) a further book, *Still Happy Though Married*. The fact that the forgetful Mr Rooney demonstrates instant recall of the first title seems to suggest that its implied presupposition – that the married state is a potential obstacle to happiness – might well hold some personal applicability for him.

A further humorous reference to a clergyman occurs in *Happy Days*, where Willie reads from his newspaper the death announcement: 'His Grace and Most Reverend Father in God Dr Carolus Hunter dead in tub' (*HD*, p. 26). This draws from Winnie the wistful exclamation: 'Charlie Hunter!', and a recollection of having sat upon the reverend's knees in a garden. She then proceeds to recall her first kiss: 'A Mr Johnson, or Johnston, or perhaps I should say John*stone*'. The combination of Hunter and Johnson is intriguing, given Beckett's early and profound interest in Samuel Johnson.[4] Johnson's feared headmaster at Lichfield Grammar School was the Reverend John Hunter (with whom Johnson kept in touch for years afterwards), and Hunter's eldest surviving son at the time of his death was the Reverend Charles Hunter. The fate of being found 'dead in tub' may be insignificant, but the Reverend Charles Hunter did indeed suffer a premature death in 1744, at the age of thirty-four, being engaged to be married at the time. The Johnsonian frame of reference is further developed when one observes that, in the French version, the donor of the kiss is not Johnson, but 'Demoulin...ou Dumoulin...voire Desmoulins'. Mrs Desmoulins was a widow who came to join the coterie living permanently at Johnson's London home. Moreover, although Johnson himself does not feature in *Human Wishes* (the abandoned play Beckett began to prepare in the late 1930s on the subject of Johnson and Mrs Thrale), Mrs Desmoulins does figure prominently in the fragment.

Interestingly, in the holograph draft of Act 1 of *Happy Days*, held at Ohio State University, Beckett considers (and then partially strikes out) a further clerically-flavoured newspaper announcement. Here, the Willie-character (called 'B' at this stage) reads out: 'Rocket strikes Erin. Six hundred and ninety priests survive'. In Beckett's ironically upturned formulation, the disaster lies not in the felling, but in the survival, of so many priests.

Prayers

In the short text *Assez*, the 'il' on whom the narrative concentrates is viewed as a murmuring companion, but one who 'voulait que tout soit entendu et jusques aux éjaculations et bribes de patenôtres qu'il lançait au sol fleuri' (*TM*, pp. 37–8). This is a rather rare occurrence, within the later writing, of someone having recourse to set prayer formulae such as the Pater Noster. Nagg, in *Fin de partie*, does begin gabbling 'Notre Père qui êtes aux...' (*FP*, p. 76), but is quickly silenced by Hamm, and Winnie, in *Happy Days*, concludes her inaudible morning prayer with a conventional doxology: 'For Jesus Christ sake Amen' (*HD*, p. 16). Apart from these odd examples, there are on the whole, in contrast with Beckett's earlier writing, far fewer references to, or inclusions of, prescribed or liturgical prayers. There are, however, a number of aspirations or attempts to pray, as well as actual, hapless prayers, uttered in adversity, often with not much faith in their potential efficacy, like the 'prière pour la prière quand tout fait défaut' referred to in *Comment C'est* (*CC*, pp. 55–6).

At the first level are vociferations such as 'Christ!', 'My God!', or 'Jesus!' There are many such examples to be found within the drama and later prose, and their function tends to be almost entirely expletory or exclamatory, like the frenzied 'Jesus! Jesus!' of Mrs Rooney, toiling along the country road in *All That Fall* (*CSPL*, p. 17). It is likely that these kinds of articulation provide their own remedy: the voicer has let off steam, registered protest or surprise. Linked with these are the phatic expressions emitted to demonstrate hope against the odds, such as the 'God grant not', 'God forbid', and 'Please God not' voiced respectively by Flo, Ru, and Vi in *Come and Go* (*CSPL*, pp. 194–5).

In some cases, however, these utterances have a vocative or connective element: they appear to be addressed to another, or others, beyond. One notable example of this is the invocation constructed in *All Strange Away*: 'Imagine other murmurs, Mother mother, Mother in heaven, Mother of God, God in heaven, combinations with Christ and Jesus, other proper names in great numbers say of loved ones for the most part' (*CSPR*, p. 122) (an enumeration which undergoes a partial reprise later in the text). Nevertheless, the uncertain pulses of this prayer, alternately pessimistic and optimistic, half-hearted and heartfelt, seem to cancel each other out and return the supplicant to where he started, amid 'a mere torrent of hope and unhope mingled and submission amounting to nothing'.

Beyond the search for a formula is the pure cry of pain which emanates from desperation, frustration, or misery. Krapp calls it a 'yelp to Providence' (*KLT*, p. 58). Such a prayer is often called a 'miserere', since this is the opening word of the Latin translation of Psalm 51: 'Have mercy upon me, O God, according to thy lovingkindness'. Indeed, on three handwritten postcards held at Reading University Library (RUL MS 4123), Beckett includes among the notes he has made upon *The Divine Comedy* the opening words of the miserere, which are chanted by the souls passing before the Pilgrim.

Clearly, the miserere expresses a perception of wretchedness. The problem is that a miserere uttered in the presence of others does not always enlist their sympathy. Hence, the misery of Job is increased by the relentless counter-arguments of the attendants upon his dung-heap, who 'comfort' him in terms such as: 'Happy is the man whom God correcteth' (Job 5: 17), and: 'If thou return to the Almighty, thou shalt be built up' (Job 22: 23). However thoroughly slumped upon the dungheap, one can always slump further, as Winnie knows only too well. So too does Mrs Rooney, who clearly perceives herself to be the fellow of Job. When Mr Rooney asks her to count the steps they are labouring up, she replies: 'Not steps, Dan, please, I always get them wrong. Then you might fall on your wound and I would have that on my manure-heap on top of everything else' (*CSPL*, p. 30).

In *En attendant Godot*, Estragon has by Act 2 already lengthily bewailed his plight to Vladimir, from whom he receives the exclamation: 'Tu as bientôt fini de te plaindre? Tu commences à me casser les pieds, avec tes gémissements' (*EAG*, p. 63). It is shortly after that dismissal that Estragon, at his wits' end, roars out his prayer: 'Dieu aie pitié de moi!' (*EAG*, p. 68), followed shortly by 'De moi! De moi! Pitié! De moi!'. It is the miserere *par excellence*, a bellow from his guts, and Vladimir is now anxious to associate himself with it: 'Et moi?'. Both men are perhaps also subliminally aware of what Psalm 51 appears to posit as a precondition of, or at least an accompaniment to, such clemency: namely, repentance. Hence, the psalmist proclaims; 'I acknowledge my transgressions: and my sin is ever before me' (Psalm 51: 3). Vladimir has already floated the idea: 'Si on se repentait?' (*EAG*, p. 5). However, neither man has a clear apprehension of what they could repent of, and the plan is aborted.

As with the unspecified repentance, Estragon flirts with the idea of a generalised thanksgiving. In the English translation, the terms in which this is couched are more pointedly directed than in the French original towards a religious context: 'Well? If we gave thanks for our mercies?' (*WFG*, p. 64). He has just enquired: 'Then what are we complaining about?', and is no doubt speculating upon the efficacy of a charm offensive upon the Almighty as a variant upon the miserere. The problem is that the 'mercies' of which he speaks are, like Winnie's 'great mercies', not perceptible. It is generally possible to find someone worse off than oneself – Vladimir and Estragon have witnessed Lucky's abjection, and Winnie can with dread imagine herself mute and companionless – but this is a grimly negative method of arriving at a conviction of 'mercies', and the word cannot but hang heavy with irony when mouthed by either camp.

What prayer there is in this later writing, therefore, is generated mainly by instincts towards supplication, rather than by praise, thanksgiving, or contrition. After all, worship and thanks seem to belong more naturally to a domain of relationship with God, in which prayer arises spontaneously, like conversation. Within Beckett's writing there is never a sense of interchange or fulfilment within prayer. Indeed, dispositions of prayer are sometimes adopted, only to fade away. In *Fragment de théâtre I*, A kneels before B, crossing his hands and lowering his head, but is driven to reply 'Non' when B exclaims in horror: 'Bon Dieu! Vous n'allez pas prier tout de même!' (*PS*, p. 32). Towards the end of Act 1 of *Happy Days*, after referring to her thankfulness, Winnie suddenly experiences a kind of mental fly-past of all her orisons: 'bow and raise and the head, bow and raise, always that' (*HD*, p. 56). Thus assessed, the prayer-wheel seems to grind to a halt, clogged by long and fruitless repetition. Similarly, when in *Fin de partie* Clov and Nagg are prompted by Hamm – 'Prions Dieu' (*FP*, p. 75) – to join him in attempted contact with the Deity, the experiment proves futile. All report blank encounters, and abandon their attitudes of prayer, while Hamm gives vent to his spleen against the *Deus absconditus*: 'Le salaud! Il n'existe pas!' (*FP*, p. 76). This definitive declaration is immediately rendered provisional, as already examined, by Clov's extension of the time-frame – 'Pas encore' – which restores God to a position of waiting in the wings. Nonetheless, it is interesting that, in the first typescript of the draft held at Ohio State University, a further line is to be seen, interjected between the two remarks, namely: 'Toujours pas'. This has the effect of expanding the time-frame still further, to the past, for 'toujours pas' hints at a history of repeated effort, always in vain.

It might be argued that there is at least one example of apparently answered prayer in Beckett's drama, since, only a split second after the roared miserere from Vladimir and Estragon, Pozzo and Lucky return, prompting from a grateful Vladimir the remark: 'Ça tombe à pic. Enfin du renfort!' (*FP*, p. 69). Yet the arrival, like most other events in the play, seems haphazard and coincidental. Moreover, can the arrival of Pozzo and Lucky be deemed an answer to prayer? In a sense, it can, since it provides a diversion when the games are running out. But, in the words of *Company*, it leaves Vladimir and Estragon 'in a very short time as chill and dim as before' (*NO*, p. 23).

In general, whether the prayer of the supplicant be a cry for help, a generalised petition, or a prayer of intercession, there is always a doubt attaching to its potential efficacy. As such, it resembles the 'vague supplique' reportedly addressed to Godot, to which he gave no guarantee of attention, other than 'qu'il verrait' (*EAG*, p. 12). The best Winnie can manage is an aspiration that 'prayers *perhaps* not for naught' (*HD*, p. 22; my italics), and the woman in *Not I* can only continue to pray by sheer persistence rather than by conviction: 'prayer unanswered...or unheard...too faint...so on...keep on...trying...not knowing what...what she was trying' (*CSPL*, p. 222).

Accordingly, prayer is in many cases regarded as something which is part of past habits, now renounced. Hence, Winnie reveals in Act 2 of *Happy Days* that: 'I used to pray. I say I used to pray. Yes, I must confess I did. Not now. No no' (*HD*, p. 66). Moreover, the narrator in *Comment C'est* reveals that he used at one time to pray for damned souls: 'Quand je pense aux âmes au tourment au vrai tourment aux vraies âmes qui n'y ont jamais droit au sommeil on parle du sommeil j'ai prié une fois pour elles d'après une vieille vue elle a jauni' (*CC*, p. 56).

This latter example again relegates prayer to a former epoch. However, it also illustrates that prayer is not treated entirely with cynicism in Beckett's writing. Not only are these previous spasms of prayer still present in the memory, but also their mainspring sometimes remains associated, in movements of compassion, with the causes of the most marginalised. In these cases, the imagination extends even towards those commonly represented as beyond help. St Augustine, for instance, issues a stern condemnation, in *The City of God*, of those misguided enough to pray for the souls in hell: 'They that before death are not engrafted into Christ, are afterward reputed as associates of the devil: and therefore the same cause forbids [the Church] to pray for the reprobate souls then, as stops her from praying for the apostatical angels now; and the same reason there is why we pray for all men while living, and yet will not pray for the wicked, nor infidels, when they are dead'.[5]

Le Vitrier in *Eleutheria* breaks this taboo (and widens its applicability) by sinking to his knees and beseeching ostentatiously: 'Pitié, pitié pour ceux qui rampent dans les ténèbres' (*E*, p. 137). In a more sustained example, the narrator in *Comment C'est* flouts Augustine's advice by praying, not without wry humour, for these victims of their own self-indulgence: 'En ta clémence de temps à autre qu'ils dorment les grands damnés ici des mots illisibles dans les plis puis rêver peut-être du bon temps que leur valurent leurs errements pendant ce temps les démons se reposeront dix secondes quinze secondes' (*CC*, p. 56). The voice in *Company* demonstrates a similar concern for a creature cut off from the mainstream, the hedgehog he has 'rescued' from the cold by placing it in a hutch: 'Kneeling at your bedside you included it the hedgehog in your detailed prayer to God to bless all you loved' (*NO*, p. 24).

The effect of prayers for the damned is not, of course, open to assessment. More sinisterly, the hedgehog who found himself the focus of ministration and prayer in fact quickly ends his days as 'mush' and 'stench' (*NO*, p. 24), buried alive within the hutch which was supposed to be his salvation. Prayer, then, is not seen in these instances to prompt divine intervention: succour for human beings remains within human hands. This may be productive of a range of reactions, as described in *Comment C'est*: 'maudire Dieu ou le bénir et attendre montre en main' (*CC*, p. 62). Nevertheless, in *Footfalls*, the gentle proffering of prayer by daughter to mother produces one of the most tender passages in Beckett's writing, and returns the benefit of such vigils to human ownership: 'Dress your sores? Sponge you down? Moisten your poor lips? Pray with you? For you? Again' (*CSPL*, p. 240).

Popular Piety

References to popular piety and to liturgy are similarly reduced in number in the later writing. *All That Fall* is something of an exception, but the clear presence of a worshipping community in this play derives from its more obvious geographical specificity, a feature which makes it unique among Beckett's plays. Mr and Mrs Rooney appear to be regular churchgoers, although seemingly deriving little benefit from it. Indeed, Mrs Rooney lists churchgoing, along with 'fat and rheumatism and childlessness', among the factors which have combined to make of her 'a hysterical old hag' (*CSPL*, p. 14). Neither does she entertain any illusions about automatic linkages between churchgoing and charity. Hence, when Miss Fitt agrees reluctantly to take Mrs Rooney's arm because 'it is the Protestant thing to do', Mrs Rooney reminds her that 'pismires [ants] do it for one another', as well as slugs (*CSPL*, p. 23).

Miss Fitt's very name suggests an outsider, a person unlikely to be immersed in charitable solidarity. She is shocked when Mrs

Rooney, reminding her that: 'Last Sunday we worshipped together. We knelt side by side at the same altar. We drank from the same chalice' (*CSPL*, p. 22), reproaches her for not immediately recognising her. For Miss Fitt, the communion service is not about community. When she attends church, she is 'oblivious to my co-religionists'. Amusingly, this abstractedness also extends to the sexton, when he approaches her pew for a contribution to the plate. It is a waste of time for him to pause, for, explains Miss Fitt: 'I am alone with my Maker'. It is for the struggling Mrs Rooney to slice into Miss Fitt's self-centred complacency by an ironic appropriation of her co-traveller's own expression: 'If you would help me up the face of this cliff, Miss Fitt, I have little doubt that your Maker would requite you, if no one else' (*CSPL*, p. 23). Her choice of possessive pronoun – 'your', rather than 'our' – acknowledges the alienation she feels from Miss Fitt's cosy spiritual absorption in God. Her own needs are immediate, and physical: 'Your arm! Any arm! A helping hand! For five seconds! Christ what a planet!'

Miss Fitt is not, however, alone in her distractedness. When she reveals to Mrs Rooney: 'I suppose the truth is I am not there, Mrs Rooney, just not really there at all' (*CSPL*, pp. 22–3), she finds a parallel in May/Amy, in *Footfalls*, who asserts that, during Evensong, 'I saw nothing, heard nothing, of any kind. I was not there' (*CSPL*, p. 243). Within May's narrative, Mrs Winter disputes this. She had distinctly heard Amy say 'Amen': 'How could you have responded if you were not there?' Amid the multiple layers of consciousness, Amy is there and not there. Significantly, the word Amy is said to utter is one of assent: 'Amen', which means 'So be it'. Amy's voice and body are, resignedly, present. She is perceptible or audible to her mother. Yet Amy's own experience of the event is of absence. In a more humorous context, her psychological absence is matched by that of Krapp, in *Krapp's Last Tape*. Physically present once at Vespers, 'like when I was in short trousers' (*CSPL*, p. 62), Krapp recalls how he 'went to sleep and fell off the pew' (*CSPL*, p. 63).

Nevertheless, Krapp is haunted by the Vespers hymn 'Now the day is over', and twice begins to sing it before being interrupted by coughing. This popular hymn, generally classified as being 'For the Young', was composed by the Rev. Sabine Baring-Gould (1834–1924), who is best-known for the words of the hymn 'Onward Christian Soldiers'. (It is normally sung to 'Eudoxia'. However, since Krapp engages on two notes at the close of the second line –

'Night is drawing nigh-igh' – he should probably sing it to 'German', or 'Newland').

The text of the hymn is allied to Proverbs 3: 24: 'When thou liest down, thou shalt not be afraid: yea, thou shalt lie down, and thy sleep shall be sweet', and consists of an aspiration for a peaceful sleep, protected by God, with the prospect of a fresh and new morning to come. The idea of retiring peacefully and sinking into a sweet sleep is not readily associated with the restless and sometimes cantankerous Krapp. Soon after his reprise of the hymn, he tells himself: 'Ah finish your booze now and get to your bed. Go on with this drivel in the morning. Or leave it at that. Leave it at that. Lie propped up in the dark – and wander' (*CSPL*, p. 63). Beckett soon decided that the hymn was better omitted in production. Nevertheless, the hymn's recognition of the cycles and rhythms of human existence, and of the interleaving of past, present, and future, seems to offer a transfiguring reflection of the cyclical temporal structure on which *Krapp's Last Tape* is based.

It appears, then, that although formal liturgies appear for the most part to fall on deaf ears in Beckett's later writing, the poignant charge of a particular hymn can prove to be extremely resilient to the passage of time. Even Mrs Rooney is susceptible to it. When Miss Fitt starts to hum John Henry Newman's great hymn 'Lead kindly light' (*CSPL*, p. 24), Mrs Rooney joins in with it. (Her metrical distribution – 'encircling gloo-oom', and 'ho-ome' – indicate that she is singing it to the tune 'Lux Benigna'). Again, the hymn is peculiarly suited to the circumstances. Mrs Rooney is indeed being led, though perhaps finding in Miss Fitt a more grudging than kindly light. The recurrent line 'Lead Thou me on' – (rendered by Mrs Rooney as 'tum tum me on') – is an aspiration which addresses not only all the difficulties in locomotion which feature so prominently in the play, but also Mrs Rooney's nagging temptation to succumb to 'wasting slowly, painlessly away, [...] drifting gently down into the higher life' (*CSPL*, p. 21).

In keeping with her individualistic instinct, Miss Fitt stops humming as soon as Mrs Rooney joins in, and threatens to take her arm away. Mrs Rooney, however, is trying to recall whether 'Lead kindly light' or 'Rock of Ages' was sung on the *Lusitania*, or alternatively on the *Titanic*. Both hymns construct God as a source of security: the first as guiding light for the pilgrim's steps, and the second as a cleft rock in which to take shelter. Both putative choirs were, however, on sinking ships, and Mrs Rooney, herself on the point of sinking, appears unaware of the irony: 'Most touching it must have been' (*CSPL*, p. 24).

There are still a few references to other elements of popular piety in the later writing, although these too are much diminished in number. In *Embers*, the words 'Santa Cecilia' issue from the Italian music master (*CSPL*, p. 98). Appropriately in the context, the Roman martyr St Cecilia is the patron saint of music, because of the legend that she sang her own interior music to God while instruments played at her own reluctant wedding to a young pagan. Clearly, given the aggressive demeanour of the music-master, the phrase is used here not as an invocation, but as an expostulation. Another conventional expression, though here attributed to one presumably fired by a more genuine religious impulse, occurs in *Eh Joe*, where the woman's voice reminds Joe of the newspaper death announcement, that of the pale young girl who loved him: 'On Mary's beads we plead her needs and in the Holy Mass' (*CSPL*, p. 205).

The church calendar is still occasionally cited to stake out given passages of time. In *Comment C'est*, the narrative voice refers to 'mes saisons et mes fêtes il me dit Pâques éternelles puis d'un bond la Toussaint pas d'été cette année-là' (*CC*, pp. 24–5). A sudden jump from the Easter season to the feast of All Saints (1 November) would be to elide more than half the year. However, knowledge of these relevant liturgical dates is here optionally deployed, since the second half of the above statement – 'pas d'été cette année-là' – elucidates the first. It also makes clear that the principal significance in the chosen feasts is temporal, not devotional. Indeed, in the corresponding passage in the English translation, it is not the Easter season which is mentioned, but that of Lent.

Similarly, when A and B in *Fragment de théâtre II* are discussing the date of the full moon, A reads out from his pocket diary the printed note 'Notre-Dame l'Auxiliatrice' (*PS*, p. 39), which happens to fall on the same day. The English translation reads 'Our Lady of Succour' (*CSPL*, p. 78). This is probably a half-hearted reference to the well-established cult of 'Our Lady of Perpetual Succour', which is celebrated in Ireland on 27 June.[6] The date does not quite match the date of the 'twenty-fifth tomorrow' mentioned by A. More important, however, is the profound irony in the fact that the suicide (assisted or otherwise) of C is anticipated for that day: a day which, it is assumed, will be devoid of the Marian succour which the coinciding feast proclaims.

THEOLOGY AND SPIRITUALITY

Jeremy Taylor

It is notable that, whereas Beckett's early fiction contains many references to theologians and spiritual writers, his drama and later fiction is almost entirely stripped of such references. Indeed, an exception to this – the play-fragment 'Human Wishes' – predates by many years the first of Beckett's stage-plays, and may well have been abandoned when Beckett found that the wealth of preparatory research he had accumulated militated against the dramatic structuring of the text.[7]

The theologian cited in 'Human Wishes' is Rev. Jeremy Taylor (1613–1667), one-time domestic chaplain to Charles I of England, and eventually Bishop of Down and Connor, and the text in question is the twin work *The Rule and Exercises of Holy Living*, and *The Rule and Exercises of Holy Dying*. *Holy Living* and *Holy Dying* were published one year apart (1650 and 1651), but are often published within the same volume. The long-lasting popularity of the works probably derives from the fact that they constitute not only works of spiritual and scriptural meditation, but also practical manuals on everyday living, drawing on a wide range of classical and Christian authors. *Holy Dying*, for example, contains not only reflections on death as a phenomenon, but also psychological advice to the sick.

Beckett was somewhat sceptical about Taylor's overall project. Indeed, he reported to Thomas MacGreevy in 1933 that he had 'read Jeremy Taylor and Leibniz. Why two books, Holy Living and Holy Dying, when one would have done the trick. Surely the classical example of literary tautology'.[8] While it is true that there is a certain amount of overlap between the two books, there is nevertheless a much greater concentration in the second volume upon demeanour in sickness, and cultivation of the dispositions before death.

It is from Section 1 of the second volume, *The Rule and Exercises of Holy Dying* that Beckett quotes, at length, in 'Human Wishes'. It is appropriate within the context of the play that Miss Carmichael should be reading extracts from the volume, since Dr Johnson (in whose home the play is set) was himself an admirer of Taylor's work.

The passages selected by Miss Carmichael to read aloud are those which contain an extended consideration of the omnipresence of death. Taylor is not unusual in using a litany of possible manners of death as a means of impressing upon the reader the importance of preparing for death. Thomas à Kempis, for example, uses a similar listing in his chapter 'On Thinking of Death' in *The Imitation of Christ*: 'How many are deceived and snatched unexpectedly from the body. How often have you heard people say that one died by the sword, another was drowned, another fell from a high place and broke his neck, another collapsed while eating, another met his end at play, one by fire, another by steel, another by plague, another died by brigandage; and so the end of all is death, and the life of man like a shadow suddenly passes away' (*IMI*, p. 55).

The listing given by à Kempis is worthy but rather lacklustre. What is unusual about Taylor's listing is its vivid and picturesque detail: a feature which characterises all of Taylor's writing and which provides one reason for its popularity. Taylor is perfectly able and willing to furnish the requisite scriptural allusion. The one he selects in the opening pages of *Holy Dying* is the Letter of James. It is the same source-passage as that which Beckett himself accesses (as noted earlier) within *How It Is*: 'For what is your life? It is even a vapour, that appeareth for a little time, and then vanisheth away' (James 4: 14). However, Taylor's breathless text is enlivened by a multitude of other classical and literary allusions, all jostling to enhance what could be a most gloomy topic. On the first page alone, he begins with a quotation from Lucian – 'A man is a bubble'[9] – and then develops the theme fungally: 'He comes into the world like morning mushrooms, soon thrusting up their heads into the air, and conversing with their kindred of the same production, and as soon they turn into dust and forgetfulness'. However, the bubble is still floating in the vicinity of the text, and Taylor re-captures it: 'The young man dances like a bubble, empty and gay, and shines like a dove's neck, or the image of a rainbow, which hath no substance'.

When Taylor proceeds to enumerate the diverse ways in which death may intervene unexpectedly, he achieves his effect not by the listing alone, but by the variety and even eccentricity of its components, together with a robust recourse to contrast and anecdote. He tells of victorious generals dying during the drunken celebrations of their triumphs, of brides dying while being dressed 'for uneasy joy' (Taylor, p. 303), and of Aeschylus being killed by the fall of an oyster, an overhead eagle having mistaken his bald head for a stone on which to break open the shell (Taylor, p. 304). It is immediately after the oyster tale that Taylor embarks upon the passage read out by Miss Carmichael in 'Human Wishes': 'Death meets us every where, and is procured by every instrument, and in all chances, and enters in at many doors' (Taylor, p. 304). After this prologue, the author sets up a series of striking antitheses, to demonstrate that, while death may ensue in one set of circumstances, it may equally well ensue in an opposite set. Hence, Miss Carmichael pursues her reading: '[...] by a full meal or an empty stomach; by watching at the wine or by watching at prayers; by the sun or the moon' (*HW*, p. 165). Two of the antitheses are queried by the listener, Mrs Williams, and confirmed by the reader. The first is: 'by the aspect of a star and the stink of a mist' (where presumably, in the latter case, asphyxiation by fog is meant). In the textual run-up to the second, in order to provide the maximum impact, Beckett simplifies Taylor's text somewhat, so that 'by water frozen into the hardness and sharpness of a dagger, or water thawed into the floods of a river' (Taylor, p. 304) becomes 'by water frozen or water thawed' (*HW*, p. 165).

There then follows the startling conjunction of: 'by a hair or a raisin'. In response to Mrs Williams's enquiry, Miss Carmichael conjectures that: 'Perhaps a horse-hair is meant, Madam'. The raisin is not discussed. Miss Carmichael then proceeds to round off the list, using Taylor's formulation: 'by every thing in Providence and every thing in manners, by every thing in nature and every thing in chance' (Taylor, p. 304). Taylor's subsequent text does not enlarge further upon the deathly agents, and the menace of the hair and the raisin thus remains unexplicated. Beckett, the careful and discriminating reader, here dramatises his own puzzlement at the passage. Perhaps the fact that the play-fragment tails off shortly after this is symptomatic of a more chronic difficulty: Beckett had during his research been collecting more and more data upon Johnson and his circle. The presence of such exhaustive detail possibly generated a creative impasse, of which the completion of the Taylor listing is a minor mirroring. The way forward was not clear. Taylor, warmly garrulous, clearly did not agonise very much about the textual bridges or sequencing. For Beckett, however, the historical and intellectual furniture he had amassed upon Johnson was too encumbering. He had not yet developed the creative strategy which begins from nothing and works to something. Instead, he had begun with everything and failed to produce anything: anything, at least, which satisfied him.

Images of God

Implicit in theology is a concern not only with revelation – the concept of God's self-manifestation to humankind – but also with imagery: the verbal or visual structures which believers have evolved in order to understand or communicate their perceptions of God. Since knowledge of God cannot be constructed on the basis of observables, it must then try to find expression in human realities, symbols, or formulae – (or, within the apophatic tradition, in their suspension or dismissal).

Within Beckett's drama and later fiction, there are still vestiges of such formulations, which either hang in the air or meet with rebuttal. In *Comment C'est*, for example, a number of key concepts in Christianity – Christ the Lamb, bearer of the world's sin; Christ the miracle-worker; the Trinity; the Holy Spirit symbolised by the dove ('le pigeon'[10]) – are run through the consciousness with a vague but largely hopeless nostalgia: 'l'agneau noir des péchés du monde le monde nettoyé les trois personnes c'est vous dire et cette croyance l'impression depuis lors dix ans onze ans cette croyance que j'aurais eue l'impression depuis lors un temps énorme que j'allais la rattraper le manteau bleu le pigeon les miracles il comprenait' (*CC*, p. 110).

Later, the question of whether God is in heaven is posited, or recalled, but not answered: 'comment savoir la vie là-haut la vie ici Dieu aux cieux oui ou non' (*CC*, p. 116). The question of whether or not this hypothesised God is defined by love is approached with much less hesitation. The formulation is a well-known one. It is stated, for example, in the First Letter of John – 'God is love; and he that dwelleth in love dwelleth in God, and God in him' (1 John 4: 16) – and re-echoed in hymnody. It is notable, then, that one paragraph in *Company* ends with a clear rejection of this equation: 'God is love. Yes or no? No' (*NO*, p. 42). This is despite the fact that, two lines earlier, the aspiration: 'Could he but smell his creator' seems to keep the idea of a creator in play.

This contrast points to an interesting feature of Beckett's writing as a whole: namely, that it exhibits much less readiness to exclude the possibility of a God than it does to dismiss some of God's rumoured properties. To that extent, Beckett could be seen to be operating a kind of reverse apophaticism. Apophatic theology proceeds on the assumption that God is not any of the things – 'Being', 'Life', 'the Good' – that he is called. This could well describe

Beckett's starting-point. But whereas the apophatic tradition would presuppose an array of positive or neutral attributes to suspend, the skittles which Beckett takes aim for are those which concern God's very desirability or benevolence. These are attributes which, despite its reluctance to name them, apophatic theology would take for granted, for, if they are not taken for granted, then the whole basis for wishing to enter into communion with such a being is put at issue.

The woman of *Not I* also mouths the phrase 'God is love', following it on two occasions with 'tender mercies...new every morning' (*CSPL*, pp. 221–2; 223). These sentiments are embraced in John Keble's morning hymn 'New Every Morning', which celebrates 'new mercies, each returning day', a hymn which itself echoes the Book of Lamentations: 'It is of the Lord's mercies that we are not consumed, because his compassions fail not. They are new every morning: great is thy faithfulness' (Lamentations 3: 22–3). The phrase 'tender mercies' emanates from yet another source: namely, the mention in Luke's Gospel (within Zechariah's prophecy) of 'the tender mercy of our God; whereby the dayspring from on high hath visited us' (Luke 1: 78), and the Letter of James: 'Ye have heard of the patience of Job, and have seen the end of the Lord; that the Lord is very pitiful, and of tender mercy' (James 5: 11).

The Hebrew word for 'mercy' is one of the commonest words used in the Old Testament to describe the kindness and fidelity of God, in his covenant with his people. It is closely linked with the notion of love, and is indeed translated as 'loving kindness' in some translations of the Bible. Within the New Testament, it continues to denote God's dynamic purpose for mankind, as well as the idea of clemency for wrongdoing. Yet, in the context of *Not I*, words such as 'love' and 'mercy' seem shockingly ironic. The woman's life-experience appears to be one of continually thwarted impulses to speak. When ordered to speak, in the courtroom, she feels paralysed, 'waiting to be led away' (*CSPL*, p. 221), and, when she does speak, the stream of words seems to dissociated from her brain. She cannot own them as if they were a product of her self, for she cannot say 'I'. As such, there seems no way forward for her other than to reel back her mind, as she does at the close of the play, and begin again. As Simone Weil states in her observations on 'Le Moi': 'Rien n'est pire que l'extrême malheur qui du dehors détruit le je, puisque dès lors on ne peut plus le détruire soi-même. Qu'arrive-t-il à ceux dont le malheur a détruit du dehors le je? On ne peut se représenter pour eux que l'anéantissement' [Nothing is worse than extreme unhappiness which destroys the 'I' from the outside, since from then on you can no longer destroy it yourself. What happens to those whose 'I' has been destroyed from without by unhappiness? One can imagine only annihilation for them].[11]

Though the woman in *Not I* speaks of having been brought up 'with the other waifs' to believe in a merciful God, her perception – that of being punished for her sins – constantly belies it. This is really a central disjuncture which Beckett's writing dramatises: that the God whose hypothesised existence can never be entirely relegated constantly fails to meet expectations. After all, notions of 'love' and 'mercy' have very little meaning if they are only infrequently applied: in order to have impact, they must be constant. For someone to be deemed 'loving' and 'merciful', they must not just assume these qualities on occasion; they must incarnate them. This is the crucial test which the God-candidate fails within the Beckettian scenario.

Moreover, this is the central doubt which structures, for example, *En attendant Godot*. Just as Vladimir worries about the 'bad thief' and the 'good thief' – (according to popular credence, only the 'good thief' was assured of mercy) – and its possible implications in the more widespread economy of salvation, the Boy mentions that, while he is associated with the goats, and is not beaten by Godot, his brother is associated with the sheep, and is the recipient of beatings. (Curiously, it is the souls to be chastised who are associated with goats in the judgement parable in Matthew's Gospel, while the virtuous souls, placed on the Father's right hand, are associated with the sheep [Matthew 25: 32 ff]). This discrimination in favour of one group rather than another is also reflected in the luckless Lucky's monologue. Having cited a conventional image of 'un Dieu personnel quaquaquaqua à barbe blanche', he observes chillingly that this God 'nous aime bien *à quelques exceptions près*' (*EAG*, p. 37; my italics).

In one text, *To Simplician – on Various Questions* (Book 1), St Augustine attempts to deal with the paradox of the differentiated fates of the 'good thief' and the 'bad thief' by inserting it into a disquisition about grace and free will. As far as the 'good thief' is concerned, Augustine argues, 'good works would have followed if after receiving grace he had continued to live for a time among men. They certainly did not precede so that he might have merited that grace, for he had been crucified as a robber, and from the cross was translated to paradise'.[12] Augustine does show himself aware of the difficulties presented by these two parallel but contrasting human beings, but his attempt to resolve the matter at the close of his text by recourse to God's inscrutability may seem cavalier to modern ears: 'Why then does he deal thus with this man and thus with that man? [...] Only let us believe if we cannot grasp it, that he who made and fashioned the whole creation, spiritual and corporeal, disposes of all things by number, weight and measure. But his judgments are inscrutable and his ways past finding out. Let us say Halleluia and praise him together in song; and let us not say, What is this? or, Why is that? All things have been created each in its own time' (*To Simplician*, p. 406).

Beckett's people cannot possibly 'say Halleluia', for, within their conception of God – of a Being who, while holding all the cards, apparently distributes them arbitrarily – there is clearly no scope for confidence and repose, or even for an interface between creator and created, eternal and temporal. As Hamm snarls in *Fin de partie*: 'Mais réfléchissez, réfléchissez, vous êtes sur terre, c'est sans remède!' (*FP*, p. 91). Simone Weil voices a similar insight with regard to the incompatibility of time-bound creatures, and timeless creator: 'Il faudrait que l'avenir fût là sans cesser d'être l'avenir. Absurdité dont seule l'éternité guérit' (*La Pesanteur*, p. 29) [We want the future to be there without ceasing to be future. An absurdity which only eternity can cure.]

Simone Weil's writing is indeed of some applicability here, since her best-known work, *Attente de Dieu* (sometimes translated as *Waiting for God*) does bear at least titular resemblance to *En Attendant Godot*. Weil (1909–43), of Jewish background, was a brilliant philosophy student and teacher who had, at different times of her life, experience of agnosticism, of anti-religious sentiments, and of a fascination with Catholicism. Giving up teaching in favour of factory work, she eventually died in England, probably worn out by self-neglect. Weil was emphatic in her literary tastes. Admiring, for example, Valéry and Koestler, she had no time for authors in whom she detected the slightest hint of self-importance, such as Hugo or Corneille. For her, only a style stripped down to the bare essential was congenial. Had she lived, she would surely have responded positively to Beckett.

Weil's theology of waiting, if it may be so called, is not a matter of passivity but of attentiveness. Seeing God as distant in his infinity, she has no aspiration towards cosy familiarity with the Godhead.

Indeed, like Beckett's creatures, she grapples with a cruel world in which God's intervention is sought but never obtained. Winnie in *Happy Days* has even come to conceive of God as a divine joker, pulling tricks at her own expense. As she says bravely: 'How can one better magnify the Almighty than by sniggering with him at his little jokes, particularly the poorer ones?' (*HD*, p. 42). Nell, in *Fin de partie*, reveals more of the weariness built into the effort of laughing at unhappiness: 'Nous en rions, nous en rions, de bon coeur, les premiers temps. Mais c'est toujours la même chose' (*FP*, p. 34). The Old Testament figure of Job takes an even more wintry view of God's role in human suffering, stating at one point: 'If the scourge slay suddenly, he will laugh at the trial of the innocent' (Job 9: 23).

Weil herself quotes this remark of Job, and her comment on it seems perfectly in tune with the Beckettian perspective: 'Ce n'est pas un blasphème, c'est un cri authentique arraché à la douleur. Le livre de Job, d'un bout à l'autre, est une pure merveille de vérité et d'authenticité. Au sujet du malheur, tout ce qui s'écarte de ce modèle est plus ou moins souillé de mensonge' [This is not a blasphemy, it is a genuine cry wrenched out of pain. The Book of Job is from end to end a pure marvel of truth and authenticity. As far as misfortune is concerned, anything which departs from this model is in some degree tainted with deception].[13]

Within this clearsighted evaluation of human wretchedness, Weil maintains that an attitude of waiting is the only desirable option: 'Il faut rester immobile, attentif, et attendre, sans bouger, en appelant seulement quand le désir est trop fort' [We must remain still, attentive, and wait, without moving, only calling out when the desire becomes too strong] (*Attente*, pp. 210–11). On one level, this describes the situation (willed or otherwise) of Vladimir and Estragon. They have kept their appointment, as Vladimir observes: 'Nous ne sommes pas des saints, mais nous sommes au rendez-vous. Combien de gens peuvent en dire autant?' (*EAG*, pp. 71–2).

Once there, they persist in waiting. It is all they can do. As Weil presents it: 'Nous ne pouvons pas faire un seul pas vers [Dieu]. On ne marche pas verticalement. Nous ne pouvons diriger vers lui que notre regard. Il n'y a pas à le chercher, il faut seulement changer la direction du regard. C'est à lui de nous chercher' [We cannot take a single step towards (God). We cannot walk vertically. We can only direct our eyes towards him. It is not a case of seeking him, we must simply change the direction of our glance. It is up to him to look for us] (*Attente*, p. 215).

However, if it is up to God to look for mankind, the perception of many in Beckett's oeuvre is that he does not exert himself sufficiently in that direction. A look may be all that is required, but a repeated look towards God without assurance of an answering one requires a strong and consistent faith. For Simone Weil, the spiritual journey towards the gaze of God is both risky and secure; in order to embark upon it or experiment with it, 'la foi est la condition indispensable' [faith is an indispensable condition] (*Attente*, p. 87). However, this is a paradox which is not easily accommodated within the Beckettian world.

Many of Beckett's people are profoundly aware of the importance of being perceived, even if the surveying glance is indiscernible, or one-sided. The Man in *Play* asks: 'Am I as much as ... being seen?' (*CSPL*, p. 157), and Estragon enquires of Vladimir: 'Tu crois que Dieu me voit?' (*EAG*, p. 68). The answer Estragon receives is revelatory: 'Il faut fermer les yeux'. Only by shutting his eyes, according to Vladimir, will Estragon have a chance of seeing that he is being seen. Yet, when Estragon does shut his eyes, he topples over, losing his balance. Bodily realities cannot be sidestepped in favour of spiritual ones. The hitches in the God/mankind communication are, it seems, manifold.

Even if one could feel convinced of being seen, it would not be possible to be certain of the tenor of that glance. Within this atmosphere of uncertainty, there is no means of knowing whether God is monitoring human conduct and finding it wanting, or, alternatively, whether his glance has been withdrawn. In *Film*, O tries to evade being the object of the gaze of others. Accordingly, he covers the parrot's cage, evicts the cat and dog, tears up the family photographs. It is notable, however, that the wall-print of God the Father, 'the eyes staring at him severely' (*CSPL*, p. 167) is the victim of a much more vehement disposal than the rest, for not only does O tear down the print from the wall and rip it up, but he also 'throws down the pieces and grinds them underfoot'. In *Happy Days*, there may be more than a little wishful thinking in Winnie's perception at the beginning of Act 2: 'Someone is looking at me still. Caring for me still' (*HD*, p. 64). That 'someone' is, however, unspecified. If present, the viewing eye is invisible. It could simply be an insect, like the ant who passed in the first Act, or as in the suggestion made to Joe by the woman's voice in *Eh Joe*: 'Why don't you put out that light? There might be a louse watching you' (*CSPL*, p. 202).

The result of these repeated disappointments – of glances never met, of prayers never heard – is often a hardening of attitude on the part of the aspiring communicant with God. Hence, the being in *Lessness* 'will curse God again as in the blessed days' (*CSPR*, p. 153), and the woman in *Mal Vu Mal Dit* 'en veut alors au principe de toute vie' (*MVMD*, p. 7).

This cursing of God is rarely countervailed in Beckett's writing by a blessing of God. Yet, as the Book of Job demonstrates, cursing provides a kind of continuity of engagement. It represents sparks and interferences in the current, but not cessation. Beckett's people seem, despite their resentments and wrestlings, unable to stamp out the God-hypothesis definitively. Perhaps it constitutes the needed folly with which 'What is the Word' grapples: 'folly for to need to seem to glimpse afaint afar away over there what –

what –

what is the word –

what is the word' (*ASWT*, p. 134).

4

Rats, Crosses and Pain

There are very many rats in Beckett's work, scuttling insidiously in and out of textual crevices. On one level, their self-sufficient but predatory activity provides a kind of wary companionship to the humans with whom they live cheek by jowl. In many contexts, rats receive a very bad press, being seen as symbols of evil, or 'imps of Satan'. In Beckett's writing, they are by no means as uncomplicatedly evil as their widespread reputation suggests. Nonetheless, they are largely uncomfortable presences, and their watching bodies are constituted within Beckett's writing as centres of sinister, unpredictable energy.

This chapter examines the forces of darkness, cruelty, and pain which thread throughout Beckett's work, as well as the postures which Beckett's people adopt in reaction to those forces. It explores the templates which are held up to structure that experience, including the model of Christ's crucifixion, the notion of punishment, and the envisioning of purgatory and hell within the perspective of Dante.

RATS

Wherever there are human beings, there are almost always large colonies of rats. They are omnivorous and omnipresent. When the narrator in *L'Innommable* says of Worm's environment that 'un rat n'y vivrait pas, pas une seconde' (*LI*, p. 140), he is making an extreme statement about its bleakness. Rats are intelligent, strong, and prolific. One breeding pair can produce a third of a billion offspring and descendants within three years. The narrator in *Dream of Fair to Middling Women* notes, appropriately, that 'a low capital in the crypt of the Basilica Saint-Sernin in the most beautiful city of Toulouse is carved to represent a rat gnawing its way into a globe' (*DFMW*, p. 9). In complementary fashion, an illustration in the Book of Kells depicts two rats performing a tug-of-war over a eucharistic host, and Chapter 2 has already examined Beckett's long and humorous exploration, in the draft notebooks of *Watt*, of the theological implications of this sacrilege. From the macro-level of the globe to the micro-level of the communion wafer, rats will happily trim their incisors on most substances, from soap to concrete.

Within Beckett's writing, rats are the underbelly of the body of habit: the constant, largely invisible but sometimes audible accompaniment to human affairs. In *Comment C'est*, a flashed memory from the past is likened to a 'petit rat sur mes talons' (*CC*, p. 23), for it gnaws, and commands attention. The presence of rats is mostly discerned when activity is stilled, and the individual is silent within his or her environment. In *Molloy*, the becalmed narrator looks with distaste on the zeal which invades his fellow human beings every morning: 'C'est le matin qu'il faut se cacher. Les gens se réveillent, frais et dispos, assoiffés d'ordre, de beauté et de justice, exigeant la contrepartie. Oui, de huit ou neuf jusqu'à midi, c'est le passage dangereux' (*ML*, p. 89). From noon onwards, however, the bustle has waned, and peace descends. It is then that 'chacun compte ses rats'. The image is deceptively neutral. In the English version – 'Each man counts his rats' (*BT*, p. 62) – it is reminiscent, in contrary fashion, of the phrase 'to count one's blessings'. Counting one's blessings, like counting one's rats, requires concentration, but whereas the enumeration of blessings is self-managed to produce optimism, the counting of rats is productive of disquiet and uncertainty. Blessings can be manufactured; rats can only be disclosed. Indeed, one visible or audible rat probably represents scores of invisible ones. (Where counting rats is concerned, it has been estimated that, in properties in which rats are seen occasionally at night, there is probably a population of between 100 and 500.)

Moreover, contact with rats may produce not only unease, but disease (bubonic plague, typhus, rabies, etc.). The narrator in *L'Innommable* recalls this when realising he has wrongly maligned the flies: 'Les mouches [...] pourraient m'apporter le typhus. Non, ça c'est les rats' (*LI*, pp. 78–9). The association with pestilence is also evoked in *Molloy*, when the narrator describes the creeping human re-emergence on the streets at twilight. In this instance, rats are discarded as a comparator in favour of toads, who are equally slithery, but less noxious: 'nauséabond sans être pestilentiel, moins rat que crapaud' (*ML*, p. 90).

The rat most commonly described by Beckett seems, on the evidence of its described habits, to be the common brown rat, or

Norway rat, which often nests in lofts and attics in the autumn. This can be a disturbing experience for adjacent humans (indeed, the colloquialism 'to have rats in the attic' means 'to be of unsound mind'). It was precisely at that time of year that Beckett visited his cousin Peggy Sinclair in Laxenburg, near Vienna, in 1928. As James Knowlson's biography points out,[1] Beckett stayed in accommodation whose layout exactly matched the lodging-place of Belacqua as described in *Dream of Fair to Middling Women*. In the novel, Belacqua is solitary in his lodgings as far as human companionship is concerned. At night, however, the breeding rodent activity is persistently noticeable: 'At night, to be sure, the rats, galavanting and cataracting behind the sweating wall-paper, just behind the wall-paper, slashing the close invisible plane with ghastlily muted slithers and somersaults' (*DFMW*, p. 15). Eventually, he begins to anticipate it: 'He thought of the rank dark room, quiet, *quieted*, when he would enter, then the first stir behind the paper, the first discreet slithers'.

This model – the surrounding quiet, punctuated by the restless movement – will later be recruited to figure 'the mind achieving creation': 'There, insistent, invisible rat, fidgeting behind the astral incoherence of the art surface' (*DFMW*, pp. 16–17). Towards the end of his stay, Belacqua begins to be infected with the rats' agitation: 'He fidgeted by night in the dark room and the rats were with him, now he was one of them. He was anxious with their anxiety, shuffling and darting about in the room' (*DFMW*, p. 26). A similar access of fitful comradeship with rathood is described in *Watt*: 'For after these there would be no more rats, not a rat left, and there were times when Watt almost welcomed this prospect, of being rid of his last rats, at last. It would be lonely, to be sure, at first, and silent, after the gnawing, the scurrying, the little cries' (*W*, p. 81). After repeated exposure to rats, the narrator in *La Fin* can report that he was able to overcome his fear of them: 'Il y avait trop longtemps que je vivais parmi les rats, dans mes logements de fortune, pour que j'en eusse la phobie du vulgaire. J'avais même une sorte de sympathie pour eux. Ils venaient avec tant de confiance vers moi, on aurait dit sans la moindre répugnance. Ils faisaient leur toilette, avec des gestes de chat' (*NTPR*, p. 105).

Fox, in *Pochade radiophonique*, is even reported to have spoken about his 'rats à poche', although A speaks contemptuously of the value of any revelation concerning pouched rats or other fauna (*PS*, p. 80). These rats seem to present no serious threat. If the 'rats à poche' are kangaroo rats, these are tiny, desert rats which burrow underground in search of cooler temperatures. The English translation – 'fodient rodents' (*CSPL*, p. 122) – has the double advantage of a pleasing semi-rhyme and a similar connotation to the 'rats à poche', for 'fodient' means 'digging' or 'burrowing'.[2]

In *Murphy*, the mutually intrusive movement patterns of human beings and rats are again mentioned, this time to illustrate the split between mind and body: 'Motion in the world depended on rest in the world outside. A man is in bed, wanting to sleep. A rat is behind the wall at his head, wanting to move. The man hears the rat fidget and cannot sleep, the rat hears the man fidget and dares not move. They are both unhappy, one fidgeting and the other waiting, or both happy, the rat moving and the man sleeping' (*MP*, pp. 64–5). Beyond these examples of uneasy coexistence of habit and habitat, however, can be found more sinister and incursionary instances.

Amongst the most cunning and tenacious of animals, some battle-scarred old rats have been known to kick traps around from a safe distance until these release their bait. Indeed, the 'musty trap' in Belacqua's lodgings (*DFMW*, p. 18) never appears to catch a representative specimen. Constantly 'controlled' by human beings, rats have their own ways of gaining the upper hand. As the narrator remarks in *Comment C'est*: 'Chaque rat a sa blütezeit' (*CC*, p. 14).

In *L'Innommable*, the role of the Promethean vulture, gnawing at the liver of its victim, is taken over in the narrator's imagination by an elderly and bloated rat: 'Et si je parlais pour ne rien dire, mais vraiment rien? Ainsi j'éviterais peut-être d'être grignoté comme par un vieux rat rassasié, et mon petit lit à baldaquin avec, un berceau, ou bien je me ferais grignoter moins vite, dans mon vieux berceau, et les chairs arrachées auraient le temps de se recoller, comme dans le Caucase, avant d'être arrachées à nouveau' (*LI*, p. 27). The rat is indeed an appropriate stand-in for the Causasian vulture. When assured of a food supply, rats will stay on the spot, becoming progressively lazier in their marauding. The narrator in *Comment C'est* even alleges that the rats have grown blasé about the opportunities he offers: 'des rats non cette fois plus de rats je les ai écoeurés' (*CC*, p. 28). A further reference to rattish predation occurs in *Watt*, where the overgrown state of Mr Knott's garden provides a warning to obese passers-by to 'turn about, and retrace their steps, unless they wished to be impaled, at various points at once, and perhaps bleed to death, or be eaten alive by the rats' (*W*, p. 155).

Whereas the climbing rat (*rattus rattus*) will retreat on being confonted by a human being, the brown rat can be extremely aggressive. Able to jump up to a height of three feet, the brown rat, when poked with a stick, is liable to leap up and bite its human aggressor. Indeed, in *Fin de partie*, Clov cannot worst the rat he finds in his kitchen with a single blow. When Hamm summons him, he reports that he has only half-killed the creature. Having ascertained that the rat is sufficiently incapacitated to be unable to crawl away, Hamm instructs Clov in a grimly revelatory moment: 'Tu l'achèveras tout à l'heure' (*FP*, p. 75). The rat will have to carry on dying while Hamm conducts his prayer meeting.

It is some time before Clov returns to his kitchen, saying: 'Si je ne tue pas ce rat il va mourir' (*FP*, p. 90). Far from dying, however, the rat has made his escape. Hamm conjectures that 'il n'ira pas loin' (*FP*, p. 93). He has, however, managed to go further than either Clov or Hamm. Indeed, perhaps he has already crept to a crevice from which he can view Hamm, thus fulfilling silently the latter's fantasies: 'Toutes sortes de fantaisies! Qu'on me surveille! Un rat! Des pas! Des yeux!' (*FP*, p. 92). If so, he may even stay to watch or participate in Hamm's death, like the vigilant rats evoked in *L'Innommable* – 'Je souffre mal aussi, même ça je le fais mal aussi, comme une vieille dinde mourant debout, le dos chargé de poussins, guettée par les rats' (*LI*, p. 46) – or in *Molloy*: 'ma poule grise était [...] par terre, dans un coin, dans la poussière, à la merci des rats' (*ML*, p. 173). The rat's presence might thus not be unwelcome, for he would at least constitute a (half-)alive witness of Hamm's demise, unlike the stuffed dog who, far from being, as Hamm fondly believes, 'en train de m'implorer' (*FP*, p. 59), has in fact slumped onto its side. Having never been alive except in Hamm's imagination, it is less of an enhancement of the company than the rat envisaged by the narrator in *Company*: 'A dead rat. What an addition to company that would be! A rat long dead' (*NO*, p. 22).

If Beckett's people can eventually acquire tolerance of the brown rat, the same is not true of the water rat, dead or alive. The voice in *L'Innommable*, imagining himself at one point in a waterbound environment, recognises his secondary status to the rats: 'Je suis maître à bord, après les rats' (*LI*, p. 176). Moreover, if rats are primary on board ship, they are also primary when disembarking. Popular wisdom has it that rats desert a ship which they know to be about to sink. The narrator in *Comment C'est* acknowledges this with an elliptical 'adieu rats naufrage' (*CC*, p. 58); the vessel, it seems, is his own body.

The water rat is firmly demarcated from its brown brothers by the narrator in *La Fin*, living temporarily at the riverside: 'Les rats avaient du mal à arriver jusqu'à moi, à cause de l'inclinaison de la coque. Ils en avaient pourtant bien envie. Pensez donc, de la chair vivante, car j'étais quand même encore de la chair vivante. [...] Mais il s'agissait de rats d'eau, d'une maigreur et d'une férocité exceptionnelles' (*NTPR*, pp. 104–05). This reputation is confirmed by the narrator of *L'Innommable*, who considers that water rats would be far more persuasive when set upon Worm than any other kind: 'Moi à leur place je lui lâcherai les rats, rats d'eau, de cloaque, ce sont les meilleurs, oh pas trop, une douzaine, une quinzaine, ça le déciderait peut-être, à décoller, et quelle introduction, à ses futurs attributs' (*LI*, p. 140).

Furred for entering the water, with an underfur which seems to protect the outer fur, a drowned rat is a shocking, bedraggled sight. In *Mercier et Camier*, Mercier uses the rat simile – disputed by Camier, who substitutes the referent of a drenched dog – to describe their fate in the rain: 'Nous allons nous faire saucer comme des rats, sans notre parapluie' (*MC*, pp. 43–4). Moreover, the image of a drowned rat, seen from the towpath as it floats along in the water at sunset, is a recurrent memory for Voice B in *That Time*: 'The bits of flotsam coming from behind and drifting on or caught in the reeds the dead rat it looked like came on you from behind and went drifting on till you could see it no more' (*CSPL*, p. 231).

Rats are seen in popular legend, as mentioned earlier, as agents of Satan. It is striking, however, that they are on at least two occasions aligned with God, or a creative force, within Beckett's work. God does not benefit from the comparison. In *Company*, the narrator refers to a smell 'such as might have once emitted a rat long dead' (*NO*, p. 42), and later associates this with the creator: 'Unless the crawler smell. Aha! The crawling creator. Might the crawling creator be reasonably imagined to smell? Even fouler than his creature'.

A more sinister reference by far, however, occurs in *Watt*. It has long been observed that rats' omnivorousness extends to their own kind, and that rodent cannibalism is rampant under certain conditions. There is therefore nothing fanciful about the episode of the black water rats in *Watt*: 'Our particular friends were the rats, that dwelt by the stream. They were long and black. [...] And then we would sit down in the midst of them, and give them to eat, out of our hands, of a nice fat frog, or a baby thrush. Or seizing suddenly a plump young rat, resting in our bosom after its repast, we would feed it to its mother, or its father, or its brother, or its sister, or to some less fortunate relative' (*W*, p. 153). Moreover, this manipulation is said to have something deific about it: 'It was on these occasions, we agreed, after an exchange of views, that we came nearest to God'. There could hardly be a more calmly devastating indictment of God. If rats are indeed to be aligned with the Devil, then God is only a rat's whisker away from his opponent.

CROSSES

In the episode just cited from *Watt*, there is a neat passing-on of the parcel of evil, from rat to God. In that reading, the malevolence is not resident in the rat. We know from metatextual data that rats will readily eat one another. Yet any 'natural' repugnance at this cannot be translated into culpability on the part of the rat, for the rat is merely following its, equally 'natural', promptings. Moreover, the baby rat who is eaten by its relatives is here presented as the casualty of a human intervention masquerading as tenderness. Once that transposition is effected, the human responsibility is then handed on again, this time to God, whose patterns of behaviour the narrator claims to be emulating.

Most theologians would recognise that the existence of innocent suffering and evil in a world they claim to have been created by a loving and provident Deity is one of the thorniest areas with which they have to deal. As far as wilful viciousness is concerned, this is often laid at the door of original sin endemic in human beings since the Fall. This, for Beckett, is too neat an explanation, as he explained in a 1931 letter to Thomas MacGreevy. He had just visited the painter Jack Yeats, who 'wanted a definition of cruelty, declaring that you could work back from cruelty to original sin. No doubt. But I don't think it is possible to define cruelty because somehow or other it would have to be separated from all the concomitant pointers in order to be apprehended. Can one imagine a pure act of cruelty? The old question!'.[3]

Within Beckett's work, as the rat-episode in *Watt* exemplifies, distress and violence are observed, sometimes minutely, but not accounted for. Just as the narrator in *Watt* witnesses, apparently dispassionately, the crunching demise of one rat in the jaws of another, the inter-human brutality to be found in Beckett's work simply happens. It is rarely explicated in terms of cause or motivation, is sometimes disturbingly routinised, and is mostly devoid of the prospect of mitigation or spiritual comfort. In Beckett's three torture-plays – *Quoi Où*, *Catastrophe*, and *Pochade radiophonique* – the reasons for the apprehending of the victim, and the nature or utility of the information that he may or may not divulge, are never made explicit. More important, it seems, are the power relationships between the hierarchy of torturers, the obsessive monitoring of their victim, and the studied calmness of their application or authorisation of violence and humiliation upon the body of the detainee.

Other works contain instances of a similar divorce between cause and effect, when cruelty is observed or implemented, without any connection having been established with the factors giving rise to it. The sadism detailed in *Comment C'est* is apparently perpetrated arbitrarily, against weaker and unresisting victims. The scissoring of butterflies' wings is even undertaken with an eye to aesthetic disposition of the pieces: 'Je découpais aux ciseaux en minces rubans les ailes des papillons l'une puis l'autre et quelquefois pour varier les deux de front je remettais en liberté le corps au milieu jamais aussi bon depuis' (*CC*, p. 13). Yet perhaps even 'sadism' is an inaccurate term, since this also implies a motivation, a pleasure taken, in the infliction of pain. The torture administered to Pim in *Comment C'est* is calculatedly applied, and yet it is as drab and undramatised as any other gesture of interaction. Moreover, it is in an obscure zone of emotional ambiguity – 'amour peur d'être abandonné un peu de chaque' (*CC*, p. 104) – that the 'lessons' take place: 'prends l'ouvre-boîte dans ma droite le descends le long de l'échine et le lui enfonce dans le cul pas le trou vous pensez bien la fesse une fesse il crie je le retire coup sur le crâne il se tait c'est mécanique' (*CC*, p. 105).

This unresolved and paradoxical encounter of reciprocity and individualism is also present in *L'Innommable*, when the narrator, musing upon his oppressors, observes: 'Nous sommes beaux, tous tant que nous sommes, serions-nous logés à la même enseigne, non, périsse pareille pensée, nous sommes beaux chacun à sa manière personnelle' (*LI*, p. 142). Despite this 'manière personnelle', there is a merging and interchangeability about these external agents. They have become implicated in a task, but have lost touch with the parameters of that task: 'On ne dirait pas les mêmes gens que tout à l'heure, pas? Que voulez-vous, eux non plus ne savent pas qui ils sont, où ils sont, ce qu'ils font, ni pourquoi ça marche si mal' (*LI*, p. 142).

Similarly, when Estragon is beaten overnight, he is no more aware of the identities of his ten assailants than he is of their motivation. As he tells Vladimir: 'Je ne faisais rien' (*EAG*, p. 51). Vladimir himself has just been singing the round about the dog being beaten to death with a ladle, the same song which occurs in *L'Innommable*, after the wonderful rhyming summary of life's searing rites of passage: 'histoires de berceau, cerceau, puceau, pourceau, sang et eau, peau et os, tombeau' (*LI*, p. 152).

It is in this context of pain, violence, and victimisation that a distinction emerges in Beckett's work between the figure of God, and that of Christ. Rather than being blurred with the Father, in a triumphalist Godhead, Christ is overwhelmingly discerned in kenotic mode: emptied, made destitute, and available for suffering of the worst kind. This is not the divine Son who merely went through the motions; rather, it is the visualisation which results from taking seriously the hymn to Christ in Paul's Letter to the Philippians: '[He] made himself of no reputation, and took upon him the form of a servant, and was made in the likeness of men: and being found in fashion as a man, he humbled himself, and became obedient unto death, even the death of the cross' (Philippians 2: 7–8).

It is on this level – that of the cross – that Christ begins to function in Beckett's work, not as a human prototype, but as a human exemplar. In other words, in undergoing crucifixion, he does not illuminate or redeem other scenes of execution: he merely offers the possibility of alignment or comparison with them. This is the case, for example, in *Comment C'est*. Having already referred in generalised fashion to 'feu au rectum comment surmonté réflexions sur la passion de la douleur' (*CC*, p. 59), the narrator later focuses more particularly on the nailed hands associated with Christ's Passion: 'ses ongles sa mort qui percées les paumes de part en part put enfin les voir qui sortaient enfin de l'autre côté et peu après ayant ainsi vécu fait ceci fait cela serré les poings toute sa vie ainsi vécu mourut enfin' (*CC*, pp. 82–3). Moreover, an allied image intervenes even more strongly in the closing paragraphs of the work: 'aplati sur le ventre oui dans la boue oui le noir oui là rien à corriger non les bras en croix pas de réponse LES BRAS EN CROIX pas de réponse OUI OU NON oui' (*CC*, p. 227).

Far from being seen as the victor over a death he has willingly embraced, Christ is seen, like Estragon or Lucky, as a victim, and not a unique victim. Indeed, the traditional crucifix of St Andrew is also represented in *Comment C'est*: 'maintenant ses bras en croix de Saint-André branches supérieures angle plutôt fermé' (*CC*, p. 90). (The cross on which St Andrew was crucified was, according to tradition, in the shape of an X). Like Estragon and Vladimir, Christ is seen as a victim twice over: of a God who does not come to his help, and of other human beings who are stronger and more violent than he. For the *Godot* comrades, Christ is indeed most accessible in his stripped and victimised role, since these are circumstances to which they can relate. Estragon does not recognise the salvific potential of Christ, for, when Vladimir refers to 'le Sauveur', he enquires: 'Le quoi?' (*EAG*, p. 6). Nevertheless, as examined in the previous chapter, he does identify with Christ in terms of poverty and loss, admitting to Vladimir: 'Toute ma vie je me suis comparé à lui' (*EAG*, p. 47).

The image *par excellence* of that victimisation is of course the crucifixion itself. This is evoked in *En attendant Godot*, notably in the discussion concerning the two thieves. Later, however, the explicit textual reminder is reinforced by visual reminders. Hence, after the climactic efforts of his monologue, itself referring to the 'divine apathie' of God the Father (*EAG*, p. 37), the sagging Lucky is propped up by the arms, between Estragon and Vladimir. His exhausted form, gazing out towards the audience, with the men on each side of him, provides just as compelling a crucifixion tableau as the one in the Second Act, when it is Pozzo's turn to be thus picked up and supported 'entre les deux, pendu à leur cou' (*EAG*, p. 77). Once erected between them, Pozzo enquires: 'Vous n'êtes pas des brigands?', thus drawing Estragon and Vladimir into even closer association with the 'deux brigands, l'un à droite et l'autre à gauche' described in Matthew's account of the crucifixion.[4] Added to this is the constant presence of the tree, always proffering its possibilities as a gibbet, though a mean and possibly ineffectual one, unlike the 'Glorious Tree' cited in Christian hymnody.

Play also offers a scene of three sufferers, each gazing to the front and fixed in joint but individual agony. The man in the middle, impossibly divided between his two women, both abuses and is abused. *Fin de partie* offers similar correspondences, although Hamm here does not share the spotlight with fellow sufferers at his shoulders. Instead, he gravitates, in his immobilised status, towards a magnetic central position, like that described by Christ: 'And I, if I be lifted up from the earth, will draw all men unto me' (John 12: 32).

In this pivotal role, all eyes would be glued on him (even those of the stuffed dog), and all ears tuned to his parables of the starving man. Hence, he insists: 'Mets-moi bien au centre!' (*FP*, p. 42). Moreover, by calling 'Père! Père!' at the close of the play (*FP*, pp. 111–12), he affiliates himself, as widely noted by commentators, with the crucified Christ, who died calling to his Father (see Luke 23: 46: 'And when Jesus had cried with a loud voice, he said, Father, into thy hands I commend my spirit'). Thus, Hamm fulfils the modificatory discourse of Clov at the opening of the play: 'Fini, c'est fini, ça va finir, ça va peut-être finir' (*FP*, p. 15), itself evoking Christ's last words as reported by John: 'When Jesus therefore had received the vinegar, he said, It is finished: and he bowed his head, and gave up the ghost' (John 19: 30).

Beckett's eye for the dramatic potential of crucifixion images is also apparent in an early undated fragment of abandoned theatre from the pre-*Fin de partie* period, consisting of a dialogue between a couple called Ernest and Alice.[5] Ernest spends his time lying in a crucified position on a mechanical cross, which is alternately hoisted and lowered according to the time of day. For much of the fragment, he wears a veronica-like handkerchief over his face. In addition, he wears a champagne-bucket around his neck, which, as he reminds his companion in humorously homophonic fashion, he likes to think of as a chalice: 'C'est un calice, Alice'. This is a vessel for the sweat and tears he claims to shed for the 'rachat universel', but, more prosaically, he also finds it useful as a spittoon and ashtray.

Ernest's attendant, Alice, addresses Ernest as 'mon petit Jésus', and her position at the foot of the cross creates visual parallels with conventional artistic representations of the scene. At the close of the fragment, Alice begins to cleanse Ernest's crossbound feet with salted water, and finally his mother arrives, mounts on a stool, and prepares to wash his face. The presence of Christ's mother at Calvary is mentioned in John's Gospel (John 19: 25), and the arrival of Ernest's mother thus tends to suggest linkages between Alice and Mary Magdalene. It is at this point, however, that the play ends, weighed down by its own over-explicit and heavy-handed structure of reference. This cross would undeniably be a striking theatre image. Nevertheless, its impact is undermined by the near-buffoonery of the surrounding interactions.

If the crucifixion is to be glimpsed in visual tableaux in Beckett's drama, it is no less resident in images to be found in the prose work. Moreover, as a configuration or posture, it lends itself to an astonishingly wide range of applications. In many of these, the figure of Christ is overlaid with that of another person or animal. In *More Pricks Than Kicks*, the observation that Belacqua 'dots his i's now and crucifies his t's to the top of his bent' (*MPTK*, p. 185) serves to denote a pained meticulousness, while in *Dream of Fair to Middling Women* Belacqua is seen at one point lying on his back at the day's end, in such a position that 'the spread flexed arms were the transepts of a cross on the bolster' (*DFMW*, p. 52). Moreover, the 'bare tree, dripping' on which he gazes is again suggestive of the prototypical tree of crucifixion. Later, as he anticipates the sight of the Alba at the forthcoming party, he visualises her bare back, in its scarlet party dress, as 'a cross-potent, pain and death, still death, a bird crucified on a wall. This flesh and bones swathed in scarlet, this heart of washed flesh draped in scarlet' (*DFMW*, p. 205). In *Le Calmant*, it is bats, with their outstretched arms, who are drawn into affiliation with the crucifixion: 'Je pénétrai dans la ville [. . .], sans avoir vu personne, seulement les premières chauves-souris qui sont comme des crucifiées volantes' (*NTPR*, p. 45).

After being freed from the rocking-chair by Celia, Murphy 'lay fully prostrate in the crucified position, heaving' (*MP*, p. 20), while Watt is repeatedly seen 'crumpling back into his post-crucified position' (*W*, p. 139) during his interactions with Mrs Gorman. In *Bing*, the focus is unremittingly on the motionless white body, with its 'mains pendues' and its legs 'collées comme cousues'. In prevalent depictions of the Crucifixion, the two legs of the victim are indeed depicted as being fastened with one single nail, and thus dragged forcibly together. Moreover, past injuries to the body in *Bing* are apparent in the reference to 'invisibles cicatrices' and to 'chairs blessées' (*TM*, p. 64).[6]

Representations and reminders of the crucifixion, in the form of large crosses elevated in the countryside or small ones worn about the person, also make their appearance. In *Mercier et Camier*, Camier draws attention to a distant cross over the tomb of a nationalist: 'En pleine tourbière, non loin de la route, mais trop loin pour qu'on pût en lire l'inscription, une croix fort simple s'élevait' (*MC*, p. 167). The two men are fleetingly intrigued by this cross, rather as Beckett was sufficiently struck by a cross he came across near Enniskerry to mention it in a 1937 letter to Thomas MacGreevy: 'I was on the Big Sugarloaf on Saturday and yesterday found in a field near Enniskerry a lovely small Celtic cross with still the dim low relief of a Christ crucifed with head duly inclined to the north'.[7]

A further example of a simple, undecorated cross is the 'bog-oak crucifix' pressed to the bosom of the dying Mrs Quin in the manuscript draft of *Watt* (UTA, Notebook 1). By then, her married life appears to her to have been 'one long draw-sheet', and it is a shorthand reference to this which opens the Addenda of the published version (*W*, p. 247).

Much more elaborate crucifixion memorabilia are sported by Moll in *Malone meurt*. Not only does she wear 'en guise de boucles d'oreilles deux longs crucifix d'ivoire qui se balançaient éperdument au moindre mouvement de sa tête' (*MM*, pp. 138–9), but she has also had a crucifix carved into one of her teeth: 'une canine longue, jaune et profondément déchaussée, taillée à représenter le célèbre sacrifice, à la fraise probablement' (*MM*, p. 150).

When Macmann enquires with regard to her two earrings: 'Pourquoi deux Jésus?', she is able to reveal that the crosses on her ears represent those of the two thieves, while the one between them – i.e. on her tooth – is that of Christ. Perhaps Moll can be deemed uniquely qualified to intone the well-known hymn: 'God be in my head and in my understanding; [...] God be in my mouth and in my speaking'. Moreover, in a sentence puzzlingly omitted in the English translation, she describes her ritual ministrations to the tooth, which consist of five applications of oral hygiene per day, to represent the five wounds of Christ: 'Je la brosse cinq fois par jour, dit-elle, une fois pour chaque blessure'.

What is striking about this kind of sustained engagement with the crucifixion is its often trauma-free context. This is apparent, for example, in a very detailed sketch drawn by Beckett within the draft material for his abandoned play 'Human Wishes'.[8] This doodle occupies more than half a page, and contains in its middle section a very detailed crucifixion scene featuring three crosses, as well as many witnesses and passers-by. On the left cross is a grey figure with a half-smile, while the right cross is occupied by a snarling figure with pointed ears and erect hair-bristles.

The middle cross – that of 'Christ' – bears a Chaplinesque figure with bow tie and bowler hat. Despite his exaggeratedly splayed fingers and toes, the figure looks almost relaxed in his spreadeagled posture. His passivity seems to participate in that 'choseté' which Beckett discerned in the brutalised Christs painted by Georges Rouault, and which he described in his essay 'Peintres de l'empêchement'.[9] (Beckett retained his interest in Rouault. In the manuscript draft for *Watt* [UTA, Notebook 3], he records in a note [later struck through] which seems to date from the first week in May 1942 – just a few months before he and Suzanne fled from Paris – that he had just seen the latest Rouault paintings in a small but well presented exhibition. He also refers, in a 1958 letter to Thomas MacGreevy,[10] to the funeral of Rouault, which had just taken place.) Rouault's (often clownlike) Christs cannot be said to be devoid of the signs of distress, but they are remarkable for their omission or downplaying of the wounds of execution, and Beckett's doodle follows this bloodless trend.

However, if Beckett's visual and textual treatment of crucifixion can seem casual and even dismissive, the sheer weight of crucifixion references to be found in his writing seems to demonstrate the iconic power they maintain in his consciousness. His letters to Thomas MacGreevy, and the notebooks he kept while in Germany, all testify to the close attention he gave to paintings depicting religious subjects such as the crucifixion, the deposition, or the entombment. Moreover, the lingering over other elements of the crucifixion event in his fictional writing seems to indicate a more long-lasting preoccupation with the spectacle than a simple image-flare.

This is not to say that the means of crucifixion are elided or overlooked. Indeed, in *Comment C'est*, the narrator states: 'Je vois chaque paille on tape trois ou quatre au moins marteaux ciseaux des croix peut-être' (*CC*, p. 139). Nevertheless, this preoccupation does not take the form of empathetic contemplation of the preliminaries or mechanics of crucifixion. In the doodle just cited, there is no crucifying agent to be seen, and no evidence of clearly-defined authority figures in the vicinity. There is on the left of the crosses an individual holding what looks like a sponge on the end of a stick, in probable acknowledgement of the accounts within all four Gospels of the Roman soldiers administering vinegar to Christ in this manner just before he died. However, even he does not wear a recognisable military uniform.

This is, of course, merely a doodle in a private notebook. Nevertheless, such off-duty musings can be revelatory. Moreover, the doodle is characteristic of other crucifixion references in the oeuvre in not expressing curiosity about how and why the victim arrived at his predicament. As already suggested, the casualties of violence and decay in Beckett's work are seen not so much as end-products of a logical cycle of events but rather as individuals caught up in the grip of a present ill whose provenance and progression can only be surmised.

This is not to downplay the suffering involved. Admittedly, Estragon appears to compare Christ's acute suffering unfavourably with his own chronic suffering, affirming that, in Christ's homeland, 'on crucifiait vite' (*EAG*, p. 47). Moreover, despite acknowledgement of the significance of Christ's outburst: 'My God, my God, why hast thou forsaken me?' (Matthew 27: 46), an underlying resentment is often to be detected in Beckett's work against that same Christ who, in the Johannine account only, utters the words: 'It is finished' (John 19: 30), as if rubber-stamping a debt paid in full. Murphy even interprets these last words as a 'parthian shaft' (*MP*, p. 44), as if the utterance were not so much an exhausted consummation but a parting shot to all those whose sufferings are still in swing.

Nevertheless, Beckett does clearly give weight to the Gospel accounts which, while allowing the trauma of the physical assault to speak for itself, make explicit also the concomitant psychic distress of Christ. It is on this level that the narrator in *Molloy* accesses the crucifixion as a metaphor for the extreme of psychological torture he experiences upon seeing his mother's image blur with those of his haglike partners in copulation: 'Et Dieu me pardonne, pour vous livrer le fond de mon effroi, l'image de ma mère vient quelquefois se joindre aux leurs, ce qui est proprement insupportable, de quoi se croire en pleine crucifixion' (*ML*, pp. 78–9).

It is clear from the versatility of the crucifixion referent within Beckett's writing that, despite his scepticism about its role in any eschatological hypothesis, it retains a strong symbolic potency, functioning not as a hermetic memorial but as a multi-functional template. A by-product of this may be to uncover fresh levels of meaning in the 'original' crucifixion event. Moreover, the simplicity of the crucifix image is often embedded in a web of connotation, revealing the author's familiarity with the entirety of the Passion narratives, and not just with their culminatory point. In *Malone meurt*, the episode concerning the Louis family is a tissue of references to death, from the death and burial of the mule, to the slaughterhouse transactions, and the mention of rabbits who die of fright prior to being knocked on the head. At the heart of all these operations is the family kitchen, where, in the light of a lamp, a crucifix hangs on a nail: 'Elle alluma la lampe à sa place sur le dessus de cheminée, à côté du réveille-matin, flanqué à son tour d'un crucifix pendu à un clou' (*MM*, p. 65).

The fact that the crucifix is hanging on a nail is on one level pragmatic and functional. Yet Beckett's simple account belies the profound irony that Christ hung on nails just as his image is now hanging on a nail, and that paintings spotlight his torment just as the lamp illumines the crucifix. The same image in the context of *Mal Vu Mal Dit* is even more rich in subtextual echoes, even though the suspended object is a buttonhook rather than a crucifix: 'En argent terni il pend pisciforme par le crochet à un clou. Il oscille sans cesse à peine. Comme si la terre tremblait sans cesse à cet endroit' (*MVMD*, p. 21). Here, the buttonhook is 'pisciform', thus bringing to mind the concept of Christ the Fish, which, inspired by the acrostic referred to in Chapter 2, has been part of Christian tradition from earliest times. Again, the fish-shaped hook hangs on a nail, and is said to be trembling, as if the earth was quaking, in accordance with Gospel accounts of the earth shaking at the moment of Christ's death: 'And, behold, the veil of the temple was rent in twain from the top to the bottom; and the earth did quake, and the rocks rent' (Matthew 27: 51).

If Christ is the Fish, he is also the Lamb. Within Christian tradition, his immolation coincides with that of the Passover lamb (see 1 Corinthians 5: 7). He is thus the Pasch, or paschal sacrifice, and *Mal Vu Mal Dit* seems to acknowledge this element by focusing at one point upon the lamb, destined for slaughter, which follows the woman: 'Agneau de boucherie comme les autres il s'en détacha pour s'attacher à ses pas' (*MVMD*, p. 45). Distinguished from his cohort, the lamb seems to be part of an ancient tradition: 'Les faits sont si anciens. Boucherie à part il n'est pas comme les autres'. Resonating with the spring lamb and the spring flowers – 'Seuls quelques crocus encore. Au temps des agneaux' (*MVMD*, p. 12) – is that 'après-midi d'avril. Descente faite' (*MVMD*, p. 72), which recalls the taking-down of Christ from the cross after his death at the ninth hour (mid-afternoon).

There are other references in Beckett's work to the slaughter of lambs. (See, for example, the imagined ovine carnage in *Molloy*: 'Il fit entrer en moi une perplexité de longue haleine, rapport à la destination de ces moutons, parmi lesquels il y avait des agneaux, et je me demandais souvent s'ils étaient bien arrivés dans quelque vaine pâture ou tombés, le crâne fracassé, dans un froissement des maigres pattes, d'abord à genoux, puis sur le flanc laineux, sous le merlin' [*ML*, p. 38]).

Perhaps the most striking and explicit use of the metaphor is, however, in the final line of the poem 'Ooftish': 'It all boils down to blood of lamb' (*CP*, p. 31). The Yiddish word 'Ooftish' is an invitation to put money down on the table, as reflected in the first line of the poem: 'offer it up plank it down'. However, the poem is a devastating parody of the doctrine that sufferings can be 'offered up', and united with Christ's sacrifice, for the sake of purification or of remission of the punishment due to sin. The place of Christ's execution, Golgotha, is mentioned as early as the second line: 'Golgotha was only the potegg'. As 'potegg', Golgotha merely dissolves into a huge cauldron of human misery: 'cancer angina it is all one to us / cough up your T.B. don't be stingy'.

When Beckett sent the typed poem to MacGreevy, prior to publication, it was entitled 'Whiting'. Here, the referent is not fish, but bleaching, for 'whiting' used to refer to rendering linen cloths white. It seems likely that Beckett had in mind the text from Revelation: 'He said to me, These are they which came out of great tribulation, and have washed their robes, and made them white in the blood of the Lamb' (Revelation 7: 14). In this understanding, everything is gathered up into the purifying blood of the Lamb. In 'Ooftish', *nothing* 'boils down to blood of lamb'. The litany of human distress recited in the poem – 'anything venereal is especially welcome' – is not elided or accounted for. It remains, as an aching, bursting hernia of ills.

As previously examined, the memory of Golgotha is never suppressed in Beckett's work. At times it is appropriated by the narrator – (perhaps unsurprisingly from the pen of an author who was born on Good Friday) – as in *Company*: 'You first saw the light and cried at the close of the day when in darkness Christ at the ninth hour cried and died' (*NO*, p. 45). At other times, it functions as an emblem of future as well as past suffering. In *Mal Vu Mal Dit*, the quivering nail is ever ready to serve again: 'Et seul de l'autre très seul le clou. Inaltéré. Bon pour le resservice. A l'instar de ses glorieux ancêtres. Au lieudit du crâne' (*MVMD*, p. 72). The 'lieudit du crâne' is Golgotha, the Place of the Skull. Golgotha may be 'only the potegg' in the human pain-pot, but its status as an 'egg' implies a promise or threat of more to come.

PAIN AND PUNISHMENT

Clearly, one does not have to look far for pain in Beckett's work, whether it be Clov's cry: 'J'ai mal aux jambes, c'est pas croyable' (*FP*, p. 66), the 'pain of bones till no choice but up and stand' in

Worstward Ho (NO, p. 102), or the spinningly multiplicatory 'douleur laquelle entre toutes' of *Comment C'est (CC*, p. 50).

Often, as already noted, the pain is deep but unfathomable. There is also within Beckett's work, however, a resilient thread connecting pain and punishment. Reeling under the weight of distress, Beckett's people still sometimes find their minds turning over hypotheses of merited suffering. Like Kafkaesque detainees, they protest, but then try to identify what unconscious sin they might have committed. In a notable passage in *Comment C'est*, the prone narrator waits not for the onset of sleep (for the relief it would bring is felt to be undeserved), but for the onset of pain, the sure guarantor of his continuing existence: 'fermer les yeux enfin et attendre ma douleur qu'avec elle je puisse durer un peu encore et en attendant / prière pour rien au sommeil je n'y ai pas encore droit je ne l'ai pas encore mérité' (*CC*, p. 55).

It is difficult to know whether the deep effect which Dante's *The Divine Comedy* had on Beckett was attributable to its partial echoing of a religious upbringing he had already received, or whether, conversely, Beckett's love of the poem accounts for his frequent advertence to the scenes of expiation and come-uppance which it foregrounds. Perhaps each factor continued to reinforce the other; at any rate, Beckett's rational scepticism, which no doubt obtained with regard to many of the theological concepts expounded in the text, did not provide an obstacle to his emotional and aesthetic response to the poem. The three zones of post-death destinations are, after all, recounted by Dante not so much as static modes of being, but rather in terms of a journey, and through the eyes of one seeing them prematurely, and being traumatised by many of the spotlit scenes in them. There is an inbuilt dynamism in the text which sweeps the reader along in a series of vivid images rather than in an accumulation of doctrinal expositions.

What seems certain is that, although familiar with all three Canticles of *The Divine Comedy*, he gravitated more readily to *Inferno* and *Purgatory* than to *Paradise*. In his 1930s 'Whoroscope' notebook (RUL MS 3000), Beckett noted down several phrases or short passages which had struck him from the *Inferno*. Thus, for example, he jotted down the phrase 'fuor della queta, nell'aura che trema' [out of the quiet into tempestuous air].[11] This line, from Canto 4, is the one immediately preceding the Pilgrim's descent into the fearful darkness of the Second Circle of Hell, where he will witness the sufferings of the damned.

Indeed, these preliminary canti of the *Inferno*, with their sense of foreboding, seem to have fascinated Beckett just as did the preliminary canti of the *Purgatory*. In *Le Calmant*, the narrator describes attempting to speak to the young boy who is holding a goat by the horn, at the harbour. Yet all that emerges from his mouth is a rattling noise, 'rien que l'aphonie due au long silence, comme dans le bosquet où s'ouvrent les enfers, vous rappelez-vous, moi tout juste' (*NTPR*, p. 50). This is a direct reference to Canto 1 of the *Inferno*, where the Pilgrim, having woken to find himself in a dark wood, makes out 'a figure coming toward me / of one grown faint, perhaps from too much silence' (*INF* 1: 62–3). This figure is the shade of Virgil, who will accompany the Pilgrim on his path through Hell and Purgatory. Presently, the pair will reach the vestibule of Hell, where they will view the doom-laden inscription above the gate leading to Hell: 'Abandon every hope, all you who enter' (*INF* 3: 9). It is this message which surfaces in the often hell-ridden atmosphere of *Comment C'est*: 'abandon ici effet de l'espoir ça s'enchaîne de l'éternelle ligne droite' (*CC*, p. 72).

It is at this spot that the 'sighs and cries and shrieks of lamentation', wafting from 'the starless air of Hell' (*INF* 3: 22–3), first reach the Pilgrim's ears, in a manner not far removed from the distant howling laughter of the damned described in *Mal Vu Mal Dit*: 'D'ici le rire des damnés' (*MVMD*, p. 68). These are the cries of shades who are condemned to linger for ever in the vestibule of hell; they are in a tormented no-man's-land because of their cowardly refusal to make positive decisions for good or evil during their lifetime. Virgil describes them as 'those sad souls who lived a life / but lived it with no blame and with no praise' (*INF* 3: 35–6). These shades also find a place in *Comment C'est*: 'tant mieux tant pis ce genre en moins froid à la bonne heure hélas ce genre en moins chaud joie et peine ces deux-là le total de ces deux-là divisé par deux et tiède comme dans le vestibule' (*CC*, p. 67). As well as citing the 'vestibule' in a clear Dantean frame of reference, Beckett also manages to evoke the passage in the Book of Revelation concerning those who are tepid: 'So then because thou art lukewarm, and neither cold nor hot, I will spue thee out of my mouth' (Revelation 3: 16). This reference to the lukewarm is particularly noticeable in the 'luke like in outer hell' which appears in the corresponding passage of the English translation (*HI*, p. 48).

Crossing the River Acheron, Virgil and Dante reach the First Circle of Hell, known as Limbo. Though not tormented, the virtuous shades here must live in a state of unfulfilled desire, since they were not baptized, or they lived before the advent of Christ. Here are to be found many Greek thinkers admired by Beckett: Thales (referred to in the poem 'Serena I'), Democritus, Empedocles, Heraclitus. It is in zones akin to this one that many of the confined beings of Beckett's drama appear to dwell (although Michael Robinson presents an important caveat in stating that part of the suffering of Beckett's people derives from their uncertainty about their whereabouts in terms of present or potential salvation[12]).

In *Fin de partie*, Hamm even rests his hand against the outer wall, remarking: 'Au-delà c'est...l'autre enfer' (*FP*, p. 41). In this further hell would perhaps be found those who are, as Lucky describes, 'dans le tourment dans les feux' (*EAG*, p. 37), or shackled to an ever-present torturer, as described in *Comment C'est*: 'Je vais rester là oui collé contre lui oui à le martyriser oui éternellement oui' (*CC*, p. 154), in a hell where there is 'pas un seul privé de bourreau' (*CC*, p. 192).

The chilling last line of Canto 4 of *Inferno* – 'I come into a place where no light is' (*INF* 4: 151) – prepares the reader for the encompassing darkness of the punitive circles of Hell. It is in the following Canto 5 that the famous encounter of the Pilgrim with Paolo and Francesca occurs. Beckett appears to have been affected, as countless other readers have been, by this episode. In an early article he deemed it 'imperishable'.[13] Now that they are both suffering in hell for the passion which resulted in their death at the hands of Francesca's husband (Paolo's brother), Francesca tells the Pilgrim: 'There is no greater pain / than to remember, in our present grief, / past happiness' (*INF* 5: 121–23). It is an impotent misery familiar to many in the Beckettian world, notably Nell in *Fin de partie*: 'Pourquoi cette comédie, tous les jours? [...] Ah hier!' (*FP*, pp. 29–30).

Francesca tells the Pilgrim that the sexual phase of the love between herself and Paolo ensued when they drew together to read a book. She concludes her speech with the words: 'That day we read no further' (*INF* 5: 138). Beckett, struck no doubt by the economy and poignancy of this phrase, subtly incorporates it into *Comment C'est*, where he precedes it with a reference to a hellish thrusting of a burning spike into the rectum, and then transforms it into a cessation not of reading but of prayer. The cross-textual echo perhaps emerges most effectively in the English translation: 'dream come of a sky an earth an under-earth where I am inconceivable aah no sound in the rectum a redhot spike that day we prayed no further' (*HI*, p. 40).

It is not, of course, difficult to find parallels between the specialised torments and environments of *Inferno* and the episodes of torture in *Comment C'est*. For example, the repeated clawing with the fingernails on Pim's back and other parts is reminiscent of the frenzied scratching at sores and scabs in Canto 29, and the adhesion of the butting and abutting bodies in *Inferno* Canto 32 – 'Wood to wood with iron was never clamped / so firm!' (*INF* 32: 49–50) – is paralleled in the yoked poses of *Comment C'est*: 'collés ensemble à ne faire qu'un seul corps dans le noir la boue' (*CC*, p. 189). Not only does the recurring mud of *Comment C'est* remind of the mire and slime of the River Styx, as evoked, for example, in Canto 7 of *Inferno*, but the unremitting nature of the onslaught is also emphasised. Just as Virgil explains to the Pilgrim that 'all the gold that is or ever was / beneath the moon won't buy a moment's rest / for even one among these weary souls' (*INF* 7: 64–6), the narrator in *Comment C'est* ponders upon that same unmitigated misery: 'quand je pense aux âmes au tourment au vrai tourment aux vraies âmes qui n'y ont jamais droit au sommeil' (*CC*, p. 56).

In revealing that he had once prayed for these souls – 'j'ai prié une fois pour elles d'après une vieille vue elle a jauni' (*CC*, p. 56) – the narrator reveals a movement of pity allied to that felt sometimes (to the exasperation of Virgil) by the Pilgrim. In Canto 20, for example, the Pilgrim views the procession of weeping soothsayers. Their heads have been twisted round, so that 'the tears their eyes were shedding / streamed down to wet their buttocks at the cleft' (*INF* 20: 23–4), as cited by Mrs Rooney in *All That Fall*: 'The perfect pair. Like Dante's damned, with their faces arsy-versy. Our tears will water our bottoms' (*CSPL*, p. 31). In Dante's poem, the Pilgrim himself weeps at the sight of these grieving remnants of humanity, and is informed by Virgil: 'In this place piety lives when pity is dead' (*INF* 20: 28). The line in the original Italian is: 'Qui vive la pietà quand'è ben morta', thereby obtaining a pun, since 'la pietà' in Italian means both 'pity' and 'piety'. Belacqua intones the first four words, 'Qui vive la pietà', at one point in *Dream of Fair to Middling Women* (*DFMW*, p. 148). Moreover, in *More Pricks Than Kicks*, Belacqua expresses to his Italian teacher his admiration for what he calls this 'superb pun': ' "Is it not a great phrase?" he gushed' (*MPTK*, p. 18). Beyond his pleasure in the linguistic ambiguity, however, Belacqua proceeds to undermine the central precept of the formula. As he carries the lobster (later revealed to be alive) in the parcel, he muses upon a counter-argument: 'Why not piety and pity both, even down below? Why not mercy and Godliness together? A little mercy in the stress of sacrifice, a little mercy to rejoice against judgment' (*MPTK*, p. 20).

Hence, Beckett engages with *The Divine Comedy*, but also submits its expositions to his critical faculties (as with Beatrice's disquisition upon the spots on the moon, which Belacqua regards as an 'impenetrable passage' [*MPTK*, p. 9]). He does not scruple to record his reservations or to move the referent into a different tone or context. A similar shift occurs in *Textes pour rien VI*, where the narrator records his surprise at how the shades in *Inferno* and *Purgatory* constantly talk about themselves in the past tense: 'Je fus, je fus, disent ceux du Purgatoire, ceux des Enfers aussi, admirable pluriel[14], merveilleuse assurance' (*NTPR*, p. 157). The Dantean residents of Purgatory and Hell do indeed retain memories of their lives on earth, often rehearsing them, in the past tense, for the Pilgrim's ears. A very similar observation made in *Pochade radiophonique* elaborates the contention a little further with reference to Purgatory, when A enquires of D whether she has read the *Purgatory* of the 'divin Florentin' (*PS*, p. 72). Finding out that she has only skimmed *Inferno*, he remarks of *Purgatory*: 'Là tout le monde soupire, Je fus, je fus. C'est comme un glas. Curieux, n'est-ce pas?' In the face of D's incomprehension, A explains that he would have expected these souls to be oriented towards the future rather than the past: 'Eh bien, on s'attendrait plutôt à "Je serai", non?'. In contrast with the inhabitants of Hell, these souls do at least have a future to contemplate which will be infinitely happier than either their present or their past.

The narrator in *Textes pour rien VI* goes on to illustrate what he means by 'merveilleuse assurance', in the context of *Inferno*: 'Plongé dans la glace, jusqu'aux narines, les paupières collées de larmes gelées, revivre ses campagnes, quelle tranquillité, et se savoir au bout de ses surprises, non, j'ai dû mal entendre' (*NTPR*, p. 157). These exemplars are no doubt Dante's traitors, frozen into the plain of ice in Cantos 32 and 33 of *Inferno*. Among these is Count Ugolino, who gives a long account of his imprisonment and death, and thus demonstrates this tendency to 'revivre ses campagnes'. The ever-reeling memory, and the present incapacity to alter or amend the deeds or omissions it has recorded, constitutes a further ingredient of these souls' torments. Those souls who, in Beckett's words, have 'les paupières collées de larmes gelées' are the ones who betrayed their own guests. They have been blind ever since the freezing of their first tears: 'for the tears they first wept knotted in a cluster / and like a visor made for them in crystal, / filled all the hollow part around their eyes' (*INF* 33: 97–9).

In *Textes pour rien VI*, however, the narrator is evoking these predicaments only to differentiate them from his own. In his perceptions, the Dantean souls at least have the benefit of a clear sense of finitude versus infinitude. They can review their past life as temporal and provisional, while being in no doubt of the everlasting nature of their present ordeal. This knowledge might more predictably be seen as an additional agony, since there is no prospect of remission. Yet the groping subjectivity of *Textes pour rien VI* cannot see it as such. For him, the desired state is one in which uncertainty is brought to an end: 'Ah être fixé, savoir cette chose sans fin, cette chose, cette chose, ce fouillis de silence et de mots, de silences qui n'en sont pas, de mots qui sont des murmures. Ou savoir que c'est encore de la vie, une forme de vie, vouée à finir' (*NTPR*, p. 158).

Therefore, although Dante's rivetting and exhausting anatomisation of Hell and Purgatory provide unforgettable models for Beckett, there is no easy transposition to be made between the Dantean formulation and the Beckettian experience. Beckett's people conceive of hell and purgatory in searching, mobile ways, as exemplified by the narrator in *L'Innommable*: 'Puis un petit enfer à ma façon, pas trop méchant, avec quelques gentils damnés à qui accrocher mes gémissements, une chose qui soupire de loin en loin et au loin par éclairs la pitié en flammes attendant l'heure de nous promouvoir en cendres' (*LI*, pp. 32–3).

What Beckett's narrator is envisaging here is a kind of amalgam of Hell and Purgatory, for it is peopled by 'damnés', and yet it has an element of movement and purgatorial expectation: 'attendant l'heure'. In a sense, he is able to share the doubtful privilege of Dante the Pilgrim, who is enabled by the intermediary of his guide to acquire a 'laissez-passer' from Hell to Purgatory. The dead who inhabit these zones of punishment or purgation are completely sealed off from one another, for, in accordance with their theological construction, Hell and Heaven are termini whereas Purgatory is a place of transition. Moreover, although Purgatory represents to its inhabitants of fair to middling virtue a place of penal detention, it is also a place of hope, since the only possible progress is forward to

Heaven: there can be no relapse into Hell. As Beckett remarks in his *Dante . . . Bruno. Vico.. Joyce,* there is in Dante's 'conical' purgatory 'absolute progression and a guaranteed consummation' (*DBVJ*, p. 33). It is no doubt with this model in mind that Beckett is able to refer in *Dream of Fair to Middling Women* to 'the gay zephyrs of Purgatory, slithering in across the blue tremolo of the ocean with a pinnace of souls, as good as saved' (*DFMW,* p. 113). 'En attendant', however, 'on this earth that is Purgatory' (*DBVJ*, p. 33), there is no such assurance to be had. In Dante's world, the allocation of zones is time-specific (consequent upon the moment of death) and once-for-all; in Beckett's world, such an allocation is temporary and shrouded in mystery. In *Malone meurt,* the narrator has to surmise his present status on the basis of hypotheses: 'Au fond, si je ne me sentais pas mourir, je pourrais me croire déjà mort' (*MM,* pp. 14–15).

Le *Dépeupleur* shares in this indefinability. There are many characteristics of this enclosed cylindrical space which seem to affiliate it with an intermediate zone between hell and purgatory. There is a source of light, but the light is prevalently dim and yellowish, like the 'hellish half-light' referred to by W1 in *Play* (*CSPL,* p. 152). The text cancels (but thereby evokes) a sulphurous characteristic in it: 'Ce qui frappe d'abord dans cette pénombre est la sensation de jaune qu'elle donne pour ne pas dire de soufre à cause des associations' (*LD,* p. 32). Sulphur (brimstone) is indeed yellow, and its 'associations' are with hell, because of the ready combustibility of the mineral. Moreover, the statement some half-way through the text that 'à la sensation de jaune s'ajoute celle plus faible du rouge' (*LD,* p. 34) may incite comparison with the 'reddish glow' which the Pilgrim sees diffused from hell (*INF* 8: 74–5).

Nevertheless, the disposition of the cylinder, with its elaborate arrangement of crevices, suggests the terraces of Dante's *Purgatory.* Moreover, the fact that the desired impetus is always upwards, by means of ladders, means that the rising movement aligns the exertions of the inhabitants with the ascent of Mount Purgatory rather than with the descent into Hell. In *Purgatory,* the soul addresses its sins in systematic fashion, purging one capital sin at one level before climbing to the next ledge. This intermittent movement is reflected in the stop-start dynamic of the cylinder: 'Tous se figent alors. Leur séjour va peut-être finir. Au bout de quelques secondes tout reprend' (*LD,* p. 7). In *Purgatory,* the climb is often arduous, the path narrow, or the space restricted (in contrast with the wide gate leading to Hell). In Canto 10, for example, Virgil and the Pilgrim have to squeeze through a 'needle's eye' in order to attain a ledge where there is 'room / for three men's bodies laid out end to end' (*PUR* 10: 23–4). Similarly, access to the niches and alcoves of Beckett's cylinder is precariously achieved, by means of sometimes rickety ladders. Once there, the niche is 'd'ampleur variable mais toujours suffisante pour que par le jeu normal des articulations le corps puisse y pénétrer et de même tant bien que mal s'y étendre' (*LD*, pp. 10–11).

The cylinder differs from other enclosed communities, such as ant-hills, in that the categorisation of its inhabitants is based not upon function but upon movement or lack of it, propensity to search or lack of it. However, these characteristics are impermanent and may be interchangeable. Very often, there are interactions (as in much of Beckett's writing) between those who are active and those who are non-active, those who are searching and those who have for the moment renounced movement. One such moment is the scrutiny of the woman at the north by 'le chercheur'. This slumped woman has frequently been inspected by searchers who draw apart her hair and raise her head, so that her body is bared to the gaze as far down as the crutch: 'Les cheveux de la vaincue ont été maintes fois relevés et écartés et la tête soulevée et mis à nu le visage et tout le devant du corps jusqu'à l'entre-jambes' (*LD*, p. 51). This episode may be compared with the exposure by Virgil of the Siren, who has mesmerised Dante's 'chercheur', the Pilgrim. Only when Virgil 'seized the other, ripped her garment off, / exposing her as far down as the paunch' (*PUR* 19: 31–2) is the Pilgrim enabled to move on.

Many purgatorial resonances cluster, of course, around the person of Belacqua, in *Dream of Fair to Middling Women*, *More Pricks Than Kicks*, and occasionally in later texts. These have already been extensively analysed by commentators and will not be examined again here. However, it is important to recall that Belacqua is not an inhabitant of Purgatory proper, but of Ante-Purgatory. As such, he is not subject to the highly structured purgatorial routine which characterises the mainstream experience. Ante-Purgatory is a kind of waiting-room for those souls who have delayed their repentance until the last minute. Guilty of having made God wait, they have been sieved out for extra waiting. Hence, in *Comment C'est*, Belacqua is observed to be 'basculé sur le côté las d'attendre' (*CC*, p. 37). In the meantime, however, being sealed off from the remedial exertions of Purgatory proper, the inhabitants of Ante-Purgatory live a mobile existence in which they roam by day and rest by night. Indeed, although Belacqua is, in accordance with his Dantean namesake, said to be 'bogged in indolence' (*MPTK*, p. 39), he does not truly possess the knack of long-term and permanent withdrawal. He even finds that his 'little acts of motion [...] certainly did do him some good as a rule' (*MPTK*, p. 39).

Belacqua aside, it may be observed that the habitat of the Ante-Purgatorial assignees, on the open slopes of Mount Purgatory, is no more or less hospitable than the country roads on which many a Beckettian wayfarer trudges, and their oppressive sense of waiting, as in Beckett's narratives, may temporarily be alleviated by song, rest or conversation. Indeed, what Murphy calls his 'Belacqua fantasy' is said to be 'just beyond the frontiers of suffering, it was the first landscape of freedom' (*MP*, p. 48).

Nevertheless, as the previous analysis has suggested, there is no possibility of imposing a Dantean template upon the complex impulses of the Beckettian text, even if this were thought desirable. Thus, although a similar intensity of physical and mental suffering is perceptible in Beckett's work, the ills which assail humankind are not transactions within a divine economy. In the *Divine Comedy* universe, the mental and the physical are wedded together, with every punishment tailored to the nature of the sin, so that a physical assault has 'meaning' within the psyche of the recipient. In the Beckettian universe, on the other hand, kicks and caresses are for the most part arbitrary, and perplexedly apprehended.

This perplexity leads by very roundabout ways to the notion of punishment, and the recurrent conviction in the Beckettian fictional world that the speaker is being judged for crimes as yet unknown, as reported, for example, in *Malone meurt*: 'L'idée de châtiment se présenta à son esprit [...]. Et sans savoir exactement quelle était sa faute il sentait bien que vivre n'en était pas une peine suffisante ou que cette peine était en elle-même une faute, appelant d'autres peines, et ainsi de suite' (*MM*, p. 109).

Within this haphazard scheme, the punishment neither fits nor follows the crime. It cannot, because there is no consciousness of any crime to begin with. Instead, therefore, as the foregoing quotation from *Malone meurt* illustrates, the primary experience is of unfathomable, meaningless suffering: the 'damnation obscure' of which the narrator speaks in *L'Innommable* (*LI*, p. 36). The secondary experience is a *post hoc* rationalisation which experiments with the idea that this suffering might be a chastisement, and that this chastisement might have been prompted by a misdeed. However, since the afflicted person is aware of no particular misdemeanour of sufficient magnitude, the process is constantly short-circuited, even while the pulses generating it remain sparking within the mind. The primary experience of suffering, physical and psychological, finds numerous manifestations within Beckett's writing. Those undergoing it may ponder about the identity of their aggressor, as does the voice in *Textes pour rien VIII*: 'Mais qui ai-je donc pu offenser aussi gravement, pour que je sois puni de cette façon incompréhensible' (*NTPR*, p. 170). Sufferers may also try out various guilt-related hypotheses to account for the ferocity and longevity of their tribulations. The narrator in *L'Innommable* conjectures that 'on m'a donné un pensum, à ma naissance peut-être, pour me punir d'être né peut-être, ou sans raison spéciale' (*LI*, p. 39). In *Textes pour rien V*, a similar linkage between guilt and simply being alive is established by the reference to 'cette instance obscure où être est être coupable' (*NTPR*, pp. 145-6).

Related speculation arises in *En attendant Godot*, when Vladimir proposes: 'Si on se repentait?' (*EAG*, p. 5). When asked, however, he is uncertain of what misdeed would attract this repentance: 'On n'aurait pas besoin d'entrer dans les détails'. It is for Estragon to propose that most far-reaching (though most irremediable) fault: 'D'être né?'. In so doing, he prefigures the desperate miserere he will utter later in the play, for the miserere psalm goes on to state: 'Behold, I was shapen in iniquity; and in sin did my mother conceive me' (Psalm 51: 5). Moreover, it is a cry of repentance and a purging 'with hyssop' which that psalm promulgates as the route to 'joy and gladness' (v. 8). Vladimir and Estragon are unable, however, to participate in that swing between shame and joy, for Vladimir's laughter at Estragon's suggestion is immediately curtailed by a bout of pain.

Just as Vladimir opines that, to be forgiven, 'on n'aurait pas besoin d'entrer dans les détails', the perception of many of Beckett's paining individuals is that the punishment allotted to them is somehow detached from the details of their supposed crimes. The woman in *Not I* does not enter into the details either: she simply speculates upon 'that notion of punishment...for some sin or other...or for the lot...or no particular reason...for its own sake...thing she understood perfectly...that notion of punishment' (*CSPL*, p. 217).

Clov, too, appears to have become habituated to the long history of what he supposes to be punishment, even while buckling under it: 'On ne peut plus me punir' (*FP*, p. 16). Moreover, he envisages a kind of monitoring of his reactions to punishment; his learning to 'suffer better' might, he wonders, induce his tormentor(s) to grow weary of their prey: 'Je me dis – quelquefois, Clov, il faut que tu arrives à souffrir mieux que ça, si tu veux qu'on se lasse de te punir' (*FP*, p. 108). The narrator in *Comment C'est* voices a similar perception: 'pas que je crie cela tombe sous les sens puisqu'on m'en punit aussitôt' (*CC*, p. 99). If further punishment results when the victim cries out, however, it is liable to occur all the same when the victim remains silent, as stated in *L'Innommable*: 'C'est pour se taire qu'il faut du courage, car on sera puni, on sera puni de s'être tu, et pourtant, on ne peut pas faire autrement que de se taire, que d'être puni de s'être tu, que d'être puni d'avoir été puni, puisqu'on recommence' (*LI*, p. 180).

Whatever the stance adopted, it appears impossible to outguess the putative punisher. Like Kafka's Joseph K, the captive is forever shadow-boxing with an opponent who is one step removed. Indeed, the context is often that of the courtroom, a courtroom in which no direct contact can be made with the judge. The woman in *Not I* seems unable to justify herself in court: 'that time in court... what had she to say for herself... guilty or not guilty... stand up woman... speak up woman... stood there staring into space' (*CSPL*, p. 221).

Even where a 'confession' of crime is undertaken, it is perceived by its hearers as incomplete or unsatisfactory. Never can a whole life be accounted for in one final confession, as the voice in *L'Innommable* notes: 'C'est comme une confession, une dernière confession, on la croit finie, puis elle rebondit, il y a eu tant de fautes, la mémoire est si mauvaise, les mots ne viennent plus, les mots se font rares' (*LI*, p. 208). It appears from the transcript of the tortured suspect's words in *Pochade radiophonique* that he has begun a process of confession. The sample given involves a sworn statement concerning the welfare of a mole: 'Quand j'ai eu savonné la taupe, [...] je ressors dans la tourmente et la remets dans son donjon avec son plein poids de vers blancs, à ce moment-là le petit coeur battait encore je le jure, ah mon Dieu mon Dieu' (*PS*, pp. 69–70). The incident is related to that 'confessed' in *Company*, when a hedgehog is put into 'an old hatbox with some worms', and, with 'a last look to make sure all is as it should be', left for 'days if not weeks', and then discovered to have dissolved into a stinking mush which the narrator has 'never forgotten' (*NO*, pp. 23–4).

The confession – shown in both these similar instances to be a traumatic revisitation of the memory – is, however, insufficient for the authorities of *Pochade radiophonique*, for the brutal interrogation continues. Perhaps all that is needed is a victim, as the voice owns in *L'Innommable*: 'Il faut accuser quelqu'un, il faut trouver quelqu'un, il faut un coupable, [...] il faut une victime' (*LI*, p. 208). The link between the required form of words and the fruitless one remains tenuous and apparently arbitrary: 'Les mots continuent, les mauvais, les faux, jusqu'à ce que l'ordre arrive, de tout arrêter, ou de tout continuer' (*LI*, p. 138). The punisher punishes; the complementary role of the punished is simply to suffer. Hence, the narrator's internal ear hears it being said of him: 'Il n'a pas besoin de raisonner, seulement de souffrir' (*LI*, p. 135).

Moreover, the degree and frequency of punishment are deemed to be calculated to achieve the keenest effect. 'L'affaire est épineuse', states the narrator (*LI*, p. 134), the pun subtly adverting to the crown of thorns pressed upon that other, more famous, victim. Like Christ in torment, to whom the words of the psalmist are often applied: 'I am a worm, and no man; a reproach of men' (Psalm 22: 6), the victimised voice in *L'Innommable* assumes the name of Worm. Moreover, just as Philip preaches to the eunuch in the Acts of the Apostles (Acts 8: 32–5) that Christ had fulfilled the words of Isaiah – 'As a sheep before her shearers is dumb, so he openeth not his mouth' (Isaiah 53: 7) – Worm says of himself that he is 'muet, sans comprendre, muet, sans l'usage d'autre parole que la leur' (*LI*, p. 137).

As Worm, the voice in *L'Innommable* invites comparison not only with Christ as suffering servant, but also, within Christian tradition, with the physical body (whereas the soul is often designated by a winged creature such as a butterfly or dove). Indeed, the Book of Isaiah concludes with a terrifying description (echoed later by Christ in Mark 9) of the Gehenna where the body burns but is not consumed, a place 'where their worm dieth not, and the fire is not quenched' (Isaiah 66: 24).

The Worm of *L'Innommable*, though persistently oppressed, nevertheless has accesses of hope that the judgement upon him may not be irreversible. He is even capable of imagining the process of judgement which 'they', his oppressors, will undergo: 'Il s'en iront peut-être, un jour, un soir, lentement, tristement, en file indienne, jetant de longues ombres, vers leur maître, qui les punira, ou les épargnera, il n'y a que ça, là-haut, pour ceux qui perdent, la punition, le pardon, les deux, c'est eux qui le disent. Qu'avez-vous fait de votre matériel?' (*LI*, p. 130). This latter question concerning the management of material brings this scenario into close affiliation with Christ's parable of the talents, in which the master of the household distributes varying numbers of talents (a unit of currency) to his servants, and then departs on a journey. On his return, he demands to know what the servants have done with the material given to them. The judgement is severe: those who have doubled their holdings are rewarded, while the servant who has merely hoarded his talent for safekeeping – hardly a grievous offence – is cast 'into outer darkness' (Matthew 25: 30).

The biblical text then develops out from the particular parable of the talents into a generalised description of the final judgement of the nations, with Christ separating the sheep from the goats and sending the former to reward, the latter to punishment. There are, in this presentation, only two groups and two outcomes, just as the voice in *L'Innommable* envisages only punishment or forgiveness.

The narrator of *Textes pour rien VIII* hopes, however, that the intermediate, purgatorial zone will be available for him, a conditional pardon for his unidentified crimes: 'Qu'on me gracie, si je suis coupable, et me laisse expier, dans le temps, en allant et venant, chaque jour un peu plus pur, un peu plus mort' (*NTPR*, p. 170). Purity here is allied to death, just as guilt is elsewhere allied to life. The problem is that the way to the court is obscure, and the manner of its workings indecipherable. It may even reach its verdict in the absence of the accused, as envisaged in *Textes pour rien V*: 'Je comparaîtrai peut-être devant le concile, ce sera la justice de l'amour suprême, sévère comme de juste, mais sujette à d'étranges indulgences, il sera question de mon âme, j'aime mieux ça, on demandera peut-être pitié pour mon âme, il ne faut pas manquer ça, je ne serai pas là, Dieu non plus, ça ne fait rien, nous serons représentés' (*NTPR*, p. 149).

Perpetually on bail, in jail, or on trial, the Beckettian sufferer is never acquitted. Even to throw oneself on the mercy of the court requires a sitting, and an opportunity to be heard. In a situation where the scales of mercy seem always to be weighted in favour of condemnation, the supreme dispenser of justice is always out of earshot, or conceivably watching from afar through a one-way mirror. Perhaps, given his remoteness, he is even powerless to help, as the voice in *L'Innommable* conjectures in a noteworthy web of propositions: 'Qu'est-ce que j'ai fait à Dieu, qu'est-ce qu'ils ont fait à Dieu, qu'est-ce que Dieu nous a fait, il ne nous a rien fait, nous ne lui avons rien fait, nous ne pouvons rien lui faire, il ne peut rien nous faire' (*LI*, p. 165).

Meanwhile, God's worm-creature writhes on the end of the line. He is blind and mute, but he can at least writhe in writing, since writhing and writing are only an aspirate or aspiration apart. Nevertheless, in these conditions, the heavens recede, and pain prevails: 'Ils sont trop difficiles, ils demandent trop. Ils veulent que j'aie mal à la nuque, preuve irréfutable d'animation, tout en entendant parler du ciel. Ils me veulent savant, sachant que j'ai mal à la nuque, que les mouches me dévorent et que le ciel n'y peut rien changer' (*LI*, p. 111). This is a God who is either callously present, obtusely absent, or haplessly paralysed. Evidence of a hypothesis rumoured to be held by some – that of a loving Providence – remains unavailable to the Beckettian witness.

5

Solitude, Stillness, Silence and Stars

The preceding chapter explored those elements, found recurrently within Beckett's oeuvre, which cast shadows over hypotheses of a loving Deity. Many of Beckett's people have to labour within an environment in which cruelty, fear, and pain are endemic: a disfigured creation in which concepts of grace, providence, and hope are as remote as a reliable bicycle.

Nevertheless, to leave the analysis at that point would be to curtain off even what light might filter through the north-facing windows of Beckett's work. As Eric Griffiths wrote in an obituary of Beckett: 'We hear much about the "infernal" or the "purgatorial", less of the paradisiacal Beckett. But his late work often imagines places of calm, of cool or chill refreshment, lit with an inexplicably constant light'.[1] That this book contains 'less of the paradisiacal Beckett' is appropriate, for there are indeed fewer such impulses to be found. Moreover, if 'paradise' is deemed to be based upon effulgence and apotheosis, then Beckett's work must be said to be devoid of it.

There is, however, a kind of nightlight to be discerned from time to time which undermines the onset of unrelieved blackness. As St John of the Cross, that luminous tenebrist, wrote in his *Ascent of Mount Carmel*: 'However dark a night may be, something can always be seen; but in true darkness nothing can be seen'.[2] Something similar is described by the narrator in *L'Innommable*: 'La nuit la plus profonde se laisse percer à la longue, jusqu'à un certain point, je l'ai entendu dire, sans l'aide d'autre lumière que celle du ciel noirci et de la terre elle-même' (*LI*, p. 22). This light issues, significantly, from both sky and earth. It is not reliant upon the heavens, although it may also be found there. Moreover, in Beckett's work, it is most often discerned in conditions not so far removed from those sought by the spiritual pursuant: solitude, stillness, and silence. These are key ingredients of the desert experience once sought by cenobites such as St Antony of Egypt. However, while Flaubert's account of teeming sensations, *La Tentation de Saint Antoine*, is seen through Brueghel's restless eyes, Beckett's desert experience is to be found in much sparser circumstances: the 'pang of light' of *Dream of Fair to Middling Women* (*DFMW*, p. 28) or the 'calme de vide' of *Mal Vu Mal Dit* (*MVMD*, p. 36).

SOLITUDE

'Art is the apotheosis of solitude', wrote Beckett in *Proust*, since 'the only possible spiritual development is in the sense of depth' (*P*, p. 64). The linking of art, solitude, and depth which Beckett discerns in Proust is no less applicable to his own concept of the writing endeavour. Further, his statement assumes the pivotal importance of 'spiritual development'. Later in the essay, Beckett will dissociate himself from d'Annunzio's 'horrible pomegranates of "Il Fuoco"', bursting and bleeding, dripping the red ooze of their seed, putrid on the putrid water', in favour of the 'Proustian stasis' which is 'contemplative, a pure act of understanding, will-less' (*P*, p. 91). The statement is a rather disingenuous one, for some of Beckett's early poetry would provide a congenial setting for d'Annunzio's pomegranates. (See, for example, the 'great mushy toadstool, / green-black, / oozing up after me' of 'Enueg I', or the 'plush hymens on your eyeballs' of 'Serena III' [*CP*, pp. 12; 25]).

Exaggeration serves the purpose of contrast, however. What Beckett is reacting against in d'Annunzio is the lushness, the self-indulgence, inhering in the writing. It is not so much the inclusion of physical, sensuous elements in d'Annunzio's novels that he objects to, as the heavy, unrestrained use of them. What he admires in Proust, on the other hand, is the recognition that 'the artistic tendency is not expansive, but a contraction' (*P*, p. 64), and that it is responsive to a domain which lies beyond word, gesture, or object.

That 'contraction' was, for Beckett, a rigorous one. It involved a privileging of solitude, of silence, and of stillness. These characteristics – always prized within Beckett's writing from the outset – remained important throughout the oeuvre, and out of them developed writing which was increasingly stripped and renunciatory. The punning monastic motto – 'O beata solitudo! O sola beatitudo!' [O blessed solitude! O only happiness!] – is one which, in more subdued terms, would not be entirely alien to Beckett's narrators.

Moreover, Beckett's interlocutors sometimes testify to the manner in which Beckett appeared to be all of a piece with this ascetic dynamic. For example, E. M. Cioran wrote of him in 1976: 'One can very easily imagine him, a few centuries back, in a bare cell unsullied by any decoration, not even a crucifix'.[3] Cioran even quotes in this connection a Buddhist requirement that one seeking enlightenment must be like 'a mouse gnawing a coffin', seeing in Beckett that very 'solitude and subterranean obstinance' which would be necessary in such an enterprise (Cioran, p. 334). Of course, there are circumstances in which even coffins are a luxury. Hamm is told abruptly by Clov, towards the end of *Fin de partie*, that there are no more coffins (*FP*, p. 102), and Beckett seems to have been struck by the graveside austerity embraced by the Carthusians – that most solitary of religious orders – who are said by Molloy, on the occasion of the burial of Lousse's dog, to be buried in the earth 'tel quel, sans boîte ni enveloppe d'aucune sorte' (*ML*, p. 47). In comparison with such gestures of ultimate poverty, Teddy the dog, buried with his collar and lead on, has a lavish funeral.

Within this perspective of radical down-sizing of human baggage, Beckett wrote to Thomas MacGreevy in 1934 that 'perhaps it is the one bright spot in a mechanistic age – the deanthropomorphizations of the artist. Even the portrait beginning to be dehumanised as the individual feels himself more and more hermetic and alone and his neighbour a coagulum as alien as a protoplast or God'.[4] This is not so much the expression of an artistic anorexia which aims to reduce all human manifestations to the proportions of a Giacometti figure, but rather a resistance to unexamined assumptions about 'human nature', and about societal hierarchies.

Of course, the existence of this correspondence, and of many other testimonies of lasting friendships, proves that Beckett was, on a personal level, far from implementing the stance which he perceived in Proust's work: 'For the artist, who does not deal in surfaces, the rejection of friendship is not only reasonable, but a necessity' (*P*, p. 64). Nevertheless, the act of artistic creation itself must, for Beckett, be carried out in solitude, as expressed also by Leonardo da Vinci (with whose Notebooks Beckett was familiar): 'If you are alone you belong entirely to yourself; if you are accompanied even by one companion you belong only half to yourself'.[5]

The stated imperative of solitude may all too easily be mistaken for a kind of elite individualism which sets the artist apart, to commune with the superior insights vouchsafed to him or her. (D'Annunzio's writing study in his last and most self-indulgent house – Il Vittoriale, in Gardone – is one such shrine to the Singular Artist). Beckett's conception of solitude, on the other hand, is an unadorned one, not bound to particular spaces inside or outside, and having more in common with Valéry's 'île intérieure'.[6] Indeed, Anthony Cronin confesses to wondering whether, when Beckett spent so much time playing golf in his youth, 'he was turning the golf course into some sort of open-air hermit's cell'.[7] He was certainly responsive to a self-contained solitude within landscape, as might be illustrated by the beautiful description of the solitary flight of the hawk in *Malone meurt*: 'Il aimait le vol de l'épervier et savait le reconnaître entre tous. Immobile il suivait des yeux les longs vols planés, l'attente tremblante, les ailes se relevant pour la chute à plomb, la remontée rageuse, fasciné par tant de besoin, de fierté, de patience, de solitude' (*MM*, p. 27).

There is a kinship here between hawk and watcher, a recognition of shared impulses to solitude. There are, after all, many phoney or reluctant solitudes. (Victor Hugo set up an elaborate mirror system on the staircase of his house in Guernsey, so that, from the solitude of his eyrie at the top of the house, he could nevertheless monitor the arrivals and departures below). Such half-hearted solitude will normally betray the one lauding it. Hence, Beckett criticised Rilke in an early review for 'the overstatement of the solitude which he cannot make his element'.[8]

The writers and painters whom Beckett most admired were those in whose output such solitariness was not asserted, but simply transparent. Two such were the van Velde brothers. In Beckett's eyes, their work rejected the so-called universals of beauty, goodness, and truth, in favour of a restrained but expansive dynamic of solitude: 'Que deviendra, dans cette foire, cette peinture solitaire, solitaire de la solitude qui se couvre la tête, de la solitude qui tend les bras?'.[9] In that latter image – a remarkable one – of the solitude with outreaching arms, there is a bridge created between 'solitaire' and 'solidaire', those phonetic brothers but semantic strangers which so haunted Albert Camus.[10] This is a solitude which, while intensely personal, is not above shouting from afar, conceivably to be heard.

There is no self-evident virtue in solitude. It may all too easily blur into self-centredness or excessive solipsism. As the rather disillusioned hermit states in Dr Johnson's *The History of Rasselas*, 'the life of a solitary man will be certainly miserable, but not certainly devout'.[11] From time to time there is a brief (if unconvincing) acknowledgement of this argument in Beckett's work. For example, the voice in *L'Innommable*, traversed by loneliness, muses: 'Il reviendra, me tenir compagnie, seuls les méchants sont seuls' (*LI*, p. 186), and the narrator in *Comment C'est* styles himself 'un monstre des solitudes', a curiosity whose skin would be prized by explorers (*CC*, p. 18). However, it is notable that neither of these instances relate directly to the narrator's self-image: the first is applied to another, and the second is applied to himself when viewed by others. Hence, the 'monstre des solitudes' is monstrous only to those who derive their identity from the collectivity, just as Valéry's Monsieur Teste is only regarded as 'un monstre d'isolement' by the local priest (*Monsieur Teste*, p. 49).

Nevertheless, just as solitude is not a positive value in its own right, neither is it a state in which everyone feels at ease. As 'Le Solitaire' chants in Valéry's play: 'La panique devant zéro.... Le rien fait peur'.[12] Dr Johnson, in whose life and work Beckett was so thoroughly immersed, had an ambiguous attitude towards solitude, in that, while seeing its spiritual value, he feared its effect. It is noteworthy, then, that Beckett should choose to copy down in his 'Whoroscope' notebook (RUL MS 3000), amongst some jottings from *The History of Rasselas*, the words 'dreading moment when solitude should deliver him to tyranny of reflection'. This phrase occurs when Imlac is discoursing on what lies within the minds of people in society: 'Believe me, prince, there was not one who did not dread the moment when solitude should deliver him to the tyranny of reflection' (*Rasselas*, p. 58).

These words, as Beckett recognised, have a particular resonance in Johnson's own life, for, while cognizant of the need for solitude when undertaking personal prayer and meditation, Johnson when isolated was recurrently prey to mental disturbance. Thus, although a great admirer of Jeremy Taylor, he could not emulate Taylor's eloquent and ironic contemplation of such phenomena as death and judgement. Appropriately, it is in a sermon on marriage that (despite his tendency to absent himself from his wife Tetty) Johnson's dread of solitude most clearly emerges. Here, citing the 'gloom of solitude', he states that: 'In solitude perplexity swells into distraction, and grief settles into melancholy; even the satisfactions and pleasures, that may by chance be found, are but imperfectly enjoyed, when they are enjoyed without participation'.[13]

This propensity to melancholy in solitude is no less apparent in Johnson's *Prayers and Meditations*, the greater part of which were written after the death of his wife. Here, in amongst the breast-beating over the paucity of improvement he discerns in his own zeal, and the rather endearing renewal of resolutions (constantly broken) to rise earlier and to avoid idleness, Johnson repeatedly prays for his own psychological disquiet to be eased, or turned to good purpose. In 1784, for example, Johnson penned a prayer 'against inquisitive and perplexing thoughts'. The prayer implores God to 'enable me to drive from me all such unquiet and perplexing thoughts as may mislead or hinder me in the practice of those duties which Thou has required. [...] Teach me [...] to withdraw my mind from unprofitable and dangerous inquiries, from difficulties vainly curious, and doubts impossible to be solved'.[14]

Beckett was very conscious of this characteristic in Johnson, and wrote of it in 1937 to Thomas MacGreevy: 'The 18th Century was full of ahuris – perhaps that is why it looked like the age of "reason" – but there can hardly have been many so completely at sea in their solitude as [Johnson] was or so horrifiedly aware of it – not even Cowper. Read the *Prayers and Meditations* if you don't believe me'.[15]

A feeling of being 'at sea in solitude' is not so rare a phenomenon. Even Beckett admitted, in answer to a question from Charles Juliet in 1975 that, while he thrived on solitude for weeks at a time, this had not always been the case: 'Plus jeune, je n'aurais pas pu supporter de rester seul pendant autant de jours' [When I was younger, I couldn't have put up with being on my own for so many days].[16] Yet Beckett's use of the emphatic word 'ahuri' (idiot; dazed person) in his letter to MacGreevy demonstrates his alienation from such uneasiness. For Johnson, the unshackling of the imagination is, as Imlac puts it, one of the 'dangers of solitude' (*Rasselas*, p. 143). For Beckett, however, the process is on an altogether different footing: namely, that the freeing of the imagination is desirable, and that such freeing is best fostered by solitude. Moreover, far from hanging heavy, solitude is all too soon curtailed. Hence, the nightmare for Fox in *Pochade radiophonique* is not just that he is being forced under torture to relive painful memories, but also that he can never light upon the confession formula which would secure his release back to his 'chères solitudes' (*PS*, p. 80).

For connoisseurs of solitude such as Beckett's narrators, there are differing modes of solitude. There is one kind which is purely pragmatic, as evoked in *Dream of Fair to Middling Women*: 'Ah solitude, when a man at last and with love can occupy himself in his nose!' (*DFMW*, p. 23). This cosy, nose-picking solitude has more to do with being temporarily out of people's sight, however, than with solitude as an existential mode.

The kind of solitude towards which Beckett's narrators aspire is not a singular settling into oneself. Rather, it is a condition in which to attain a mobile exploration of the self, a confluence of plural solitudes. Solitude is not something to be managed or domesticated. Hence, in the first of the 'Six Poèmes', the journeying within solitude, both its familiarity and its strangeness, is indicated by the lines: 'ma solitude je la connais allez je la connais mal / j'ai le temps c'est ce que je me dis j'ai le temps' (*CP*, p. 55).

In *Dream of Fair to Middling Women*, the property of being 'untouched by the pulls of the solitudes' refers merely to the resistance towards a static and situational solitude, for the narrator claims to dwell between 'the red solitude and the violet solitude, the red oneness and the violet oneness' (*DFMW*, p. 28). The 'red' domain may here be construed as the physical or passional, with the 'violet' (emblematic of love of truth) attaching to the intellectual or spiritual. Spurning the concept of 'oneness', or 'fake integrities', the narrator lingers in the spaces between them, for the bridge between them – 'the summit of the bow' – is itself a kind of solitude.

A similar plurality is to be found in *Comment C'est*, where the narrator affirms that 'les deux solitudes celle du voyage et celle de l'abandon diffèrent sensiblement et par conséquent méritent d'être traitées à part' (*CC*, p. 203). Neither of these solitudes is static or proprietorial, since one is found on the move, the other in a willed ceding to willlessness. They can be seen exemplified in the second part of *Stirrings Still*, where the solitary man on whom the narrative focusses is also given to wondering, like Johnson, 'if he was in his right mind' (*ASWT*, p. 120). In his state of being 'lost to suffering' (*ASWT*, p. 122), it is even the case that he can regard a cry as an 'enlivener of his solitude'. Renouncing his visual memory-hoard, he stops dead in order to 'sink his head as one deep in meditation', before finally moving on 'through the long hoar grass resigned to not knowing where he was or how he got there or where he was going or how to get back to whence he knew not how he came' (*ASWT*, p. 125). Hence, the two solitudes are here separately designated, but intermingle within the same mobile quest.

The old woman's movement patterns in *Mal Vu Mal Dit* are similarly structured. Seen primarily in solitude, except when she is followed by the lamb, the woman's movements and stillnesses seem to blend into one another, whether she is walking over the snow in the pastures, or is at her chair, which 'respire la solitude' (*MVMD*, p. 42). This chair, exuding solitude, could scarcely be further removed from Johnson's famous 'throne of human felicity' in the corner of the tavern, though both chairs afford to their occupant the opportunity, in the closing words of the Beckett text, to 'connaître le bonheur' (*MVMD*, p. 76).

Within Beckett's texts, solitude is, then, not an enclosure but a layered experience. The voice in *L'Innommable* refers to it as one of the principal elements of his life: 'Oui, dans ma vie, puisqu'il faut l'appeler ainsi, il y eut trois choses, l'impossibilité de parler, l'impossibilité de me taire, et la solitude, physique bien sûr, avec ça je me suis débrouillé' (*LI*, p. 183). Physical solitude is here seen as the constant environment for the apparently warring imperatives towards speech and silence.

The speaker in *Malone meurt* goes further: 'Je sens s'amonceler ce noir, s'aménager cette solitude, auxquels je me reconnais' (*MM*, p. 23). In this instance, the contrast between the Johnsonian and the Beckettian impulses could hardly emerge more clearly, for, whereas Johnson saw 'gloom' and 'solitude' as inextricably enmeshed, Beckett's narrator finds in 'ce noir' and 'cette solitude' a familiar home, a means towards self-knowledge. This is the gloom which Beckett rehabilitates, the 'darling gloom' (*DFMW*, p. 194) which Belacqua's girlfriends find so excluding and he finds so indispensable.

STILLNESS

If Belacqua is given to solitude, he is also attached to stillness. In *Dream of Fair to Middling Women*, he can love in the Smeraldina her 'great stillness of body', her quality of being 'quiet as a tree' (*DFMW*, p. 23). The problem is that she cannot remain so for long, for 'it was only a question of seconds before she would surge up at him, blithe and buxom and young and lusty', threatening to arouse in him thoughts of 'the poor anger of the world that life cannot be still' (*DFMW*, pp. 23–4).

The imagined assault by the Smeraldina is clearly presented here as being physically, sexually motivated, a sequel to the incident a

short while earlier, when 'she raped him' (*DFMW*, p. 18). Such incursions are dreaded by Belacqua for their ability to barricade the
road to intellectual and spiritual recollection. They contrast strongly
with the recorded episode which the ageing chronicler of *Krapp's
Last Tape* finds so mesmeric: 'We lay there without moving. But
under us all moved, and moved us, gently, up and down, and from
side to side' (*CSPL*, pp. 60; 61; 63). This erotically-charged moment
occurs, paradoxically, when the couple have just agreed to enter a
post-sexual phase of their relationship. It is the stillness of their
bodies, in the shade afforded by Krapp's leaning body, which, for a
few moments, enables them to transcend the Manichaean division
of body and spirit.[17]

Similarly, the girl evoked in Part 1 of *Comment C'est* is remembered partly for the 'immobilité de ces mains-là' (*CC*, p. 45).
Later, the couple will walk peacefully hand in hand through the
fields, but, as with Krapp's recollection, the interaction is lodged in
the past. Here, it is abruptly curtailed – 'Je ne nous vois plus la
scène est débarrassée' (*CC*, p. 47) – and the place of stillness cedes to
a solitary horse, which is 'immobile échine courbée tête basse les
bêtes savent' (*CC*, p. 48). Just as the prized solitude is sometimes to
be found outside, in the open air, the quality of stillness can also be
discerned by Beckett's narrators in elements of the natural world:
rocks, certain animals, or vegetation. This expansive tenderness is
expressed, for example, in *From an Abandoned Work*: 'Great love in
my heart too for all things still and rooted, bushes, boulders and the
like, too numerous to mention' (*CSPR*, p. 129). All too easily is the
stillness broken by human agitation, as effected by the narrator's
mother in the same text: 'If only she could have been still and let me
look at it all' (*CSPR*, p. 130). What interferes so distressingly with
his access to the contemplation of still and rooted phenomena is the
activity imposed upon him: 'One week it would be exercises, and
the next prayers and Bible reading, and the next gardening, and the
next playing the piano and singing, that was awful' (*CSPR*, p. 130).
These pursuits, policed by his mother, prompt him to accuse her of
having 'no tenacity of purpose'. Her behaviour does, of course,
exude an extreme tenacity – but of a hydra-like tendency. Thus, an
association is established between activity and capriciousness on
the one hand, and, by extension, between stillness and perseverance
on the other.

Nevertheless, beyond judgements like these, a marked penchant
either for activity or for contemplation is to some extent a matter of

temperament, as Molloy recognises with reference to the presence of desires: 'Car il semble y avoir deux façons de se comporter en présence des envies, l'active et la contemplative, et quoiqu'elles donnent le même résultat toutes les deux, c'est à la deuxième qu'allaient mes préférences, question de tempérament sans doute' (*ML*, p. 69). This differentiation is indeed reflected even within monasticism, with its division between 'active' and 'contemplative' religious, where the former devote a much higher proportion of their time to apostolic works, the latter to prayer and meditation. (In *Comment C'est*, the renunciation of desires is briefly allied with the eastern tradition: 'un oriental mon rêve il a renoncé je renoncerai aussi je n'aurai plus de désirs' [*CC*, p. 87]).

The state of stillness inevitably provides a kind of model, or re-hearsal, for the ultimate stillness, that of death. This definitive ces-sation is often contemplated with a kind of wistfulness within Beckett's work. Hence, Hamm in *Fin de partie* muses upon an irre-vocable stillness which would terminate the interventions of needs and desires: 'Si je peux me taire, et rester tranquille, c'en sera fait, du son, et du mouvement' (*FP*, p. 92). An even more intense evoca-tion of this gradual transition to immobility occurs in *Company*: 'Some object moving from its place to its last place. Some soft thing softly stirring soon to stir no more' (*NO*, p. 15).

That permanent stillness remains, however, a prospect rather than a realised state, within Beckett's writing. Instead, what still-ness can be found is temporary, an often diminishing or threatened resource, and all the more cherished for that. It is exemplified by the 'Beethoven pause' of which Belacqua is said to be fond (*MPTK*, p. 40). To live one of these oxymoronic 'moving pauses' (*MPTK*, p. 41) is to put aside intentionality, to declare oneself 'exempt from destination', but nevertheless to remain available to receive 'the faint inscriptions of the outer world'.

These 'inscriptions', the stimuli made available by passing events, feelings, or phenomena, are quite distinct from the ma-ternal predations described above with reference to *From an Abandoned Work*, for they begin, proceed, and end within the same subjectivity. The desired stillness originates in the 'pure blank movement' which is not inertia. Rather, it is an openness which refrains from spurring itself into actions prescribed either from within or from without.

There are, incidentally, significant differences between English and French in this respect. Considering, for a moment, French as the target language (since Beckett's first language was, after all, English), it seems that Beckett's use of the word 'stir' is only imperfectly rendered in French by the verb 'bouger', just as his usage of the word 'stillness' is more plurivocal than nouns like 'immobilité' or 'calme' would suggest. When translating into French the phrase 'softly stirring soon to stir no more' from *Company* (*NO*, p. 15) as 'mollement bouge pour n'avoir plus à bouger' (*CO*, p. 24), Beckett must have not only regretted the loss of the whispering alliteration, but also have felt acutely conscious of the much more definitive and pro-active ring of 'bouger'. To 'stir', within the Beckettian context, manages to make available a whole spectrum of movement, shading into non-movement. Perhaps the selection of the title *Soubresauts* for the translation of *Stirrings Still* into French was simply a compromise, in which the advantage of retaining the double sibilancy was deemed to outweigh the disadvantage of denoting a much more violent, jolting movement than is indicated in the English original.

Similarly, the word 'stillness' can (and does, within Beckett's writing) embrace without discordancy both motionlessness and motion, for it can suggest a kind of composure, self-sufficiency, or recollection, which may be found in either movement or quiescence. (Hence, to translate the 'all things still and rooted' of *From an Abandoned Work* as 'tout ce qui est fixe et à racine' [*TM*, p. 9] is to nail down the cherished element much more firmly). Great athletes can sometimes exhibit a stillness in action which is neither 'immobilité' nor 'calme', but has to do with intense presence, channelled energy, or collectedness.

Towards the end of *Molloy*, Moran is seen approaching a shepherd and his dog. He has already revealed that his leg is hurting him, but suddenly his movement towards the shepherd seems to acquire a profound and almost cinematic stillness: 'Le silence était absolu. Enfin, profond. Ce fut toutes choses considérées un moment solennel. Le temps était radieux. Le soir venait. Chaque fois que je m'arrêtais je regardais autour de moi. Je regardais le berger, les moutons, le chien et même le ciel. Mais en marchant je ne voyais que la terre et le jeu de mes pieds, le bon qui s'élancait en avant, se retenait, se posait, attendait que l'autre vienne le rejoindre' (*ML*, pp. 215–6).

The narrator in *L'Innommable*, paining and haplessly persevering, makes little distinction between hypotheses of movement or of stillness, of rolling or of rest: 'Mettons donc que je sois fixe quoique cela n'ait pas d'importance, que je sois fixe ou que roulant je change

sans cesse de place, dans les airs ou en contact avec d'autres surfaces, ou que tantôt je roule, tantôt m'arrête, puisque je ne sens rien,
ni quiétude ni changement' (*LI*, p. 33). Significantly, in this attenu-
ated environment, where stirring or coming to rest have lost the
sharp edges of their distinctiveness, it is the hypothesis of stillness
which is adopted – at least for the space of a pause.

SILENCE

St Benedict of Nursia, often dubbed the father of Western monasticism, maintained that there were two kinds of silence: *taciturnitas*
(silence relative to other sounds), and *silentium* (absolute silence).
No doubt these two modes can blend into one another, but the
distinction between a withholding of sound and a systemic silence
is a useful one in the context of Beckett's work. In a sense, it also
embraces the two characteristics – solitude and stillness – which
have gone before. Silence is not mandatory in either case, but
company and movement do not foster it as naturally as do solitude
and stillness. Hence, silence and solitude are mentioned in the same
breath in *Comment C'est*: 'long silence dix mots quinze mots long
silence longue solitude' (*CC*, p. 196). For Charles Juliet, it was these
two elements which constituted the mainsprings of *Textes pour rien*:
'Ce qui m'avait le plus impressionné, c'était cet étrange silence qui
règne dans les *Textes pour rien*, un silence qu'on ne peut atteindre
qu'à l'extrême de la plus extrême solitude, quand l'être a tout quitté,
tout oublié' [What had impressed me most was that strange silence
which reigns in the *Texts For Nothing*, a silence which one can only
attain at the extreme point of the most extreme solitude, when one's
being has left everything, forgotten everything] (Juliet, p. 12).
    Both relative silence and absolute silence are described in Beck-
ett's work, both as modes and as aspirations. The former is perhaps
more readily associated with the imperative to silence which in-
habits the imperative to speak, or the silence which is preserved in
the company of others. A prolonged silence is not always a comfortable home, particularly if it is traversed with fears of what may
ensue at its end. In a tortured text such as *Comment C'est*, the silence
may take on an uneasy quality which hastens its own curtailment:
'vivre donc sans [...] autre silence que celui que je dois rompre si je
n'en veux plus c'est avec ça que je dois durer' (*CC*, p. 19).

However, it is the second kind of silence which draws the attention of Beckett's narrators more powerfully and compulsively. This is the silence which, when sustained, can also sustain its keeper. The aspiration towards a profundity of silence is a recurrent one in Beckett's oeuvre, although its realisation can only be partial. The most that can be achieved is the kind of lingering and silent stillness which pervades Beckett's late prose writing in particular. In *Mal Vu Mal Dit*, a rhythm of silence is allowed to infuse the text – 'ce grand silence soir et nuit' (*MVMD*, p. 33) – which recalls the *magnum silentium* [great silence] observed in monastic houses throughout the night hours, from the close of Compline until the first Matins of the following dawn.

Within Beckett's writing, the shattering of profound silence may be experienced not just as loss, but as an irremediable sundering. As the narrator asserts in *L'Innommable*: 'Le silence une fois rompu ne sera jamais plus entier' (*LI*, p. 132). In this section of the novel, a distinction is made, between 'le silence gris' and 'le silence noir', which corresponds in some degree with the Benedictine distinction. The first is the silence lit by lamps. It is likely to be a temporary silence, since servants will have to return to tend the lamps. The second is the silence which ensues when the lights, left untended, go out. This 'silence noir' is a more encompassing silence. It represents a cessation of pain or importunity, and bears a close relation to the 'dark whole again. Blest dark' of *A Piece of Monologue* (*CSPL*, p. 268), or to that dark silence desired by W1 in *Play*: 'Silence and darkness were all I craved. Well, I get a certain amount of both. They being one. Perhaps it is more wickedness to pray for more' (*CSPL*, p. 156).

In that reference to 'praying for more', it is clear that a durable silence remains elusive, just as it does for the narrator in *L'Innommable*: 'Il en est du noir comme du gris, le noir ne prouve rien non plus, quant à la valeur du silence que pour ainsi dire il épaissit. Car ils peuvent revenir, longtemps après l'extinction des feux [...]. Alors tout sera à recommencer' (*LI*, p. 131).

Strung between silences, grey and black, the narrator thinks back with nostalgia to the silences of old: 'Il faut écouter, guetter les murmures des silences d'autrefois' (*LI*, p. 132). This deep, secure blanket of silence is perhaps similar to that recalled in *Krapp's Last Tape*: 'Past midnight. Never knew such silence. The earth might be uninhabited' (*CSPL*, p. 61). This silence is, however, another of the 'silences d'autrefois'. No longer attainable in such intensity, it belongs to the voice of the past, and when the tape reaches the second mention of it, Krapp switches it off, broods, and fidgets. Nevertheless, fuelled with the memories of olden silences, the Beckettian narrator can undertake the uncertain project of continuance. There may even come a time when the antique silence will return. In the meantime, as expressed in *L'Innommable*, the best tactic – the hope of salvation – is to remain still and attentive within solitary confinement: 'Et cela est un bonheur pour lui, qu'il ne puisse pas bouger, même s'il en souffre, car ce serait signer son arrêt de vie, que de bouger de là où il est, à la recherche d'un peu de calme, d'un peu de silence de naguère' (*LI*, p. 119). Perhaps, in this attitude of expectancy, the darkness will after all turn out to be azure, as envisaged towards the close of the text: 'une vie, comment me faire voir ça, ici, dans le noir, j'appelle ça le noir, c'est peut-être de l'azur' (*LI*, p. 202).

STARS

In a polyvalent sense, Beckett's people cannot 'see the light'. All they can do is trudge, as the opening words of the short text 'Neither' indicate, 'to and fro in shadow from inner to outershadow' (*ASWT*, p. 108), and 'on unknowing and no end in sight', as in *Stirrings Still* (*ASWT*, p. 125). Any light they can see ahead of them is merely a 'dim light source unknown', as in *Worstward Ho* (*NO*, p. 103).

Thus, although Dante's *Hell* and *Purgatory* proved to be significant intertextual resources in the last chapter, Dante's *Paradise*, at the climax of which the Pilgrim is repeatedly bedazzled by the 'glorious living light' which surrounds him (*PAR* 30: 49), begins to draw Dante's enterprise into sharp divergence from that of Beckett. This is not to say that Beckett's writing refrains from advertence to the third canticle of Dante's poem.[18] Nevertheless, when bright light invades Beckett's stage or page, it tends to be the 'blaze of hellish light' to which Winnie is subjected (*HD*, p. 20), or the sourceless, meaningless glare – 'Hell this light from nothing no reason any moment' – which illuminates the planes of *All Strange Away* (*ASWT*, p. 43), forcing the irradiated occupant to experiment with putting a 'black bag over his head' (*ASWT*, p. 44).

Although there is an instinctive responsiveness to light in Beckett's writing, the source and quality of the light is often unknown or unknowable. Moreover, on those occasions when illumination is laid claim to within Beckett's work, the statement encounters a re-active irony. Hence, when Clov complains of his dying light, Hamm sneers at the very idea of such an interior illumination: 'Ta lumière qui – ! Qu'est-ce qu'il faut entendre! Eh bien, elle mourra tout aussi bien ici, ta lumière' (*FP*, p. 26). In *Krapp's Last Tape*, it is the elderly Krapp who curses at the younger Krapp's claim to have seen 'the vision at last' (*CSPL*, p. 60).

Indeed, such affirmations of 'vision' do not sit easily within Beckettian surroundings. In *Malone meurt*, the exclamation: 'Quelle lumière. Serait-ce un avant-goût du paradis?' (*MM*, p. 166) is im-mediately followed by a sensation which is more infernal than ce-lestial: 'Ma tête. Elle est en feu, pleine d'huile bouillante'. A further blurring of hell into heaven is to be found in *L'Innommable*, where the narrator hypothesises about his status: 'drôle d'enfer, non chauffé, non peuplé, c'est peut-être le paradis, c'est peut-être la lumière du paradis, et la solitude, et cette voix celle des bienheureux qui inter-cèdent, invisibles, pour les vivants, pour les morts' (*LI*, pp. 120–1). Paradise, then, may linger as a concept, but there are no signposts. Unlike the approach to Dante's Paradise, where the Pilgrim sees 'the sparks of living light' erupting like brilliant fireworks (*PAR* 30: 64), the most the Beckettian wayfarer can glimpse is the 'brume dormante radieuse. Où se fondre en paradis' of *Mal Vu Mal Dit* (*MVMD*, p. 34).

In such surroundings, where all extensions are occluded, the observer must conclude: 'Seule certitude la brume' (*MVMD*, p. 61). The certitude of haze does not stifle the questions which inhabit that haze. It is significant, moreover, that the longest word-string of Beckett's final text, 'What is the Word' – 'folly for to need to seem to glimpse afaint afar away over there what' (*ASWT*, p. 134) – appears in a text whose title and recurrent refrain is itself a question. That imperative, even if designated 'folly', finds a kind of parallel in *Le Dépeupleur*, in which the cylinder-dwellers, unable to see the light, need to act *as if* they could see the light. Hence, despite the existence of two schools of thought among the inhabitants concerning the whereabouts of the outlet towards 'le soleil et les autres étoiles' (*LD*, p. 17), they are unanimous about the need to move, when in moving mode, upwards.

This phrase from *Le Dépeupleur* clearly recalls the final line of Dante's *Paradise*, with its reference to 'the Love that moves the sun and the other stars' (*PAR* 33: 145). Indeed, all three canticles of Dante's poem famously conclude with the word 'stelle' [stars], and it is the ending of *Inferno* – 'we came out to see once more the stars' (*INF* 34: 139) – which is most closely echoed in the concluding phrase of *Textes pour rien IX*: 'passer à travers, et voir les belles choses que porte le ciel, et revoir les étoiles' (*NTPR*, p. 181).

Any references to the prospect of a radiance beyond are always, however, remote and deferred. In *Malone meurt*, Macmann is able to give thanks for 'cette pluie battante et de la promesse qu'il y voyait d'étoiles un peu plus tard, pour éclairer son chemin' (*MM*, p. 110). Yet that later hour is always suspended, for 'passé un certain délai il ne peut plus rien arriver, ni venir personne, ni y avoir autre chose que l'attente se sachant vaine' (*MM*, p. 111). Moreover, as Beckett jots down humorously in his 'Whoroscope' notebook (RUL MS 3000), there are 'no stars without stripes'. For Beckett's people, these stripes are not insignia, but lashes, physical and psychological. While they are raining down, the stars will always, as for Macmann, be relegated to 'un peu plus tard'.

CONCLUSION

The previous chapter focussed upon pain, cruelty, and crucifixion in Beckett's writing, and this chapter is in no way intended to undermine or counteract the bleakness of that vision. Whereas that chapter analysed deep and intractable challenges to the equilibrium of the Beckettian individual, this chapter has proposed some modes or stances which on the whole seem to offer resting-places to those labouring individuals. As suggested, those temporary or mobile homes afforded by solitude, stillness, and silence are not exclusive to Beckett. They have a rich and varied history within a wide range of spiritual and mystical traditions. Nevertheless, a love of solitude, stillness, and silence has no necessary connection with a religious impulse, since these preferences are found in people of all faiths and none.

What can safely be observed is that, in cleaving to these stilled and silent modes of being, Beckett's people often seem to be travelling along routes similar to those upon which the neophyte or spiritual seeker would embark. Yet, even here, differentiation is needed. These values are, for example, heavily extolled by Thomas à Kempis, notably in the chapter entitled 'On the Love of Solitude and Silence' (Book 1, Chapter 20), of *The Imitation of Christ*. In amongst many other statements of similar kind, the author maintains here that 'it is praiseworthy for a religious man to be seen rarely abroad, to escape from being seen, even to have no wish to see men' (*IMI*, p. 48). Yet Beckett selects from this chapter phrases which seem to him (as discussed in Chapter 2) to represent what he calls 'an abject and self-referring quietism'.[19] It is not, he informs MacGreevy, the kind of programme to which he could consent as a structure for his life.

The Imitation of Christ is a work which constantly reiterates the message that the pleasures and triumphs of earthly life are transient, and must be set aside by the devout person in favour of preparing the soul, by repentance and humility, for heaven. A prayer in Book 3, Chapter 15, is typical in this regard: 'Grant me to die to all things in the world, and for your sake to love, to be despised, and to be unknown in this world' (*IMI*, p. 113). Not much attention is devoted in the volume to presenting a multi-facetted image of the glories of heaven. No doubt this is because the author assumes pre-existent familiarity or faith in this happy outcome, and considers that a greater emphasis upon punishment in hell will be more salutary for the thoughtless reader. Whatever the case may be, the basic assumption upon which *The Imitation of Christ* is predicated is that heaven is a sure and worthy goal of all people's desires and efforts. This is a prospect which Beckett's people can never share.

What does unite Beckett and à Kempis is a keen sense of transience. However, whereas à Kempis deals with this by extolling a claustrated individualism, the better to avoid the temptations which might fill the diminishing years with unprofitable pleasures, Beckett allows some shreds of companionship to lighten the hours of vigil. This takes the form, in *Malone meurt*, of a presence, never glimpsed, but discerned as welcoming and upbuilding: 'celui qui m'attendait toujours, qui avait besoin de moi et dont moi j'avais besoin, qui me prenait dans ses bras et me disait de ne plus partir, qui me cédait la place et veillait sur moi, qui souffrait chaque fois que je le quittais, que j'ai beaucoup fait souffrir et peu contenté, que je n'ai jamais vu' (*MM*, pp. 34–5). This portrait bears some resemblance to the parable of the prodigal son (Luke 15: 11–32), in which the son who has squandered all his money returns to the forgiving arms of his father. The crucial difference, however, is that the waiting figure in *Malone meurt* remains unseen. Moreover, the past tense in which he is described makes unclear his present availability.

This doubling effect – a detailed projection of a familiar companion, but bearing the aura of one departed – enables comparisons to be made once again between Beckett and Dante. Just as the Pilgrim addresses Virgil as 'my sweet father' (see for instance, *Purgatory*, Canto 4: 44), this figure of the spirit-guide is often enfolded in the Beckettian perspective into the figure of a trusted father. Thus, in *Company*, the voice recalls 'the giant tot in miles. In leagues. How often round the earth already. Halted too at your elbow during these computations your father's shade. In his old tramping rags. Finally on side by side from nought anew' (*NO*, pp. 11–12). A comparable visualisation is found in *Worstward Ho*: 'In the dim void bit by bit an old man and child. [. . .] Backs turned. Both bowed. Joined by held holding hands. Plod on as one. One shade. Another shade' (*NO*, p. 105).

This proximate shade is always, however, on the borders between presence and absence. The same voice which recalls the father in *Company* later records: 'Your father's shade is not with you any more. It fell out long ago' (*NO*, p. 30). Similarly, Virgil's shade, reinforcive while present, cannot survive the Pilgrim's onward progress. Virgil shrinks imperceptibly away at the gates of Paradise, leaving Dante, united with Beatrice, to observe: 'We found ourselves / without Virgil, sweet father, Virgil to whom / for my salvation I gave up my soul' (*PUR* 30: 49–51).

This ministering figure whose presence is apprehended and yet tenuous, or still awaited, is also exemplified in Beckett's drama. In *Ghost Trio*, the male figure is seen in an attitude of expectation – 'He will now think he hears her' (*CSPL*, p. 250) and in . . . *but the clouds* . . . the man's voice speaks of longing for the apparition of the woman: 'I began to beg, of her, to appear, to me' (*CSPL*, p. 260). In *Nacht und Träume*, the visitor operates at a still more remote level, only visible to the dreamer's dreamt self. Nevertheless, the gestures undertaken by the dreamt hands are not disembodied ones. They impact on the dreamer in a notably tender way, resting on his hand, his head, wiping his brow Veronica-fashion, and giving him to drink. That this rapprochement between separated beings should operate in a context suffused with solitude, stillness, and silence (but for the sound of Schubert's song *Nacht und Träume*) seems to indicate that if any faint light is to be discerned through Beckett's opaque skylights, then it must be in these conditions or not at all.

It is not surprising that several studies have in recent years drawn attention to the correspondences between Beckett's writing and the mystical tradition, of both east and west. This is justifiably the case, given Beckett's privileging of solitude and silence, and the deeply spiritual tenor of passages such as the following, from *Company*: 'What visions in the dark of light! Who exclaims thus? Who asks who exclaims, What visions in the shadeless dark of light and shade! Yet another still?' (*NO*, p. 49). Further, as critics have usefully explored, the major role of negative theology within the long tradition of mysticism has proved to be a resource richly interactive with Beckett's discourse of negativity, cancellation, and qualification. As the narrator in *Watt* points out: 'The only way one can speak of nothing is to speak of it as though it were something, just as the only way one can speak of God is to speak of him as though he were a man' (*W*, p. 74).

Within this *via negativa*, or apophatic tradition, God is considered to be unknowable. Only by 'unknowing' – disqualification of the known – can God be approached. Interestingly, the God-epithets commonly affirmed by denial in established devotion and hymnody – immortal, invisible, inaccessible, infinite, ineffable, unnamable – are those having particular resonance in Beckett's writing.

Meister Eckhart (1260–1329) – whose mystical writing Beckett discussed with Charles Juliet in 1977 (Juliet, p. 51) freely embraces the apophatic tradition: 'Mark this. No fire no light, no earth no life, no air no love, no water no place. Ergo, God is not light nor life nor love nor nature nor spirit nor semblance nor anything we can put into words'.[20] The searcher grasps for what lies beyond, but also lingers among what lies between, suspended between differentiated points such as light and darkness, knowledge and ignorance. 'God', continues Eckhart, 'is not black nor white, nor large nor small' (*Tractates*, p. 363). It is this intermediate, interstitial locus which so characterises the Beckettian consciousness within its 'grisaille' environs.

Beckett clearly immersed himself in a great deal of mystical writing when he was a young man (although informing Charles Juliet: 'Je ne les ai pas approfondis' [I didn't carry it much further] [Juliet, p. 38]). Moreover, in his 1931/2 'Dream' notebook (already referred to earlier in connection with notes made there on St Augustine, à Kempis, St John of the Cross, Julian of Norwich, etc.), Beckett includes notes on Eckhart and on Pseudo-Dionysius (also known as Denys or Dionysius the Areopagite), the fifth-century mystic. With reference to the latter, he writes that Pseudo-Dionysius 'prefers circular (meditative) movement of the mind to oblique (rational) and direct (affective/sensuous)'. This observation is duly incorporated into a descriptive passage of *Dream of Fair to Middling Women*: 'That was the circular movement of the mind flowering up and up through darkness to an apex, dear to Dionysius the Areopagite' (*DFMW*, p. 17). Indeed, Dionysius opens his best-known essay, *The Mystical Theology*, with just such aspirations, couched in the apophatic style in which his writing is steeped: 'Lead us up beyond unknowing and light, up to the farthest, highest peak of mystic scripture, [...] in the brilliant darkness of a hidden silence'.[21]

Just above this reference to Pseudo-Dionysius in the 'Dream' notebook, Beckett writes: 'the All transcending hiddenness of the all-transcending superessential, superexisting super-Deity'. These find almost identical shape, in *Dream of Fair to Middling Women*, in a reference to Belacqua's 'tilted brain' being 'flooded no doubt with radiance come streaming down from the all-transcending hiddenness of the all-transcending super-essentially superexisting super-Deity' (*DFMW*, p. 17). The passage appears to be based upon a description of the Trinity in Pseudo-Dionysius's *The Divine Names*: 'The indivisible Trinity holds within a shared undifferentiated unity its supra-essential subsistence, its supra-divine divinity, its supra-excellent goodness, its supremely individual identity beyond all that is'.[22] Clearly, this cascade of prefixion and qualification amused or appealed to Beckett.

Beckett's writing, and particularly his prose work, does often demonstrate an abiding attachment to an attitude of contemplative, will-less receptivity which does not privilege the noetic, but seems to share to a considerable degree the characteristics of the Dionysian embrace of unknowing. Pseudo-Dionysius writes in *The Celestial Hierarchy* of 'the simple ray of Light itself' to which 'we must lift up the immaterial and steady eyes of our minds'.[23] The analogy comes to mind when reading Beckett's drafts of the unpublished texts entitled 'Long Observation of the Ray'.[24] As the title suggests, this ray functions as object of sustained observation. Yet it also draws attention to its status as emanation from a source as yet unspecified. The beholder notes the faint but steady quality of the ray, reminiscent of the Dionysian ray which 'remains inherently stable and [...] is forever one with its own unchanging identity' (*The Celestial Hierarchy*, p. 146). As the eye inspects the ray in the Beckettian text, the mind ponders in one draft 'whether faintness due to that of inexhaustible source. Or to nursing of some finite blaze'. The question of causality is here broached but remains unanswered, just as, in *The Divine Names*, Pseudo-Dionysius says of 'the ray which transcends being' that 'it is of a kind that neither intelligence nor speech can lay hold of it nor can it at all be contemplated since it surpasses everything and is wholly beyond our capacity to know it' (*The Divine Names*, p. 53).

The linkage between Beckett's writing and such writers as Eckhart and Pseudo-Dionysius is clearly a fruitful one. Moreover, it was in these same terms – that of the apophatic tradition – that Charles Juliet reflected back to Beckett, in a conversation, the latter's work: 'J'apprécie que cette oeuvre n'affirme pas, mais procède par la négation, puis la négation de la négation, faisant fuser dans l'entre-deux ce qu'il importe de saisir, mais que jamais les mots ne réussissent à capter' [I appreciate that this writing does not affirm, but proceeds by negation, then by negation of the negation, fusing in the middle what needs to be understood, but which words can never capture] (Juliet, p. 33).

Nevertheless, four years later, Beckett's own comment to Juliet was rather different: 'La négation n'est pas possible. Pas plus que l'affirmation. [...] Il faut se tenir là où il n'y a ni pronom, ni solution, ni réaction, ni prise de position possibles' [Negation isn't possible. Any more than affirmation. [...] It's necessary to stand in a place where there is no possible pronoun, solution, reaction, or stance] (Juliet, p. 49). At the end of this interview, Juliet questioned Beckett about St John of the Cross, Eckhart, and Ruysbroeck. Beckett replied that what he admired in those writers was 'leur illogisme brûlant... cette flamme... cette flamme... qui consume cette saloperie de logique' [their burning illogicality... that flame ... that flame... which burns up the trash of logic] (Juliet, p. 51). This reply is in perfect harmony with a response he had given two years earlier, in which he asserted that, in the case of some mystical writing, he could identify with 'une même façon de subir l'inintelligible' [the same method of submitting to the unintelligible] (Juliet, p. 38).

The fact that this affinity should exist with certain mystics of the *via negativa* tradition is significant. Nevertheless, a caveat should be borne in mind. Just as, in the foregoing quotation from the conversation with Charles Juliet, Beckett stated his resistance, within his writing, to any kind of 'réaction', or 'prise de position', the danger is that his work may be forced into a reactive dialogue with mysticism, such that it is assessed insofar as it is perceived as using, adopting, or rejecting certain aspects of mystical belief or tradition.

It is in my view useful, if mysticism is to be applied as an intertextual resource, to extend the spectrum further, in the direction of non-belief. In this respect, the writing of Georges Bataille provides a fruitful comparator. Much of Bataille's writing is as unclassifiable as Beckett's. In Paris, Bataille and Beckett were both part of the coterie of friends which included Georges Duthuit.[25] They are very different writers, and yet both are groping towards some sort of accommodation to the religious upbringing they received, and to the religious practice they once observed but subsequently abandoned.

In a text – *L'Expérience intérieure* – which draws examples not only from mystical writers (Pseudo-Dionysius, Eckhart, St John of the Cross, St Teresa of Avila, St Angela of Foligno), but also from philosophers (Nietzsche, Kierkegaard, Descartes, Hegel), and from poets and novelists (Proust, Blake, Rimbaud), Bataille explores the mystical experience on the basis of his own agnosticism: 'Je ne sais si Dieu est ou n'est pas' [I don't know whether God exists or not].[26]

Bataille shares with Beckett a preoccupation with the passage from womb to tomb: 'Je sais que je descends vivant pas même dans une tombe, dans la fosse commune, sans grandeur ni intelligence, vraiment nu (comme est nue la fille de joie). [...] Mieux vaut me laisser voir qu'on ne peut rien faire (sauf, peut-être, involontairement, de m'accabler), qu'on s'attend à mon silence' [I know that I am going down alive not even into a tomb, but into the common pit, with no splendour or intelligence, truly naked (as a prostitute is naked). [...] It is best to allow myself to understand that nothing can be done about it (except, perhaps, involuntarily, to be overwhelmed by it), and that I am expected to remain silent] (Bataille, p. 81).

Nevertheless, despite or because of this perception, Bataille also shares with Beckett the ability to be still, to void the mind, and to contemplate the elements of his inner and outer landscape. (In 1951, Bataille published an article on Beckett entitled 'Le Silence de Molloy'. The novel clearly made a deep impression on him, a kind of fascinated horror. He sees in it 'la réalité à l'état pur: c'est la plus pauvre et la plus immanquable réalité' [reality in its pure state: it's the poorest and most unmissable reality][27]). When vision is intensified, hierarchies between objects begin to fade, and the smallest object or effect of light can fill the mind. Charles Juliet reports that,

on one occasion, Beckett said to him, after a long pause: 'La chute
d'une feuille et la chute de Satan, c'est la même chose' [The fall of a
leaf and the fall of Satan are the same thing] (Juliet, p. 48).
Similarly, Bataille describes in *L'Expérience intérieure* how significant can be
the fall of a pin: 'Le vrai silence a lieu dans l'absence des mots;
qu'une épingle tombe alors: comme d'un coup de marteau, je sur-
saute... Dans ce silence fait du dedans, ce n'est plus un organe,
c'est la sensibilité entière, c'est le coeur, qui s'est dilaté' [Real silence
takes place in the absence of words; if a pin drops then, it's like the
thud of a hammer, and I jump... In that interior silence, it's no
longer an organ, it's the whole sensitivity, the heart, which has
opened up] (Bataille, p. 30).

In this voided but never vacuous consciousness, Bataille cites
St John of the Cross as the person who 'tombant dans la nuit du
non-savoir, touche à l'extrême du possible' [falling into the night of
unknowing, goes to the extreme of what is possible] (Bataille, p. 24).
Here again, Beckett's repeated relinquishment of 'knowledge' is
comparable. His famous remark to Israel Shenker in 1956 concerning 'the experience of a non-knower, a non-can-er'[28] was reiterated
in graphic form to Charles Juliet in 1968: 'Je suis comme une taupe
dans une taupinière' [I'm like a mole in a molehill] (Juliet, p. 19).
The image of the near-blind mole, burrowing in interior darkness, is
indeed allied to John of the Cross's metaphor of the dark night, and
to its echo in Bataille: 'A contempler la nuit, je ne vois rien, n'aime
rien. Je demeure immobile, figé, absorbé en ELLE' [Contemplating
the night, I see nothing, love nothing. I remain still, motionless,
absorbed in HER (= the night)] (Bataille, p. 145).

Despite his sustained exploration within mysticism – an exploration which extends far beyond this pivotal text – Bataille rejects the label of 'mysticism'. For him, mysticism would imply a
confessional adherence which is not, for him, on the agenda. Instead, he prefers the term 'expérience intérieure', used to denote
'une expérience nue, libre d'attaches, même d'origine, à quelque
confession que ce soit. C'est pourquoi je n'aime pas le mot *mystique*'
[a naked experience, free of attachments, even by origin, to whatever confession it might be. That's why I don't like the word *mystic*]
(Bataille, p. 15). Within this experience, Bataille, like Beckett, gravitates towards the *via negativa*: 'Si je disais décidément: "j'ai vu
Dieu", ce que je vois changerait. Au lieu de l'inconnu inconcevable
– devant moi libre sauvagement, me laissant devant lui sauvage et
libre – il y aurait un objet mort et la chose du théologien' [If I said

decisively: "I have seen God", what I see would change. Instead of the inconceivable unknown – wild and free before me, leaving me wild and free before it – there would be a dead object, the thing of the theologian] (Bataille, p. 16).

More recently, the novelist and writer Jean Claude Bologne, an atheist, has presented a similar perspective, although in his case not demurring from the term 'mysticisme athée' [atheistic mysticism]. He too makes the distinction between theologians and mystics, associating the former with water, raining down to quench the fire of the latter. Having discovered 'l'incroyable richesse des mystiques chrétiens' [the unbelievable richness of the Christian mystics],[29] Bologne concluded that, insofar as mystics suspend all knowledge of God in the depths of their silence, he could identify his own experience with theirs: 'Le mystique [...] n'est plus qu'un grand silence où ne résonne pas même le nom de Dieu. C'est dans ce silence que moi, l'athée, je suis allé le rejoindre' [The mystic is nothing more than a great silence where not even the name of God resounds. It's in that silence that I, the atheist, met with the mystic] (Bologne, p. 13).

For Beckett, it was writing which led him towards silence, as he remarked to Charles Juliet: 'L'écriture m'a conduit au silence' [Writing has led me to silence] (Juliet, p. 18). Within that silence or nothingness, writing persists, even though 'rien n'est dicible' [nothing is sayable] (Juliet, p. 48). Bologne, too, discerns that same *tabula rasa* which is the only possible ground for creativity, and which forms a parallel with Beckett's renunciation of any 'prise de position': 'Le vide, le néant, est le stade ultime, où l'esprit s'est libéré de toute idée, de tout désir, de tout point de référence' [Void, nothingness, is the ultimate stage, when the spirit has freed itself from every idea, every desire, every point of reference] (Bologne, p. 91).

Thus, the deepest point of affiliation with mysticism, in Bologne's analysis, is in a shared, willed refusal to install presence where there is absence: 'Refuser de matérialiser l'impalpable, le vide, le grand néant, mais l'assumer comme tel, et y trouver l'appui de notre propre néant. Et précisément, telle a été la démarche des mystiques, croyants ou athées, orientaux ou occidentaux' [To refuse to give substance to what is impalpable, void, the great nothingness, but rather to assume it as such, and to find in it support for our own nothingness. And that has been precisely the undertaking of the mystics, believers or atheists, of east or west] (Bologne, p. 53).

Beckett voiced in *Proust* a similar distaste for all projects to make material what is immaterial, giving the example of music, which exists 'outside the universe, apprehended not in Space but in Time only [...]. This essential quality of music is distorted by the listener who, being an impure subject, insists on giving a figure to that which is ideal and invisible, on incarnating the Idea in what he conceives to be an appropriate paradigm' (*P*, p. 92). Citing Proust, Beckett reminds the reader that 'in one passage he describes the recurrent mystical experience as "a purely musical impression, non-extensive, entirely original, irreducible to any other order of impression, ... sine materia" ' (*P*, p. 93).

It is here that Bologne's analysis approaches Beckett's endeavour most closely, for he also uses the example of music within the context of mysticism. Bologne explains that he cannot respond fully to music if he concentrates merely on the notes and rhythms of the melody, but only if he banishes from his perception all internal images. Thus, he maintains, a profound difference exists between the professor of harmony on the one hand, and the exposed and engaged listener on the other. The first is the theologian, espousing the *via positiva*; the second is the mystic, wedded to the *via negativa*: 'Cette comparaison explique qu'on retrouve les mêmes thèmes chez les mystiques chrétiens médiévaux et chez des écrivains modernes qui, tout en faisant profession d'athéisme, décrivent des expériences extrêmement proches' [This comparison explains why one finds the same themes in medieval Christian mystics and in some modern authors who, even while professing atheism, describe experiences which are extremely similar] (Bologne, p. 86).

Samuel Beckett does not, in those terms, 'profess atheism' in quite such a definitive way. Nevertheless, Bologne's analysis, grounding itself in the musical referent, seems to embrace Beckett's project in a manner which does not deform or manipulate it. It leaves Beckett space to interact with mysticism, while respecting his resistance to any 'prise de position'. It is also notable that a play such as *Nacht und Träume*, in which the only sound is that of Schubert's music, is one of the most mystical (in Bologne's definition) of Beckett's plays.

Yet music, by the beauty of its immateriality, cannot help but expose, by contrast, the oppressive materiality of the ailing or paining human body. In 1933, Bataille went alone to Italy, to recuperate from illness. At Stresa, he managed to walk towards the floating bridge at Lake Maggiore, where boats were moored, and was suddenly transfixed by the sound of choral music: 'Les voix s'élevaient comme par vagues successives et variées, atteignant lentement l'intensité, la précipitation, la richesse folles, mais ce qui tenait du miracle était le rejaillissement comme d'un cristal qui se brise, auquel elles parvenaient à l'instant même où tout semblait à bout' [The voices rose as if in varying waves, succeeding one another, slowly building up towards a mad intensity, speed, and richness, but what seemed miraculous was the spurt of resurgence, like shivering crystal, which they achieved just when all seemed over] (Bataille, p. 90).

Bataille later realised that the sounds were from a sung Mass, broadcast over loudspeakers, but so beautiful and celebratory was the sound that he was momentarily immune to alienation from the dogma which predicated the music. When he returned to Paris, all euphoria dissipated: 'Je rencontrai l'horreur' [I encountered horror] (Bataille, p. 91). The triumphant sound heard at Stresa was now set in its fuller context – not just of eucharist (thanksgiving), but of sacrifice and death: 'Le triomphe saisi sur le pont de bateaux de Stresa n'atteint le sens plein qu'au moment de l'expiation (moment d'angoisse, de sueur, de doute)' [The triumph apprehended on the floating bridge at Stresa only assumes its full meaning at the moment of expiation (moment of anguish, sweat, doubt)] (Bataille, p. 92).

Writing only a few years earlier than Bataille's experience at Stresa, Beckett also contrasts the permanent beauty of music with the ugly finitude of human mortality, at the close of *Proust*, when he writes of 'the invariable world and beauty of Vinteuil, expressed timidly, as a prayer, in the Sonata, imploringly, as an inspiration, in the Septuor, the "invisible reality" that damns the life of the body on earth as a pensum and reveals the meaning of the word: "defunctus"' (*P*, p. 93). Life on earth is an imposition. Once discharged, life is defunct, finished. And the music plays on.

Notes

INTRODUCTION

1. Letter 73 (10 March 1935), TCD MS 10402.
2. Tom Driver, Interview with Beckett, in *Samuel Beckett: The Critical Heritage*, ed. Lawrence Graver and Raymond Federman (London: Routledge and Kegan Paul, 1979), pp. 217–23 [p. 220]. (Originally appeared in *Columbia University Forum* [Summer 1961], pp. 21–5).
3. James Knowlson, *Damned to Fame: The Life of Samuel Beckett* (London: Bloomsbury, 1996), p. 279.
4. Charles Juliet, *Rencontre avec Samuel Beckett* (Paris: Editions Fata Morgana, 1986), p. 50.
5. Jean Claude Bologne, *Le Mysticisme athée* (Monaco: Editions du Rocher, 1995), pp. 127–8.
6. Shira Wolosky, *Language Mysticism: The Negative Way of Language in Eliot, Beckett, and Celan* (Stanford: Stanford University Press, 1995), p. 2.
7. Simone Weil, *La Pesanteur et la grâce* (Paris: Plon, 1988), p. 50.

1 WRITING ON WRITING

1. Morton Feldman's opera, for soprano and orchestra, received its première in Rome in 1977.
2. Feldman's interview with Everett Frost appears in *Samuel Beckett and Music*, ed. Mary Bryden (Oxford: Clarendon Press, 1998.).
3. Matthew Arnold, *Essays in Criticism* (First Series) (London: Macmillan, 1910), p. 1.
4. See Anthony Cronin, *Samuel Beckett: The Last Modernist* (London: HarperCollins, 1996), pp. 202–3.
5. Giambattista Vico, *The New Science* (revised trans. of 3rd edn.), trans. Thomas Goddard Bergin and Max Harold Fisch (Ithaca, NY: Cornell University Press, 1968), pp. 313–4.
6. Samuel Beckett, 'Humanistic Quietism', in *Disjecta*, ed. Ruby Cohn (London: John Calder, 1983), pp. 68–9 [p. 68]
7. Simone Weil, *Attente de Dieu* (Paris: Fayard, 1966), p. 196.
8. This notebook from the 1930s, with the word 'Whoroscope' written across the front cover, is kept in Reading University Library at MS 3000. Its pages are unnumbered.
9. Samuel Johnson, *The History of Rasselas* (London: J. M. Dent, 1926), p. 32.
10. Letter 80 (8 September 1935), TCD MS 10402.
11. Samuel Beckett, 'Intercessions by Denis Devlin', in *Disjecta*, ed. Ruby Cohn (London: John Calder, 1983), pp. 91–4 [p. 92].

12. This passage corresponds to fragment No. 308 in Blaise Pascal, *Pensées*, ed. Louis Lafuma (Paris: Editions du Seuil, 1962), pp. 155–6.
13. Samuel Beckett, 'Recent Irish Poetry', in *Disjecta*, ed. Ruby Cohn (London: John Calder, 1983), pp. 70–6 [p. 71].
14. Samuel Beckett, '*Poems*. By Rainer Maria Rilke', in *Disjecta*, ed. Ruby Cohn (London: John Calder, 1983), pp. 66–7 [p. 66].
15. Paul Valéry, Preface to *Monsieur Teste* (Paris: Gallimard, 1946), p. 8.
16. Sir Philip Sidney, *Astrophel and Stella*, ed. Mona Wilson (London: Nonesuch Press, 1931), p. 1.
17. Carducci is referred to pejoratively in *More Pricks Than Kicks* as belonging to the group of 'old hens trying to cluck like Pindar' (London: Calder and Boyars, 1970), p. 16.
18. Giosuè Carducci, 'Satan', in *Carducci: A Selection of his Poems*, ed. and trans. G.L. Bickersteth (London: Longmans, Green & Co., 1913), p. 85.
19. Thomas MacGreevy, *Poems* (London: Heinemann, 1934), p. 35.
20. Quoted by Beckett from Devlin's poem 'Victory of Samothrace', rather than from the 'Intercessions' collection. See Denis Devlin, *Collected Poems*, ed. Brian Coffey (Dublin: Dolmen Press, 1964), p. 75.
21. Samuel Beckett, *Dante... Bruno.Vico.. Joyce*, in *Disjecta*, ed. Ruby Cohn (London: John Calder, 1983), pp. 19–33 [p. 24].
22. When Charles Juliet mentioned St Bernard to Beckett in a conversation in 1975, Beckett laughingly revealed that he had a grievance against the saint (presumably Bernard's association with the Second Crusade). See Charles Juliet, *Rencontre avec Samuel Beckett* (Paris: Fata Morgana, 1986), pp. 38–9.
23. Samuel Beckett, 'Ex Cathezra', in *Disjecta*, ed. Ruby Cohn (London: John Calder, 1983), pp. 77–9 [p. 79].
24. Samuel Beckett, 'La Peinture des van Velde ou le Monde et le Pantalon', in *Disjecta*, ed. Ruby Cohn (London: John Calder, 1983), pp. 118–32 [p. 132].
25. Tom Driver, 'Interview with Beckett', in *Samuel Beckett: The Critical Heritage*, ed. Lawrence Graver and Raymond Federman (London: Routledge & Kegan Paul, 1979), pp. 217–23 [p. 220].
26. Letter 23 (20 December 1931), TCD MS 10402.
27. Samuel Beckett, 'Peintres de l'empêchement', in *Disjecta*, ed. Ruby Cohn (London: John Calder, 1983), pp. 133–7 [pp. 135–6].
28. Samuel Beckett, 'Bram van Velde', in *Disjecta*, ed. Ruby Cohn (London: John Calder, 1983), p. 151.
29. For the first extended engagement with Samuel Beckett's interest in art, see James Knowlson, *Damned to Fame: The Life of Samuel Beckett* (London: Bloomsbury, 1996). In diaries he kept while travelling in Germany during the 1930s, Beckett mentions a host of paintings which he had studied closely, including many on religious themes.
30. Compare the faded green beret worn by the Smeraldina as recalled by Belacqua in *Dream of Fair to Middling Women* (London: John Calder, 1993), p. 4.
31. Samuel Beckett, 'Assumption', *transition*, No. 16/17 (June 1929), pp. 268–71 [p. 270].

Notes 191

32. Lawrence Durrell, 'Vega', in *Collected Poems 1931–1974*, ed. James A. Brigham (London: Faber, 1980), p. 322.
33. The line 'one with the birdless, cloudless, colourless skies' appears in one of the poems which appear in Beckett's novel *Dream of Fair to Middling Women* (London: John Calder, 1993), p. 70.
34. Benedict de Spinoza, *Tractatus Theologico-Politicus*, in *The Chief Works of Benedict de Spinoza*, Vol. 1 (revised edn.), trans. R.H.M. Elwes (London: George Bell and Sons, 1891), p. 83.
35. Benedetto Croce, *The Philosophy of Giambattista Vico*, trans. R.G. Collingwood (London: Howard Latimer, 1913), p. 78.
36. Paul Valéry, *Le Solitaire*, in *Oeuvres de Paul Valéry*, Vol. 2, ed. Jean Hytier (Paris: Gallimard, 1960), p. 394.
37. Samuel Beckett, 'Les Deux Besoins', in *Disjecta*, ed. Ruby Cohn (London: John Calder, 1983), pp. 55–7 [p. 55].
38. Letter 34 (18 October 1932), TCD MS 10402.
39. Thomas MacGreevy, 'The Catholic Element in *Work in Progress*', in *Our Exagmination Round his Factification for Incamination of Work in Progress* (Paris: Shakespeare and Co., 1929), pp. 119–27 [p. 124].
40. See MacGreevy's 'Crón Tráth na nDéithe' (parts 4 & 5), in *Poems by Thomas MacGreevy* (London: Heinemann, 1934), pp. 24–6.
41. Letter 1 (1928), TCD MS 10402.
42. Patrick Bowles, 'How to Fail. Notes on Talks with Samuel Beckett', *PN Review*, 96, Vol. 20, No. 4 (March-April 1994), pp. 24–38 [p. 26].
43. Letter 73 (10 March 1935), TCD MS 10402.
44. Samuel Beckett, 'MacGreevy on Yeats', in *Disjecta*, ed. Ruby Cohn (London: John Calder, 1983), pp. 95–7 [p. 97].
45. *Leonardo da Vinci's Note-Books*, trans. and ed. Edward McCurdy (London: Duckworth, 1910), p. 161.
46. Samuel Beckett, 'Homage to Jack B. Yeats', in *Disjecta*, ed. Ruby Cohn (London: John Calder, 1983), p. 149.
47. Samuel Beckett, 'For Avigdor Arikha', in *Disjecta*, ed. Ruby Cohn (London: John Calder, 1983), p. 152.

2 THE EARLY FICTION

1. Letter 73 (10 March 1935), TCD MS 10402.
2. The Latin edition used is *De Imitatione Christi* (Malines: H. Dessain, 1921).
3. The English translations are from *The Imitation of Christ*, ed. E.M. Blaiklock (London: Hodder & Stoughton, 1979).
4. Colin Duckworth, *Angels of Darkness: Dramatic Effect in Samuel Beckett with Special Reference to Eugène Ionesco* (New York: Barnes & Noble, 1972), p. 18.
5. Letter 67 (1 January 1935), TCD MS 10402.
6. The French original here runs: 'Passez l'éponge'. I am grateful to my colleague Walter Redfern for pointing out a pun in the French, for 'passer l'éponge' is a colloquial expression meaning 'to wipe out'.

'Passons l'éponge là-dessus' would mean 'Let's say no more about it'. This could not be more appropriate, given the fact that Mercier has just requested that the barman 'overlook this little incident' of Watt shouting out 'Bugger life!' (*MAC*, pp. 115, 114). Moreover, the sponge is one of the barman's tools of trade.

7. Letter 84 (18 October 1932), TCD MS 10402.
8. James Knowlson, *Damned to Fame: The Life of Samuel Beckett* (London: Bloomsbury, 1996), p. 36.
9. Samuel Beckett, 'Censorship in the Saorstat', in *Disjecta*, ed. Ruby Cohn (London: John Calder, 1983), pp. 84–8.
10. Blanchard Jerrold (ed.), *The Final Reliques of Father Prout* (London: Chatto and Windus, 1876), p. 38.
11. I am grateful to Fr John Buckley for this information.
12. I am grateful to James Knowlson for drawing my attention to the entry concerning Fr Prout in the first of Beckett's German notebooks, copies of which are held in Reading University Library.
13. 'Bander' in French, as Vladimir and Estragon famously quip, is a slang term for 'to have an erection'.
14. Letter 25, TCD MS 10402.
15. Letter 33 (8 October 1932), TCD MS 10402.
16. *Connemara Calling* (Dublin: Cliona Press, 1948), p. 18. I am grateful to Fr John Buckley for this information.
17. René Descartes, 'Réponses aux quatrièmes objections', in *Oeuvres philosophiques* (Tome 2), ed. F. Alquié (Paris: Garnier Frères, 1967), pp. 657–704 [p. 694].
18. I am indebted for much of the corroborative information in this section, concerning the trials of animals, to the scholarly account of E.P. Evans (1906), with which Beckett may even have been familiar. (It was republished in 1987, with a new foreword by Nicolas Humphreys: E.P. Evans, *The Criminal Prosecution and Capital Punishment of Animals* [London: Faber, 1987], and references given are to this edition).
19. I am grateful to my colleague Walter Redfern for information on Henno, probably the least known among the listing of theologians.
20. Beckett clearly has in mind here Gerard Honthorst's painting, *Girl Catching a Flea in her Nightdress*, which, in an early notebook, he includes among his notes upon R.H. Wilenski's *An Introduction to Dutch Art* (London: Faber and Faber, 1929). Beckett also notes that the painting hung in the Doria gallery in Rome. (I am grateful to James Knowlson for help in locating this reference.)
21. Letter 73 (10 March 1935), TCD MS 10402.
22. I am indebted for this information to Yoshiki Tajiri, who spotted this parallel while translating *Dream of Fair to Middling Women* into Japanese, and brought it to my attention.
23. See Julian of Norwich, *Revelations of Divine Love* (London: Methuen, 1912), p. 57.
24. I am grateful to Sr Teresa Benedicta of the Holy Spirit ODC for locating this reference for me.

25. I am grateful to Fr Iain Matthew ODC for locating this reference for me.
26. Richard Crashaw, 'The Flaming Heart upon the Book and Picture of the Seraphicall Saint Teresa', in *Steps to the Temple, Delights of the Muses, and Other Poems*, ed. A.R. Waller (Cambridge: Cambridge University Press, 1904), p. 276.
27. Vita Sackville-West, *The Eagle and the Dove* (London: Michael Joseph, 1943).
28. St John of the Cross, *The Complete Works*, Vol. 1, trans. and ed. E. Allison Peers (London: Burns, Oates & Washbourne, 1947), p. 36.

3 DRAMA AND LATER PROSE

1. 'Handbreadth' is incorrectly rendered as 'handbreath' in the edition cited.
2. I am grateful for these elucidations to Rev. Dr Michael Child.
3. R.E.R. Madelaine, 'Happy-Though-Married Hardy', *Notes and Queries*, Vol. 29, No. 4 (August 1982), pp. 348–9.
4. I have briefly discussed the possible Hunter/Johnson significance in 'Samuel Johnson and Beckett's *Happy Days*', *Notes and Queries*, Vol. 40, No. 4 (December 1993), pp. 503–4.
5. St Augustine, *The City of God* (Vol. 2), trans. J. Healey, (London: J.M. Dent, 1945), p. 344.
6. I am grateful to Br Jamie Glackin for this information.
7. These three notebooks were generously donated to the Beckett International Foundation at Reading University Library by Professor Ruby Cohn (MSS 3458–61).
8. Letter 57 (6 December 1933), TCD MS 10402.
9. Jeremy Taylor, *Holy Living and Dying* (London: Henry G. Bohn, 1850), p. 299.
10. 'Le pigeon' is a well-known pejorative term for the Holy Spirit in French anti-clerical circles, as expressed in the limerick:

> Y avait un jeune homme de Dijon
> qui avait si peu de religion
> qu'il dit 'Quant à moi,
> je déteste les trois,
> le père, et le fils, et le pigeon.

(I am grateful to Walter Redfern for supplying the above).
11. Simone Weil, *La Pesanteur et la grâce* (Paris: Plon, 1988), p. 35.
12. St Augustine, *To Simplician – on Various Questions*, Book 1, in *Augustine: Earlier Writings*, ed. John H.S. Burleigh (London: SCM Press, 1953), p. 403.
13. Simone Weil, *Attente de Dieu* (Paris: Fayard, 1966), p. 102.

4 RATS, CROSSES AND PAIN

1. James Knowlson, *Damned to Fame: The Life of Samuel Beckett* (London: Bloomsbury, 1996), pp. 83–5.
2. I am grateful to Walter Redfern for help with these references.
3. Letter 16 (3 February 1931), TCD MS 10402.
4. The edition cited here is *La Bible de Jérusalem*, 6th edition (Paris: Desclée de Brouwer, 1960), Matthew 27: 38.
5. RUL MS 1227/7/16/2. For a fuller discussion of this fragment, see Mary Bryden, 'Figures of Golgotha: Beckett's Pinioned People', in *The Ideal Core of the Onion: Reading Beckett Archives*, ed. John Pilling and Mary Bryden (Reading: BIF, 1992), pp. 45–62.
6. See David Lodge, 'Some Ping Understood', *Encounter*, Vol. 30, No. 2 (February 1968), pp. 85–9, for an analysis of *Bing's* English translation, *Ping*, including some consideration of crucifixion references.
7. Letter 126 (26 April 1937), TCD MS 10402. I am grateful to James Knowlson for help in deciphering this letter.
8. This sketch is reproduced, and discussed more fully, in my article 'Figures of Golgotha: Beckett's Pinioned People', in *The Ideal Core of the Onion: Reading Beckett Archives*, referred to above.
9. Samuel Beckett, 'Peintres de l'empêchement', in *Disjecta*, ed. Ruby Cohn (London: John Calder, 1983), pp. 133–7 [pp. 135–6].
10. Letter 210 (18 February 1958), TCD MS 10402.
11. The translation I have used throughout is that of Mark Musa, listed under 'Editions Used'.
12. 'One torment Beckett's characters have to suffer is precisely this ignorance of where they are and for how long they will remain there. Such uncertainties are unknown in the *Commedia*', Michael Robinson, 'From Purgatory to Inferno: Beckett and Dante revisited', *Journal of Beckett Studies*, No. 5 (1979), pp. 69–82 [pp. 70–1].
13. Samuel Beckett, 'Papini's Dante', in *Disjecta*, ed. Ruby Cohn (London: John Calder, 1983), pp. 80–1 [p. 81].
14. 'Ceux des Enfers aussi, admirable pluriel' is rendered in the English translation as 'in Hell too, admirable singulars'. 'Les Enfers' [the underworld] exists in English only in the singular.

5 SOLITUDE, STILLNESS, SILENCE AND STARS

1. Eric Griffiths, 'At Odds with Ends', *The Independent* (27 December 1989), p. 11.
2. St John of the Cross, *The Complete Works* (Vol. 1), trans. and ed. E. Allison Peers (London: Burns, Oates and Washbourne, 1947), p. 68.
3. E.M. Cioran, 'Encounters with Beckett', in L. Graver and R. Federman (eds), *Samuel Beckett: The Critical Heritage* (London: Routledge and Kegan Paul, 1979), pp. 334–9 [p. 338].
4. Letter 63 (8 September 1934), TCD MS 10402.

5. *Leonardo da Vinci's Note-Books*, trans. and ed. Edward McCurdy (London: Duckworth, 1910), p. 166.

6. Paul Valéry, Preface to *Monsieur Teste* (Paris: Gallimard, 1946), p. 10.

7. Anthony Cronin, *Samuel Beckett: The Last Modernist* (London: HarperCollins, 1996), p. 53.

8. Samuel Beckett, '*Poems*. By Rainer Maria Rilke', in *Disjecta*, ed. Ruby Cohn (London: John Calder, 1983), pp. 66–7 [p. 66].

9. Samuel Beckett, 'La Peinture des van Velde', in *Disjecta*, ed. Ruby Cohn (London: John Calder, 1983), pp. 118–32 [p. 132].

10. See the reference, at the close of Camus's short story, 'Jonas', to 'un mot qu'on pouvait déchiffrer, mais dont on ne savait s'il fallait y lire *solitaire* ou *solidaire*'. Albert Camus, *L'Exil et le royaume* (Paris: Gallimard, 1957), p. 176.

11. Samuel Johnson, *The History of Rasselas* (London: J.M. Dent, 1926), p. 73.

12. Paul Valéry, *Le Solitaire*, in *Oeuvres de Paul Valéry*, Vol. 2, ed. Jean Hytier (Paris: Gallimard, 1960), p. 383.

13. Samuel Johnson, Sermon 1, in *Sermons*, ed. Jean Hagstrum and James Gray (New Haven: Yale University Press, 1978), p. 3.

14. Samuel Johnson, *Prayers and Meditations*, in *The Works of Samuel Johnson*, Vol. 9 (Oxford: Talboys and Wheeler, 1825), p. 281.

15. Letter 130 (4 August 1937), TCD MS 10402.

16. Charles Juliet, *Rencontre avec Samuel Beckett* (Paris: Editions Fata Morgana, 1986), p. 47.

17. For a full discussion of Manichaean influences within the context of *Krapp's Last Tape*, see Beckett's production notebook for the 1969 Schiller-Theater production of the play, RUL MS 1396/4/16, and James Knowlson's discussion of these aspects in James Knowlson (ed.), *The Theatrical Notebooks of Samuel Beckett:* **Krapp's Last Tape** (London: Faber, 1992).

18. See John Fletcher's article, 'Beckett's Debt to Dante', *Nottingham French Studies*, Vol. 4, No. 1 (1965), pp. 41–52 for significant consideration of references to *Paradise* within Beckett's work up to *Comment C'est*.

19. Letter 73 to Thomas MacGreevy (10 March 1935), TCD MS 10402.

20. Meister Eckhart, *Tractates*, XI, 3, in F. Pfeiffer (ed.), *Meister Eckhart*, Vol. 1 (London: John M. Watkins, 1947), p. 363.

21. Pseudo-Dionysius, *The Mystical Theology*, in *Pseudo-Dionysius: The Complete Works*, trans. Colm Luibheid (London: SPCK, 1987), p. 135.

22. Pseudo-Dionysius, *The Divine Names*, in *Pseudo-Dionysius: The Complete Works*, trans. Colm Luibheid (London: SPCK, 1987), p. 61.

23. Pseudo-Dionysius, *The Celestial Hierarchy*, in *Pseudo-Dionysius: The Complete Works*, trans. Colm Luibheid (London: SPCK, 1987), pp. 146; 145.

24. RUL MS 2909 consists of a series of manuscript and typescript versions of this abandoned prose text.

25. See James Knowlson, *Damned to Fame: The Life of Samuel Beckett* (London: Bloomsbury, 1996), p. 370.

26. Georges Bataille, *L'Expérience intérieure* (Paris: Gallimard, 1954), p. 126.

27. Georges Bataille, 'Le Silence de Molloy', *Critique*, Vol. 7, No. 48 (May 1951), pp. 387–96 [p. 387].

28. Israel Shenker, 'An Interview with Beckett', in Lawrence Graver and Raymond Federman (eds), *Samuel Beckett: The Critical Heritage* (London: Routledge and Kegan Paul, 1979), pp. 146–9 [p. 148]. (First published in *The New York Times* [5 May 1956], Section II, 1, 3).

29. Jean Claude Bologne, *Le Mysticisme athée* (Monaco: Editions du Rocher, 1995), p. 28.

Select Bibliography

Note: The bibliography is a selection of books, articles, and essays containing significant reference to ideas of God or religion in the context of Beckett's writing. Frequently-quoted sources (Dante, St Augustine, etc.), denoted in the text by abbreviations, are detailed in the List of Abbreviations and Editions Cited. Other cited works are given full references in the footnotes to the chapter in which they appear.

* * *

Acheson, J., 'Madness and Mysticism in Beckett's *Not I*', *AUMLA*, No. 55 (special issue on Beckett), (May 1981), pp. 91–101.

Ackerley, C.J., 'Beckett's "Malacoda": or, Dante's Devil Plays Beethoven', *Journal of Beckett Studies*, Vol. 3, No. 1 (Autumn 1993), pp. 59–64.

Amiran, E., *Wandering and Home: Beckett's Metaphysical Narrative* (Pennsylvania: Pennsylvania State University, 1993).

Bajomée, D., 'Lumière, ténèbres et chaos dans *L'Innommable* de Samuel Beckett', *Les Lettres romanes*, No. 23 (1969), pp. 139–58.

Baldwin, H.L., *Samuel Beckett's Real Silence* (Pennsylvania: Pennsylvania State University Press, 1981).

Barge, L., 'Beckett's Metaphysics and Christian Thought: A Comparison', *Christian Scholar's Review*, Vol. 20, No. 1 (September 1990), pp. 33–44.

Barge, L., *God, The Quest, The Hero: Thematic Structures in Beckett's Fiction* (Chapel Hill: University of North Carolina, 1988).

Barjon, L., 'Le Dieu de Beckett', *Etudes*, No. 322 (1965), pp. 650–62.

Baxter, K.M., *Speak What We Feel: A Christian Looks at the Contemporary Theatre* (London: SCM Press, 1964).

Bernold, A., *L'Amitié de Beckett* (Paris: Hermann, 1992).

Brater, E., 'Noah, *Not I*, and Beckett's "Incomprehensibly Sublime"', *Comparative Drama*, Vol. 8, No. 3 (Fall 1974), pp. 254–63.

Bryden, M., 'The Sacrificial Victim of Beckett's *Endgame*', *Journal of Literature and Theology*, Vol. 4, No. 2 (July 1990), pp. 219–25.

Bryden, M., 'No Stars Without Stripes: Beckett and Dante', *Romanic Review*, Vol. 87, No. 4 (November 1996), pp. 541–56.

Buning, M., 'Samuel Beckett's Negative Way: Intimations of the "via negativa" in his Late Plays', in *European Literature and Theology in the Twentieth Century: Ends of Time*, eds. D. Jaspers and C. Crowder, (London: Macmillan, 1990), pp. 129–42.

Butler, L. St J., '"A Mythology with which I am perfectly familiar": Samuel Beckett and the Absence of God', in *Irish Writers and Religion*, ed. R. Welch, (Gerrards Cross: Colin Smythe, 1992).

Butler, L. St J., *Samuel Beckett and the Meaning of Being* (Basingstoke: Macmillan, 1984).

Coe, R.N., 'Le Dieu de Samuel Beckett', *Cahiers Renaud-Barrault*, (spec. issue on Beckett), No. 44 (October 1963), pp. 6–36. Appeared in English as 'God and Samuel Beckett', *Meanjin Quarterly*, No. 100, Vol. 24, No. 1 (1965), pp. 66–85.

Critchley, S., *Very Little... Almost Nothing: Death, Philosophy, Literature* (London: Routledge, 1997).

Cuddy, L.A., 'Beckett's "Dead Voices" in *Waiting for Godot*: New Inhabitants of Dante's *Inferno*', *Modern Language Studies*, Vol. 12, No. 2 (Spring 1982), pp. 48–61.

Davies, P., *The Ideal Real* (Cranbury: Associated University Presses, 1994)

Dearlove, J.E., *Accommodating the Chaos: Samuel Beckett's Nonrelational Art* (Durham: Duke University Press, 1982).

Dodsworth, M., '*Film* and the Religion of Art', in *Beckett the Shape Changer*, ed. Katharine Worth (London: Routledge & Kegan Paul, 1975), pp. 161–82.

Edwards, M., *Eloge de l'attente: T.S. Eliot et Samuel Beckett* (Paris: Belin, 1996).

Elam, K., 'Dead Heads: Damnation-narration in the "dramaticules"', in *The Cambridge Companion to Beckett*, ed. John Pilling (Cambridge: Cambridge University Press, 1994), pp. 145–66.

Fletcher, J., 'Beckett's Debt to Dante', *Nottingham French Studies*, Vol. 4, No. 1 (1965), pp. 41–52.

Foster, P., *Beckett and Zen: A Study of Dilemma in the Novels of Samuel Beckett* (London: Wisdom Publications, 1989).

Friedberg-Dobry, L., 'Four Saints in Two Acts: A Note on the Saints Macarius and the Canonization of Gogo and Didi', *The Journal of Beckett Studies*, No. 6 (Autumn 1980), pp. 117–9.

Friedman, M.J., 'Molloy's "Sacred" Stones', *Romance Notes*, Vol. 9, No. 1 (1967), pp. 1–4.

Graver, L., & Federman, R. (eds), *Samuel Beckett: The Critical Heritage* (London: Routledge & Kegan Paul, 1979).

Hamilton, A. & K., *Condemned to Life: The World of Samuel Beckett* (Grand Rapids: Wm B. Eerdmans, 1976).

Harries, R., 'Samuel Beckett and Christian Hope' (Drawbridge Memorial Lecture 1982), (London: Christian Evidence Society, 1982), 14 pp.

Harvey, L.E., *Samuel Beckett Poet and Critic* (Princeton: Princeton University Press, 1970).

Hokenson, J., 'A Stuttering *Logos*: Biblical Paradigms in Beckett's Trilogy', *James Joyce Quarterly*, Vol. 8, No. 4 (1971), pp. 293–310.

Hutchings, W., '"The Unintelligible Terms of an Incomprehensible Damnation": Samuel Beckett's *The Unnamable*, Sheol, and *St Erkenwald*', *Twentieth Century Literature*, Vol. 27, No. 2 (Summer 1981), pp. 97–112.

Jacobsen, J., & Mueller, W.R., *The Testament of Samuel Beckett* (London: Faber, 1966).

Juliet, C., *Rencontre avec Samuel Beckett* (Paris: Editions Fata Morgana, 1986).

Kennedy, S., 'Beckett's "Schoolboy Copy" of Dante: A Handbook for Liberty', *Dalhousie French Studies*, No. 19 (Fall-Winter 1990), pp. 11–19.

Knowlson, J., *Damned to Fame: The Life of Samuel Beckett* (London: Bloomsbury, 1996).

Levy, E.P., *Beckett and the Voice of Species* (Dublin: Gill & Macmillan, 1980).

Lodge, D., 'Some Ping Understood', *Encounter*, Vol. 30, No. 2 (February 1968), pp. 85–9.

Mercier, V., *Beckett/Beckett* (Oxford: Oxford University Press, 1977).

Morrison, K., 'Neglected Biblical Allusions in Beckett's Plays: "Mother Pegg" Once More', in *Samuel Beckett: Humanistic Perspectives*, eds. M. Beja, S.E. Gontarski & P. Astier, (Columbus: Ohio State University Press, 1983).

Onimus, J., *Beckett* (Paris: Desclée De Brouwer, 1968).

Pilling, J., *Beckett Before Godot: The Formative Years (1929–1946)* (Cambridge: Cambridge University Press, 1997).

Politi, J., 'Not (Not I)', *Journal of Literature and Theology*, Vol. 6, No. 4 (December 1992), pp. 345–55.

Rabinovitz, R., *The Development of Samuel Beckett's Fiction* (Urbana: University of Illinois Press, 1984).

Ricks, C., *Beckett's Dying Words* (Oxford: Oxford University Press, 1993).

Robinson, M., 'From Purgatory to Inferno: Beckett and Dante Revisited', *Journal of Beckett Studies*, No. 5 (1979), pp. 69–82.

Robinson, M., *The Long Sonata of the Dead: A Study of Samuel Beckett* (London: Hart-Davis, 1969).

Shainberg, L., 'Exorcising Beckett', *The Paris Review*, Vol. 29, No. 104 (Fall 1987), pp. 100–36.

Simon, A., *Samuel Beckett* (Paris: Pierre Belfond, 1983).

Solomon, P.H., 'Purgatory Unpurged: Time, Space, and Language in "Lessness"', *Journal of Beckett Studies*, No. 6 (Autumn 1980), pp. 63–72.

Weber-Caflisch, A., *Chacun son dépeupleur* (Paris: Editions de Minuit, 1994).

Wolosky, S., *Language and Mysticism: The Negative Way of Language in Eliot, Beckett, and Celan* (Stanford: Stanford University Press, 1995).

Zeifman, H., 'Religious Imagery in the Plays of Samuel Beckett', in *Samuel Beckett: A Collection of Criticism*, ed. R. Cohn, (New York: McGraw-Hill Paperbacks, 1975), pp. 85–94.

Index